Dixie Walker of the Dodgers

To Hank,

From 1 Baseball Fan
To another.

ENJOY!

Susan Walker

se4walker@yahoo.com

Fire Ant Books

Dixie Walker
of the Dodgers
The People's Choice

MAURY ALLEN with SUSAN WALKER

THE UNIVERSITY OF ALABAMA PRESS
Tuscaloosa

Copyright © 2010
The University of Alabama Press
Tuscaloosa, Alabama 35487-0380
All rights reserved
Manufactured in the United States of America

Typeface: Perpetua

∞

The paper on which this book is printed meets the minimum requirements of American
National Standard for Information Sciences-Permanence of Paper for Printed Library
Materials, ANSI Z39.48-1984.

Library of Congress Cataloging-in-Publication Data

Allen, Maury, 1932–
Dixie Walker of the Dodgers : the people's choice / Maury Allen with Susan Walker.
p. cm.
"Fire Ant books."
Includes index.
ISBN 978-0-8173-5599-9 (pbk. : alk. paper) — ISBN 978-0-8173-8358-9 (electronic)
1. Walker, Dixie, 1910–1982. 2. Baseball players—United States—Biography. I.
Walker, Susan, 1943– II. Title.
GV865.W3348A55 2010
796.357092—dc22
[B]

2009045317

To our five children, six grandchildren, and hopefully more to come. That they may discover the love, dedication, heartaches, and wonderment of my parents' lives.

To the immortal game of baseball that permitted my father, uncle, brother, grandfather, and great-uncle to express their God-given talents in the great American pastime.

And to my mom, beautiful inside and out, who was always my mentor and friend.

But most of all to my dad, who selflessly gave of himself his entire life to the game he loved: as player, manager, coach, scout, and craftsman of the players' pension plan. My fondest wish is that this book will help clear up the issues that have prevented him from obtaining the recognition he so richly deserves.

Susan Ellen Walker

To my Most Valuable Player, my wife Janet, and to our children and amazing grandchildren with deepest love and appreciation for the joy and laughter they bring to my life as I record the doings of others.

Maury Allen

Contents

Acknowledgments

The story of a baseball player's life is never the sole contribution of the author. It is the accumulation of information and insight offered by so many through the years. As Dixie Walker's one hundredth birthday is marked in 2010, it is writings from the past and revelations from the present that flesh out the full picture of this dedicated athlete and complicated man.

It is with much appreciation that I note the offerings throughout the book by the skilled journalists of Alabama who recorded Dixie Walker's early career and brought him to light as a public figure. The efforts of sportswriters in cities across America, where Dixie first played, helped shape the detailed picture of this baseball wizard.

Thanks go to the reporters of the early 1930s who saw Dixie Walker as the next Babe Ruth and chronicled his feats at Yankee Stadium and in Chicago, Detroit, and his glory in Brooklyn as the People's Choice achieved success, fame, and a little historic fortune.

Dozens of books captured his doings, and I drew from the best of them, *The Baseball Encyclopedia,* the *Elias Book of Baseball Records,* and the *Sporting News Official World Series Records, 1903–2008,* for numbers and records of his career; then on to accounts such as Frank Graham, *The Brooklyn Dodgers: An Informal History;* Leo Durocher, with Ed Linn, *Nice Guys Finish Last;* Red Barber's *1947: When All Hell Broke Loose in Baseball;*

The Dodgers by Tommy Holmes; Harold Parrott, *The Lords of Baseball;* Robert W. Peterson's brilliant work *Only the Ball Was White: A History of Legendary Black Players and All-Black Professional Teams;* and Jonathan Eig's *Opening Day: The Story of Jackie Robinson's First Season.* I also relied heavily on one of my own books, *Jackie Robinson: A Life Remembered.*

Most importantly I give thanks to the gracious offerings of many of Dixie Walker's teammates, men now in their eighties and nineties who spent so much time with me, recalling events from sixty and seventy years ago. These boyhood heroes of mine, Bobby Bragan, Clyde King, Duke Snider, Ralph Branca, Gene Hermanski, Howard Schultz, Ed Stevens, the baseball immortals such as Bob Feller and Ralph Kiner, and baseball's most significant twentieth-century figure, Players Association leader Marvin Miller, offered so much without asking anything in return.

I am also grateful to the fans of Dixie Walker, many of whom watched him break into the big leagues at Yankee Stadium and followed his career as he moved on to Chicago, Detroit, Brooklyn, and later Pittsburgh. Their memories of Dixie against that famed Bedford Avenue wall in Brooklyn were precious.

And, of course, to Susan Walker and husband, Ed, for their marvelous memories of a lifetime of connection with Dixie and Estelle Walker.

Much thanks also to the staff at the University of Alabama Press for their kindness, consideration, and total professionalism in moving this work from an author's idea to this cherished book.

Dixie Walker of the Dodgers

I

How It All Started

Leo Durocher was wearing blue silk pajamas and a golden yellow bathrobe as he stood in the kitchen of the army barracks at Fort Gulick in the Panama Canal Zone. It was the middle of the night in late March 1947. Durocher, the manager of the Brooklyn Dodgers, a team on the threshold of making history with the promotion of a Negro, Jackie Robinson, from its Montreal farm club to Brooklyn, had called his players together to put down an insurrection.

Harold Parrott had gotten word from handsome right-handed pitcher Kirby Higbe that a petition was being circulated by several of the Brooklyn players. Dixie Walker, Eddie Stanky, Hugh Casey, and Bobby Bragan—southerners all—were said to be leading a protest against Robinson's promotion to the major league team.

Walker, the oldest player on the team at thirty-six, had been with the Dodgers since 1939 and was the most popular player on the team. Known for his special clutch hitting (he had a .340 average against the hated Giants), he was called the People's Choice, or Peepul's Cherce, as it was often written in Brooklyn. He was said to be the leader of the protest against Robinson.

"I was supposed to have organized a meeting of some of the players to boycott Robinson," he told the *New York Times* sportswriter Ira Berkow in 1981, some six months before his death. "When it was announced that

Robinson would be joining the Dodgers, the team was playing an exhibition game in Panama. I was in Miami, meeting my family. We then took a boat to Havana where the Dodger training camp was that year. I met the team plane when it flew in from Panama. I heard a good deal of talk about Robinson. But I didn't know a thing about any insurrection, as it was later called. But I got a message that Mr. [Branch] Rickey wanted to see me. I went to the Hotel Nacional in Havana the next day and I sat down with Mr. Rickey in that room."

From that meeting and from a letter Walker later sent Rickey asking to be traded, Walker was identified as the center of the storm that followed Robinson's arrival in Brooklyn. Seven years before the historic *Brown versus Board of Education* ruling banned school segregation; a dozen years before the last major league team (the Boston Red Sox) was integrated in 1959; seventeen years before passage of the 1964 Civil Rights Act; and more than sixty years before an African American would be taken seriously as a presidential candidate, a young black man was added to a major league roster. And Dixie Walker would be labeled a racist. It kept him from being considered for baseball's Hall of Fame. Like Cap Anson before him, it identified him as a bigot, the leader of baseball's antiblack movement of the 1940s, and it damaged his family and friends.

When Durocher gathered his players together on that 1947 night, he had been the manager of the Dodgers since 1939. According to Durocher's 1975 autobiography, *Nice Guys Finish Last,* written with Ed Linn, he called all the players, including Dixie Walker, together for a historic meeting. Jackie Robinson was coming to the Dodgers. Durocher was all for it. Anyone who wouldn't accept the Negro as a teammate would be traded. "I hear some of you players don't want to play with Robinson and you have a petition drawn up that you are going to sign," Durocher wrote. "Well, you know what you can do with that petition. You can wipe your ass with it. Mr. Rickey is on his way down here and all you have to do is tell him about it. I'm sure he'll be happy to make other arrangements for you."

Durocher's story continues in a spirited vein. "I hear Dixie Walker is going to send Mr. Rickey a letter asking to be traded. Just hand him the letter, Dixie, and you're gone. Gone. If this fellow is good enough to play on this ball club—and from what I've seen and heard he is—he is going to play on this ball club and he is going to play for me."

Durocher died in 1991 and was inducted into baseball's Hall of Fame at Cooperstown in 1994, with his wife, Laraine Day, a former actress, on hand to accept the honor. He was suspended for a year by the baseball commissioner Albert (Happy) Chandler because of alleged immoral conduct on April 9, 1947. He was accused of a gambling involvement with actor George Raft and of violating church rules by marrying the actress. He was accused of associating with what were described as "shady characters," mostly based on complaints of the man who had once hired him, Larry MacPhail, who was running the Yankees in 1947. Robinson was officially promoted to the Dodgers on April 10, 1947.

Dixie Walker, born in Villa Rica, Georgia and raised in Birmingham, Alabama, was never seriously considered for the Hall of Fame despite a lifetime .306 average over eighteen seasons. He was married to the same woman, the former Estelle Shea, for forty-six years. They raised six children together. He spent fifty-two years in baseball as a player, coach, manager, scout, and batting instructor.

In 1981 Walker told sportswriter Berkow about his heated meeting with Branch Rickey in Rickey's office at the Havana spring headquarters of the Brooklyn Dodgers. "He really reamed me out. I was so mad at him accusing me of being a ringleader that a few days later I wrote him this letter requesting to be traded. But I did not mention Jackie Robinson's name," Walker said.

The letter was written on a piece of plain yellow paper. It was handwritten by Walker and addressed to Rickey, the president of the Dodgers, at his Brooklyn office at 215 Montague Street. Walker made two copies of the letter. He delivered one copy to Harold Parrott, the traveling secretary, and asked him to deliver it personally to Rickey when he returned to Brooklyn. He kept the second copy.

Walker wrote the date on the right-hand top of the letter in a firm hand.

March the 26th, 1947
Dear Mr. Rickey.

Recently the thought has occurred to me that a change of ball clubs would benefit both the Brooklyn ball club and myself. Therefore I would like to be traded as soon as a deal could be arranged. My association with you, the people of Brooklyn *(this was the People's Choice as author),* the press and radio has been very pleasant, and one I can truthfully say I am sorry has to end.

For reasons I don't care to go into, I feel my decision is best for all concerned.
Very truly yours,
Dixie Walker.

"When Mr. Rickey got back to Brooklyn and saw the letter he did his dead level best to say that my opposition to Robinson was the reason I wanted to be traded," Walker told Berkow in that 1981 interview. "Well, I had been with the club for nine years and I resented being the scapegoat."

Walker was traded to Pittsburgh on December 8, 1947, after Robinson had a Rookie of the Year season at age twenty-eight, after the Dodgers won the National League pennant, then lost a bitter seven game World Series to the Yankees, and after Walker passed his thirty-seventh birthday.

"He wasn't traded over the Robinson thing or the letter or any damn petition," says Ralph Branca, eighty-two, born and raised in Mount Vernon, New York, one of five surviving members of the 1947 Brooklyn Dodgers. "He was traded for the same reasons Rickey traded anybody. He thought he could make the club better and he didn't want to pay a thirty-seven-year-old guy more money."

Branca was twenty-one years old that season of 1947, in his fourth year as a member of the Brooklyn Dodgers and a twenty-one-game winner, the youngest pitcher to win more than twenty games since Hall of Famer Bob Feller won twenty-four games in 1939 at the age of twenty for the Cleveland Indians.

Walker was traded to the Pirates along with pitchers Hal Gregg and Vic Lombardi for pitcher Preacher Roe, third baseman Billy Cox, and utility man Gene Mauch. Roe and Cox would go on to be vital players in the surge of the Dodgers over the next decade. Mauch would go on to a brilliant managerial career.

"I was there, I never heard of any petition," recalls Branca. "Sure there was a lot of talk about Jackie. Why not? This was a revolutionary move for baseball. The southerners on the team, Dixie, Stanky, Bragan, Casey, and some other guys, Furillo, maybe, Lavagetto, maybe, talked about it among themselves. Nobody talked to me about it. I was a young pitcher working to get better and make a living."

Branca's twenty-one wins at the age of twenty-one for the Brooklyn Dodgers that year and an opening game start in the World Series against the Yankees were the memorable parts of his season. "I remember that season more for the year I had than for Jackie. Jackie took care of himself. I'm not saying Dixie was a pal of Jackie's but he probably didn't treat him any differently than a lot of other guys on the team did," Branca says.

Bobby Bragan, a native of Birmingham, Alabama, and longtime Texas resident, runs a charity in Fort Worth, Texas, for underprivileged children. He is ninety-one years old. He was the regular shortstop on the Philadelphia Phillies for three seasons before being traded to Brooklyn in 1943 where he played as a backup infielder and catcher into 1948.

"Sure I was against Jackie joining the club. I was from the South. That was my background. There was some talk of a petition but I never saw anything like that," he says.

After the Dodgers returned to Havana and after the Durocher meeting in the barracks, Bragan was called in to Rickey's room at the Nacional Hotel in Havana.

"Dixie was there in the room," Bragan says. "I remember that. Mr. Rickey was all over him. Heck, Dixie was the leader of the team, the senior man, he had a lot of influence on that club. Dixie's face just got red as Mr. Rickey went on and on about giving Jackie a chance. Maybe Dixie said a few words. I can't remember. But it wasn't many. This was Mr. Rickey's show. I don't think Furillo said a word. He just looked stunned. It was Dixie, me, Stanky, and Furillo in that room with Mr. Rickey. I don't know if he called any others in at any other time."

Bragan said, "When Mr. Rickey finished he asked all four of us, one at a time, if we would play any differently if Jackie was on the club. We all answered we would not. Then he asked us if we wanted to be traded. I said I did. That's just the way I felt. Dixie said he did. Stanky just put his head down. Furillo didn't say a word. He was just a kid then. I don't even know why he was there," Bragan says. Bragan died in January 2010.

Clyde King is eighty-three years old, still living in his hometown of Goldsboro, North Carolina; he has three daughters and eight grandchildren. He is a consultant with the New York Yankees, an instructor in the team's spring training headquarters at Tampa each March, and a longtime pal of Yankees boss George M. Steinbrenner. He has received a baseball check from his employers for sixty-five years, one of the longest salaried figures in the game's history.

"I was a kid pitcher still trying to make my way in the big leagues in 1947," King says. "I don't recall any petition in Havana where we trained. I looked up to Dixie Walker as a veteran player, a kind and gentle man and someone we all admired."

King said about a dozen years later he managed a minor league team playing an exhibition in Havana. The new leader of the country, Fidel Castro, was scheduled to throw out the first ball. "He came up to me and said, 'Do you know who I am?' I said, 'Of course, you are the leader of Cuba.' Then Castro looked at me and said, 'I pitched against you in 1947.' I didn't remember that. Maybe if he had pitched better I would have remembered him and he would have signed with the Dodgers. Then we wouldn't have had all that trouble with Cuba."

King says all he could remember about Robinson and Walker that spring was Rickey asking him if he would play the same, as a southerner, if Robinson was on the team. "I think Mr. Rickey asked everybody that. I told him I certainly would. I just wanted to be a big league pitcher. We went back for the season and after the second or third week, my wife, Norma, was inside the fence at Ebbets Field with the other wives waiting for us all to come out of the clubhouse. Jackie's wife, Rachel, was outside the fence, with her baby, all by herself. Norma just told her to walk a few feet down the gate and come inside with the other wives to wait for Jackie. She did. There it was, just a little southern girl taking care of the new black girl."

He remembers how much of a financial struggle it was in 1947 as a big league ball player. He made thirty-five hundred dollars in that rookie season and never made over twelve thousand dollars in his seven-year major league pitching career. "Alex Rodriguez makes more in one at bat than I made in my entire professional career," says King.

The Yankees pay A-Rod $25.2 million a year in his ten-year contract signed before the 2008 season. In 2009 he was identified as one of 104 big leaguers who failed steroid drug testing in 2003. He was with the Texas Rangers then. He later admitted he used steroids from 2001 through 2003.

Gene Hermanski is eighty-eight years old, a ten-year resident of Homosassa, Florida, after a lifetime in his native New Jersey. He played with the Brooklyn Dodgers in 1943, joined the Coast Guard, then returned to Brooklyn in 1947. He was fighting for a job in 1947.

"I had played against a lot of black players when I was in the Coast Guard playing on a navy team and during the time I played on a semi-professional team in Brooklyn called the Bushwicks. I had to use a different name, Gene Walsh, because I was already with Brooklyn and I was playing for a navy team out of Floyd Bennett Field in Brooklyn. I played against Satchel Paige, Josh Gibson, Buck O'Neil, all of the Negro League stars." Hermanski says he knew making the ball club in 1947 would be a tough chore with all the World War II vets back now and the talented youngsters, including Robinson, knocking on the big league doors. "That's all I thought about that spring, making an impression, making the club. Dixie helped me with my batting and fielding. He was always kind and helpful to me," Hermanski remembers.

What about the petition?

"There was talk, you know clubhouse gossip, about what some guys would do if Jackie came to the team. I didn't take it very seriously. It was mostly the southern players, Dixie, of course, as a veteran and Bragan, Hugh Casey, Kirby Higbe. I didn't pay much attention to it. I paid more attention to hitting the ball in spring training so I could win a job."

After Robinson did join the Dodgers it would be Hermanski who came up with one of the funniest lines that helped break the building tension around the team concerning Robinson's arrival. "It was in Cincinnati, a few weeks into the season and the rumors were flying, this time about guys threatening to shoot Jackie if he walked on the field. We actually had cops in the clubhouse and everybody was told about it," says Hermanski.

As a police officer warned the Dodgers about the possible plot, Hermanski stood up and told his teammates, "Let's all go out there wearing number 42 [Robinson's Brooklyn uniform number] and then the guy won't be able to tell us apart. He won't know who to shoot."

As he looks back sixty years or more on that spring training in Havana, Hermanski now says, "If any petition existed I didn't know about it. Nobody ever came to ask me to sign anything. I'm sure if they did come to me, they knew I wouldn't sign something like that." Hermanski recently looked at the starting lineup for that historic April 15, 1947, when Jackie Robinson's name was first included in a big league game. "I'm the only one still alive," he says. "That must mean *something*."

Duke Snider, eighty-two, a 1947 rookie that April opening day in 1947 and inducted into the Hall of Fame in 1980, never got off the bench on that significant day Robinson played at Ebbets Field for the first time. "That's what I remember about the day, not Jackie playing, but me *not* playing. When you are a kid trying to make it that is the only thing you think about when a game lineup is posted. Am I in there? I wasn't so that made me mad," he says.

Snider does remember something about a petition late in spring training.

"I think it was Hugh Casey [the famed Brooklyn relief pitcher] who came up to me in the clubhouse one day late in the spring and told me to sign this little piece of paper he had in his hand," Snider says. "I don't even think he said it was a petition. It was just a sheet of yellow paper. I just got up and walked away. 'I'm not signing anything like that.' That was it," Snider says.

Snider grew up in Los Angeles near the campus of the University of California at Los Angeles. "Everybody around my area knew who Jackie Robinson was. He had been a great star at Pasadena Junior (now City) College and then he went on to UCLA. I was out on the field there one day and here comes Jackie Robinson. A bunch of us kids recognized him and walked with him. He was playing in a UCLA baseball game and wearing baseball spikes and he was walking across the field to the track and field area. We walked with him, sat down along the edge of the track and watched him broad jump. He won the broad jump for UCLA and then he just got up and walked back to the baseball game. I think he won that for UCLA, too."

Snider says he remembers Dixie Walker fondly from that spring. "I was a left-handed hitter like Dixie was and he gave me lots of batting tips. He later became a great hitting coach for the Dodgers but you could see how much he knew about hitting even then. I guess I was a wild swinger and he tried to tell me that hitting was all about making contact. You can have the greatest swing in the world but if you don't hit the ball it doesn't matter. Dixie gave me a lot of advice about hitting the ball. As far as his attitude toward Jackie and what he might have said or done, I can't say. I was just a rookie then and rookies didn't get into deep discussions with veterans about anything, especially something as sensitive as race."

Walker may or may not have been involved in a petition to keep Robinson off the Dodgers. No one alive knows for sure. What is certain is that he felt enormous pressure from friends and family back home in Birmingham about possibly playing with a black man in 1947.

Birmingham was identified as the most racist city in America during the civil rights demonstrations and violence of the 1950s and 1960s. The police commissioner in the city in the 1960s was Eugene (Bull) Connor, a boyhood friend of Dixie Walker's and the personality most credited with the racist violence of the time. He was the police chief who ordered the howling dogs to be used on civil rights demonstrators, and he was the man who ordered the furious fire hoses blasted on American citizens. It is Birmingham where the most ghastly attack on innocent people occurred in the 1963 bombing of the Sixteenth Street Baptist Church. Four young black girls were killed and twenty-two other people were injured. Birmingham was soon called by newspaper reporters and editorialists "Bombingham."

All this would occur ten or fifteen years after Robinson integrated baseball with Walker as a teammate.

Walker told Berkow in the 1981 interview that there were pressures on him from people in Alabama not to play with Robinson. "I didn't know if they would spit on me or not," Walker said. "And it was no secret I was worried about my business because I had a hardware and sporting goods store back home." Most ball players had off-season jobs or businesses then to support themselves throughout the long winters.

Walker was more concerned about the reaction of townspeople to his playing with the Negro than others might have been for a simple reason. The store was the lifeblood of his father.

Dixie Walker's father, Ewart Gladstone Walker, had pitched in the big leagues with the Washington Senators from 1909 to 1912. He had managed for a few seasons in the minor leagues, played some semiprofessional baseball and held odd jobs as a miner and laborer.

Susan Walker recalls her mother saying her grandfather had been a heavy drinker before he worked in the hardware store. The store kept Ewart Walker away from the temptation of alcohol. He didn't run the business but he worked in it most every day, under the direction of a manager when Dixie and his brother, Harry (the Hat) Walker, were away playing baseball and at their sides during the winters.

Walker's reason for opposing Robinson's arrival in Brooklyn had something to do with the common cultural attitude of the time with few southerners forgetting the indignities of the Civil War some eighty years earlier and fewer still more loyal to the flag of the United States than to the Confederate flag flying in most towns below the Mason-Dixon line. It may have had more to do with protecting his father.

"I grew up in the South and in those days," Walker related in that 1981 interview, "you grew up in a different manner than you do today. We thought blacks didn't have ice water in their veins and so couldn't take the pressures of playing big league baseball. Well, we know now that's as big a farce as ever was. A person learns and you begin to change with the times."

Walker did not deny his racism of the 1947 season but he also pointed out something about Robinson himself that few supporters have considered or admitted through the years of the deification of the breaker of that color barrier. "Jackie was a very antagonistic person in many ways, at least I felt he was," Walker said. "Maybe he had to be to survive. The curses, the threats on his life. I don't know if I could have gone through what he did. I doubt it. But we just didn't gee and haw, like they say down here."

Over the years, Walker told Berkow, he and Robinson would meet at old-timers' games and "we sat and chatted some." Walker continued, "The other night I watched a television program and heard mention of a number of people who were important in blacks gaining advantages in America. And the name of Jackie Robinson never came up. It surprised me. I mean, how soon people forget."

A black baseball player named Vince Coleman was asked in 1986 about Jackie Robinson as the fortieth anniversary of his 1947 arrival in

Brooklyn approached. "I don't know nothing about no Jackie Robinson," Coleman replied.

Brooklyn teammate Joe Black wrote Coleman a scathing letter pointing out that there might not be "no Vince Coleman" in the big leagues were it not for Jackie Robinson.

Other black players recalled Robinson's arrival in the big leagues differently. "I remember when Jackie came through with the Brooklyn Dodgers to my hometown of Daytona, Florida," says Ed Charles, the African American third baseman of the 1969 world champion New York Mets. "Everybody in our part of town wanted to see him. Old people and small children, invalids and town drunks all walked through the streets. Some people were on crutches, and some blind people clutched the arms of friends, walking slowly to that ball park to sit in the segregated section. We watched him play that day and finally believed what we had read in the papers, that one of us was out there on the ball field. When the game was over, we kids followed Jackie as he walked with his teammates to the train station, and when the train pulled out, we ran down the tracks listening for the sounds as far as we could. And when we finally couldn't hear it any longer, we ran some more and finally stopped and put our ears to the tracks so we could feel the vibrations of the train carrying Jackie Robinson. We wanted to be part of him as long as we could."

Baseball has retired his uniform number 42 now. Times change. Robinson is clearly a historic American figure.

Dixie Walker wore uniform number 11. Not even the Dodgers of Los Angeles have retired his number. Walker never even gained early entry to the Brooklyn Dodgers Hall of Fame, enshrined now in the Brooklyn minor league baseball park in Coney Island called Key Span stadium. His stand against Jackie Robinson was the first thing many Brooklyn fans remembered about him.

He was a vital member of the first Brooklyn team to win a pennant in twenty-one years with the 1941 Dodgers. He won a batting title in 1944. He was on the 1947 pennant winners. He represented the National League players in establishing the first pension plan for big leaguers in 1947.

His legacy is clouded. Is it only an aborted petition and a withdrawn letter that will always represent Dixie Walker's contributions to the great American pastime?

2

The Lingering Legend

Susan Walker hadn't been in the New York City area for several years. She was born in Rockville Centre, New York, a leafy Long Island suburb about forty-five minutes from Manhattan depending on Long Island Railroad traffic or the whims of drivers on the ballooning Long Island Expressway.

She remembered nothing of the small village, some 3.4 square miles inside the Nassau County town of Hempstead, with a constant population somewhere around 20,000, growing to as much as 24,568 in the very latest census of 2000.

The average price of a home in 2008 among the 9,201 listed households was valued at over $500,000, and the population, according to a town study, was 90.7 percent white, 3.72 African American, 1.42 Asian, and 1.37 of those assorted indefinable "others." Some 7.7 percent of residences claimed Hispanic or Latin identification regardless of race, a typical New York suburb.

The median income of households in Rockville Centre in the latest listing from village sources was $103,315.

A famous Brooklyn and Los Angeles Dodgers baseball player, Sanford Braun, born in Brooklyn, New York, on December 30, 1935, lived in Rockville Centre from 1944 through 1949 when his mother and step-father, attorney Irving Koufax, moved back to Brooklyn. Sandy Koufax, the greatest pitcher of his time, entered the Baseball Hall of Fame in Cooperstown in 1972.

The writer-historian Doris Kearns Goodwin, a 1995 Pulitzer Prize winner, was a fanatic Brooklyn Dodgers fan as a kid growing up in the borough and continued the emotional link despite a move to Rockville Centre.

Howard Stern, the tall iconoclastic comedy-talker-storyteller-purveyor of bare-breasted women, lived in Rockville Centre as did writer Pete Axthelm; basketball player Art Heyman, a star at Duke University; Anne Meara, the female half of the Stiller and Meara comedy team; heavyweight champion Floyd Patterson; and Billy Donovan, the coach of the back-to-back NCAA basketball champions at the University of Florida.

Susan Walker knew none of this about her hometown. Why should she? She left Rockville Centre in 1947. She was four years old. Her father was a professional baseball player in Brooklyn, New York. He also owned a package liquor store on Rockville Centre's Main Street from 1940 until 1948 when the family moved away.

She was born in the Long Island village on February 16, 1943, the fourth child of Frederick (Dixie) Ewart Walker and Estelle Casey Shea Walker, "Sheazy" to old friends, during her father's occupational summers away from his hometown of Birmingham, Alabama.

"My mother was born in New York City," recalls Susan, "but she, as a result of the move, developed more of a southern accent than he had from all the years of living down South. They were married in 1936, and as soon as they settled in his home she quickly adjusted. I don't think anyone ever considered her a northern girl."

Susan's father was born in Villa Rica, Georgia, although the family soon settled in Birmingham. He, too, was always privately and publicly identified with the South. His own father, Ewart Gladstone Walker, was born in Brownsville, Pennsylvania, some twenty-two years after the end of the Civil War and chose Alabama for his home.

"I think my father could always be understood as a classic southern

gentleman. He spoke softly; he cared about manners; he ran our home
the way the traditions of so many southern generations dictated," says
Susan. "His habits were simple and elegant. He and mother would have
a quiet glass of sherry before dinner. They would talk alone in his office. At dinner he would eat in the English style, the knife in his right
hand, the fork in his left, pushing the food onto his fork. When dinner
was done he would gently get up from the table and firmly address his
daughters. 'All right, girls,' he would say, 'it's time to do the dishes.'
Then he would leave the dining room, go to the back study, light up his
pipe and read the evening newspapers."

In those summer working months, he rose early, showered, dressed
with a shirt and tie, ate two boiled eggs with a slice of toast, sipped a
cup of tea, kissed his wife goodbye, waved to the children, and drove his
only luxury, a shiny black Cadillac purchased from a Long Island show-
room near Rockville Centre to his famous summer job. If Estelle had
errands to run with the children he would often ride the Long Island
railroad and the Brooklyn subway to Ebbets Field.

Dixie Walker worked in Brooklyn from July 24, 1939, until December 8, 1947. His daughter Susan was a little more than four years
old when her father's place of summer employment was shifted from the
most populous New York City borough to the industrial city of Pittsburgh, Pennsylvania. Pittsburgh was the iron and coal center of the
United States, along the shores of three rivers—the Monongahela, the
Susquehanna, and the Allegheny. Soon after this move, the family went
home to Birmingham.

Walker may have been traded to Pittsburgh, but it was in Brooklyn,
at Ebbets Field, that Dixie Walker established his name and fame with
the baseball fans of America.

Dixie Walker was the star right fielder of the Brooklyn Dodgers, a
lifetime .306 hitter in the big leagues over eighteen seasons, a defender
of that oddly shaped wall along the Bedford Avenue landmark. He was
a three-time National League All-Star, a two-time pennant-winning
player with the Dodgers (in 1941 and 1947), and the 1944 batting cham-

pion with a .357 mark. Dixie was also a league leader in runs batted in during the 1945 season with 124 and the most popular player on the team in his time. Perhaps most importantly for players of the game, he was one of the founders of and passionate fighters for the first Baseball Players Pension Plan. Clearly, he is a Baseball Hall of Fame candidate.

Dixie was called the People's Choice by many members of the press, and it was often spelled and pronounced as the Peepul's Cherce in the language of Brooklyn natives, caught mostly in Hollywood films filled with strange characters from the borough. The term came about when a fan sitting in pitcher Hugh Casey's Brooklyn bar discussed his Dodgers with sportswriter Tommy Holmes of the *Brooklyn Eagle.* Walker's name came up. "Ahh, Dixie," said the fan, a little loopy from the brew. "He's the People's Choice." Only it sounded to the ear of Holmes, a Brooklyn native himself, like "the Peepul's Cherce." *New York Daily Mirror* sportswriter Dan Parker soon was referring to Walker in all of his columns as the Peepul's Cherce.

"You would come into the clubhouse," Hall of Fame Brooklyn shortstop Pee Wee Reese once recalled, "and you had to go past Dixie's locker in the front. He sat there on an upholstered chair in the middle of the room while the rest of us dressed on uncomfortable, hard wooden stools. You would greet him every day, 'Hi, Dixie, hi Dixie,' and he would smile back at you, 'Hi, Pee Wee.' Then you could move on to your locker. It was like greeting a mayor. I got to calling him "the Mayor—the Mayor of Ebbets Field." The fans caught on to that, too, and Walker was often referred to in sports stories as "the Mayor of Flatbush," the neighborhood in Brooklyn where famed Ebbets Field was located.

Susan Walker knew none of this. It just wasn't discussed at home.

"My mother and father lived such separate lives. He played baseball during the day. She took care of the family and the house. In those days it was mostly during the day. He brought none of it home. I never heard anything discussed at home about baseball. I remember my mother having the radio on at home and listening to Red Barber describe the games.

She listened; she knew what was happening, but it wasn't discussed with us kids. Once in a while we went to a game and sat with the families of the other players behind home plate. I was always on my mother's lap, fidgeting and squirming. The People's Choice? No, I never heard that expression in our home," she says.

Ebbets Field. Bedford Avenue and Sullivan Place. A short walk from the Prospect Park station of the BMT, the Brooklyn Manhattan Transit. Charles Ebbets and the McKeever brothers, Ed and Steve, had put up the money and the magic to create the new park, the Flatbush successor to the dilapidated Washington Park, and it finally opened, after a series of frustrating financial and political battles, on April 5, 1913. Early Brooklyn pitching star Nap Rucker defeated the hated New York Giants that day 3–2. Two future Hall of Famers, Casey Stengel, the right fielder, and Zack Wheat, the left fielder, were in the starting Brooklyn lineup. Stengel had joined the team on September 12, 1912, collected four hits in his first game in the big leagues in four at bats and was on his way to a legendary career. He was as famous for his elocution as for his playing and managing days, including three seasons, 1934 to 1936, as field manager of the Brooklyn Dodgers. In later years, Stengel often credited his pal and teammate Wheat with having taught him much about the game. After Wheat's death in 1972, Stengel loved to tell tales about the great outfielder, ending the discussion by announcing, "He's dead at the present time, you know."

The Brooklyn Dodgers always seemed to collect characters. There was a pitcher named Dazzy Vance because he was "dazzy" and the rotund manager named Uncle Robbie, Wilbert Robinson. There was the famed hitter of the late 1920s and 1930s, Babe Herman, who still holds many Dodger batting records. Herman once complained that he was being damaged by negative, comical stories about his performances instead of applauding his great skills. When a fly ball hit Herman on the shoulder instead of the glove, the writers exaggerated that the ball hit him on the head.

"If a ball ever hits me on the head," he announced, "I'll quit."

When the sportswriters insisted being hit on the shoulder was still evidence of entertainment, Herman reached into his back uniform pocket. He pulled out a cigar and said he wanted to think about that a little more.

"Do you have a light?" he suddenly asked a sportswriter.

When the man reached into his own pocket for a book of matches, Herman demurred.

"Oh, forget about it," he said. "This one is still lit."

Herman played in the big leagues from 1926 through 1937. Then he came back to the Brooklyn Dodgers as a teammate of Dixie Walker during the war, in 1945. He batted .265 in thirty-seven games at the age of forty-two. He had another claim to fame. He was a stand-in for actor Gary Cooper, batting for him when Cooper played baseball legend Lou Gehrig in the 1942 film *The Pride of the Yankees*.

In truth, veteran reporters got to know Herman quite well in his later years. He was a neighbor and close friend of Stengel's in Glendale, California, and they often shared reminiscences of days gone by. Herman was a rare bird for the baseball establishment, with unusual hobbies. He was bright, articulate, a learned student of gardening and a significant grower of orchids. His son, Robert, ran the Metropolitan Opera of New York City for many years under the direction of the famed Rudolph Bing.

Herman had a lifetime average of .324 over thirteen seasons, the highest average over that many seasons for any player not in Baseball's Hall of Fame. His image as a clown destroyed his chances for that honor. Image can be vital when it comes to Hall of Fame voting. Dixie Walker would find that out.

The Brooklyn Dodgers won pennants in 1916 and 1920. They got as high as second in 1924 but seemed to make a habit of finishing fifth, sixth, or seventh over the next fifteen years. Their image was set. They were losers. *Dem Bums.* That's what newspapers and fans called them.

Still, fans filled the small park in Brooklyn. They were passionate about their Dodgers, usually cheering for their team but booing them on occasion. A good neighborhood fight would often start when a smart-aleck Giants fan or the occasional Yankees fan used that pejorative term, bums. Bang. Kids rolling in the dirt in a Brooklyn lot. It was all right for loyal Brooklyn fans to call the team Dem Bums. But others? Never.

That all started changing in 1939. Leo Durocher was named manager of the team by the bombastic boss of the club, Larry MacPhail. Youngsters came up from the minor leagues with ability. Trades were made for talented players. Dixie Walker came to the Dodgers from Detroit in July. He batted .280 in sixty-one games. Dixie and Estelle settled into their summer home in Rockville Centre.

The fans became more involved. They could see a bright future. Hilda Chester, a rotund woman with a piercing voice and screeching cow bell, sat in the front rows of the seventy-five-cent center field bleachers. She howled at the players when they failed and screamed congratulations to them when they succeeded. Dixie Walker, guarding that wall against Bedford Avenue in right field, was one of her favorite players.

There was Eddie Bataan, the whistling man, who gained as much attention for himself with those high calls as players did for clutch hits. Then there was the Brooklyn Dodgers Sym-Phony. It was led by a man named Shorty Laurice. The Sym-Phony paraded around the stands exciting Brooklyn fans and irritating the opposition. The four or five Sym-Phony players were fans disguised as a working band using a wash board as an instrument, a harmonica, a broken metal container as a drum, a sour old horn, and anything else that would make noise. Laurice did have one legitimate bass drum and he pounded on it in a rhythmic style, especially when an opponent struck out, marching back to his dugout with head down and baseball cap pulled tight over his head.

"Every once in a while," Hall of Fame slugger Ralph Kiner once recalled, "I tried to beat them out of that last, ugly pounding of the drum after I struck out by standing on the dugout steps. They would keep hitting that drum without a real sound until I sat. I was first up one inning, struck out and stood up the rest of the inning. Then I went to left field. The Dodgers got four or five runs. When I came back to the dugout I was mad at the turn of events in the game and forgot about Shorty. Then I sat down. Boom. The sound woke up the entire neighborhood."

Ebbets Field had always been a place of great fun. The Dodgers didn't have to win to entertain the fans. All they had to do was be the Dodgers. That was always good enough with a collection of colorful characters. The characters may have been colorful. They certainly weren't colored, as the terminology of the time described some 13 percent of the population, the people of black skin, the so-called Negroes, the underbelly of the American dream.

Baseball called itself the great American pastime, a phrase pushed by the owners and perpetuated by the fawning media. The great American pastime. It was for white Americans—on the field *and* in the stands. Black Americans played in a separate if unequal league. That was the only dream they had.

"I remember when I was a kid growing up in New Jersey after my family moved up north from Alabama," said Hall of Famer Monte Irvin. "I wanted to play baseball. I loved the game. I wanted to be like Satchel Paige and Josh Gibson. Those were the names and the heroes I related to. Sure I knew about Joe DiMaggio and Lou Gehrig and the great stars in the big leagues. That was a different world. I could never play with them. That's just the way it was. I don't think I ever thought about playing in the white leagues. If you were a colored kid and you liked to play baseball you thought about playing for the Newark Eagles, the Kansas City Monarchs, the teams in your own league."

Baseball had no laws against blacks playing in the big leagues. Custom was more important than law. The custom was to sign only white players, to promote white players, to bring white players before white fans in America's stadiums.

"There never had to be any laws," a general manager once said. "Everybody knew the rules. This is the way it had always been. This is the way it would always be."

When asked why no owner or general manager would step forward in the 1920s, 1930s, and early 1940s and sign a black baseball player, an incredible pitcher like Paige, a vaunted slugger like Gibson, reported to have hit the only fair ball out of Yankee Stadium in an exhibition game there, a speedy Cool Papa Bell, he paused and whispered conspiratorially, "You want to know the real reason? You couldn't take them to your golf club and show them off."

America had been segregated in housing, in schools, in churches, in private clubs, in town swimming pools, in every measurable way since Civil War days. Blacks moved north after that conflict but they lived in separate (if unequal) sections of northern cities, not on Fifth Avenue and Park Avenue in Manhattan but in Harlem, not on Lake Shore Drive in Chicago but on the South Side, not along the Charles River in Boston but in Roxbury, once the home of Malcolm X.

Baseball mirrored America. Blacks played in their own leagues with their own players, their own traditions, their own stars. They could be seen in league games at a rented Yankee Stadium, a rented Ebbets Field, a rented Wrigley Field. Occasionally a black team would play an exhibition against a white team and the Negro League stars would gain attention for a day or two.

Connie Mack, the venerable owner of the Philadelphia A's in the 1930s and early 1940s, suggested publicly, "I wish I could sign some of them. They can play." Good for the ego of Negro League players. Not much for changing customs or increasing earning capacity.

A dark-skinned player from Cuba or Venezuela would appear in big league games and some suggested he might be darker than some Negro player in the Negro Leagues. Nothing was made of it because his name was Spanish, Adolf Luque or Alex Carrasquel or even a Brooklyn Dodger named Luis Olmo.

Rumors were rampant in the 1920s and 1930s that the greatest star in the game's history, Babe Ruth, might even have some Negro blood. His nose was as wide as the noses of blacks often were and his lips were thick and his skin was leathery and summer-tanned. The Chicago Cubs harassed the aging Bambino in the 1932 World Series and some witnesses even suggested the word "nigger" was actually shouted at the Babe to ruffle him, possibly "nigger lips," a commonly used derogatory term of the times for persons with full, thick lips such as the Babe had. He responded with the famous called home run shot off pitcher Charlie Root.

Ruth's biological background was always a small mystery. What if Babe Ruth truly integrated the game of baseball before Jackie Robinson did?

The man credited or discredited with establishing the unchallenged racism and segregation of the game of baseball for some seventy years was Adrian Constantine Anson. He was later called Cap for the many teams he captained or Pop as he aged as a nineteenth-century player from 1871 to 1897. He was born in Marshalltown, Iowa (all racists aren't southerners and all southerners aren't racists), and attended boarding school at the University of Notre Dame. He then attended the University of Iowa where his bad behavior resulted in the school asking him to leave after one semester. He began playing baseball professionally in the National Association at the age of nineteen.

Records are muddled as to the reasons for his intense racism. It is known that Cap refused to play an exhibition game against the Toledo Blue Stockings in 1883 because their catcher, Moses Fleetwood Walker, was a Negro. Walker played one season in the big leagues with Toledo in 1884 as did his brother, Welday Walker, no relation as far as researched genealogy shows to brothers Fred (Dixie) and Harry (the Hat) Walker. Anson again refused to take the field when confronted with the starting pitcher in another exhibition with the Newark Little Giants. His name was George Stovey, a Negro, and Anson refused to play this game in 1887. International league owners followed suit by passing a resolution at a league meeting forbidding the signing of Negro players.

In 1888 Cap was to play an exhibition against a Syracuse team and refused to take the field when he saw the name of Moses Walker listed again in the starting lineup. By now, a star player, team leader as captain and field manager, Anson's influence was significant. No other Negro players were brought to the big leagues, knowingly, through the remainder of the nineteenth century and into the first forty-five years of the twentieth century.

On October 23, 1945, Branch Rickey, general manager and part owner of the Brooklyn Dodgers, signed Jack "Jackie" Roosevelt Robinson to a contract with the Brooklyn organization's Montreal Royals farm team.

Rickey was born in Stockdale, Ohio, on December 20, 1881. He attended Ohio Wesleyan University as an undergraduate, where his name and reputation remain among the most distinguished alumni. He then attended the University of Michigan Law School. He was a catcher with the Ohio Wesleyan team and later coached the baseball team. In a story Rickey often told, he was chagrined when one of his players, Charley Thomas, was not allowed into a hotel room when the team arrived for a game against the University of Notre Dame at South Bend, Indiana.

Rickey compromised with the hotel clerk who allowed Thomas into Rickey's room if he would sleep on the floor. Thomas, later a successful Ohio dentist, was spotted by Rickey rubbing his hands violently as if to peel off his black skin. "Oh I wish I could make the skin white," Thomas was quoted by Rickey as saying.

Why did Rickey sign a Negro?

The Charlie Thomas tale is not enough of an explanation. Rickey had been in baseball as a player, manager, farm director and executive for most of the first half of the twentieth century. He was never previously identified with liberal causes asking for the opening of the game to blacks on or off the field. In 1945 there were no black players in baseball but there were also no black general managers, public relations directors, traveling secretaries, trainers, or farm directors. There would be an occasional janitor in a big league office, a porter on a train carrying a team, a shoeshine boy working outside a big league park. Not much had changed since Cap Anson's time.

Kenesaw Mountain Landis, baseball commissioner from 1920, in the aftermath of the Black Sox scandal, until his death in 1944, kept the game white. He was a former federal judge, hired by the owners to clean up the sport after the Chicago White Sox agreed to lose the 1919 World Series to Cincinnati. He was a North Carolinian, racist by culture, officious, arrogant, pretentious, ego-driven, and uncompromising. When the question of race occasionally arose, through newspaper stories or liberal pronouncements, Landis had the same answer, "The game is open to everybody. There are no rules against it." Then he would quickly change the subject, run his hands through his shock of white hair, and pose for more pictures.

Conditions changed quickly in the early 1940s. Liberal groups became more militant about racial equality. Blacks had fought valiantly in World War II, the same as whites, if only in segregated units. The talent was out there. Rickey noticed.

Why did he sign a Negro?

Morality? Perhaps. To make money? Perhaps. To corner the market on black players and produce a line of winners for the Brooklyn Dodgers? Perhaps. To show up the fellow owners who still went along with the unwritten code even after the death of Landis in 1944? Maybe. They didn't want to be the first in their cities to bring blacks, players or families, into those segregated private golf clubs.

Rickey would not have signed Robinson for morality alone. He had plenty of opportunity to sign a black player in St. Louis where he controlled the future Cardinals. He never did. He would say later that St. Louis was not the right town and the Cardinals were not the right team. Brooklyn was the right town, Rickey later said, and 1945 was the right time. Jackie Robinson, of course, was the right man.

Jackie Robinson was born in Cairo, Georgia, on January 31, 1919. This was a little more than nine years after Dixie Walker was born across the same state in Villa Rica, just outside Atlanta. Jackie was the fifth child of Jerry and Mallie Robinson. Jerry was a sharecropper who decided shortly after his youngest child was born that he no longer wanted to be a farmer. He wanted an easier life in the city. Jackie's sister Willa Mae would later say that her father took up with a married woman and they soon moved away together from Georgia to Florida. Jerry Robinson would show up once after Jackie had become famous. "Jack didn't have anything to do with him and that was that," Willa Mae Robinson said.

The family moved to Pasadena, California, where Mallie had relatives and soon settled in at their own home at 121 Pepper Street. A plaque now sits outside the area on the concrete sidewalk. It reads, "Jackie Robinson resided on this site with his family from 1922 to 1946." The house itself was torn down years ago in a city redevelopment program.

Jackie was soon starring in sports at Grover Cleveland School, George Washington Junior High, and Muir Technical High School. He attended Pasadena Junior College, now known as Pasadena City College, at 1570 East Colorado Boulevard in Pasadena. His brother Mack had been an Olympian in 1936, and Jackie followed as a recognized school star for his athletic performances in football, basketball, track, and his least favorite sport, baseball.

He stayed there from 1937 through 1939 and soon matriculated at the University of California at Los Angeles. He was again a star in baseball, football, basketball, and track.

After serving in the U.S. Army during World War II and completing a season with the Kansas City Monarchs in the Negro National League, he was brought to Brooklyn by Dodger scout Clyde Sukeforth in August 1945. Robinson thought he was being brought to Brooklyn for a tryout with a new Negro team called the Brown Bombers.

Sukeforth introduced Robinson to Rickey. They spent three hours together in the Brooklyn offices at 215 Montague Street in downtown Brooklyn. Rickey laid out his plan for Robinson in minute detail. Rickey knew the consequences of signing the first Negro in more than sixty years to a professional baseball contract. The last word from Rickey was that Robinson was to answer back to critics and racists with his talent, not his tongue.

"Mr. Rickey, do you want a ball player who's afraid to fight back?" Robinson asked.

"I want a ballplayer with guts enough *not* to fight back," Rickey bellowed.

The Chicago Cubs had actually won a pennant that year of 1945. Of course they had lost the World Series to Detroit with help from returning World War II home run hero Hank Greenberg. They would enter the 2010 baseball season a hundred and two years away from their last World Series title. St. Louis was second in the National League in 1945 and Brooklyn finished third under manager Leo Durocher.

Dixie Walker, the National League batting leader in 1944 and the RBI leader in 1945, had batted .300. He was at his peak as a player at the age of thirty-four with a .300 average for the fifth time in the last six seasons. He was on a team that expected to contend in the next several seasons as the World War II vets returned, the farm system developed more stars, and Rickey's deals turned out to be careful and clever. Goody Rosen, Luis Olmo, and Augie Galan each batted over .300. Hal Gregg had won eighteen games, and two young pitchers, plucked off college campuses, seemed destined for stardom. Clyde King joined Brooklyn from the University of North Carolina and Ralph Branca came to the Dodgers, via nearby Mount Vernon, New York, from New York University.

If this Robinson kid could contribute anything, the Dodgers would certainly be improved and a serious contender in 1946. Rickey had a better plan. The kid would first get his chance at organized baseball with the Montreal farm club in 1946.

The news about Robinson signing a professional contract seemed more about the social impact of a black in baseball than the baseball impact. After all, Robinson was already twenty-six years old, pretty old for a Triple A rookie and certainly too old to break into Brooklyn in 1946 or 1947. Robinson had really been a football and basketball player in college. Baseball was just a way to stay in shape for the fall sports. One big star already put the kibosh on Robinson's baseball chances.

Bob Feller, who had returned from four years of navy combat in World War II, had won five games in 1945 as he pitched again for the Cleveland Indians. He had actually pitched against Robinson a few weeks after the season ended in a Kansas City exhibition.

"He won't make it," Rapid Robert told the press. "He's too big up in the shoulders."

The press didn't chase many of the Dodgers for comment after the Robinson signing on October 25, 1945. Branca was back in school at NYU and King was at the University of North Carolina again. Goody Rosen, a rare Jewish big leaguer, avoided any controversy. Luis Olmo pretended not to speak English when called by the press. Augie Galan was on a hunting trip. Second baseman Eddie Stanky was looking for a new home for his family in Mobile, Alabama.

The phone rang one afternoon in the home of Dixie Walker at 3415 Montevallo Road in Birmingham. The People's Choice of Brooklyn, the most popular player on the team, the leader of the Dodgers, was sitting in his home office doing some paperwork. Estelle Walker answered the phone in her gentle, if recently developed, southern accent.

"Yes, I'll see if he can talk to you," one of the children remembered her saying. She walked a few feet over to where Dixie Walker seemed involved in his paperwork. She told him a reporter from the Associated Press was on the phone. He wanted to know if Dixie had heard the Brooklyn Dodgers, his team since 1939, had signed a Negro player.

"No, I haven't heard it," he told the reporter. "I've been busy here at home since the season ended. We have a lot of work to do in the house." The reporter persisted. He wanted the great star of the Dodgers, the southern gentleman from Birmingham, to make a comment he could put out on the Associated Press wires to more than fifteen hundred newspapers around the world. "Well," Walker finally said, "he's signed with Montreal. It doesn't matter to me as long as he isn't on our club."

Susan Walker, a mother of five and grandmother of six, lives with her husband, Ed, in one of the most upscale integrated communities in America, Northern New Jersey. She smiled when told of the quote attributed to her father more than sixty years ago.

"A different America," she says.

3
The Walkers of Birmingham

World War II ended in 1945. The Germans accepted unconditional surrender on May 7 and the Japanese signed their surrender documents after two atomic bomb attacks in August on their homeland on September 2 on the battleship *Missouri* in Tokyo Bay before General Douglas MacArthur.

More than 17 million men and women had served their country during those war years and now most of them were coming home. Professional baseball players, especially big leaguers, were returning as fast as they could to the playing fields across America.

Bob Feller had returned early enough that year to pitch in nine games with a 5–3 mark for the Cleveland Indians. Hank Greenberg played in seventy-eight games with a .311 average for the Detroit Tigers, including a home run on the last day of the season, helping the Tigers win the American League pennant.

Within a few months dozens of other stars—Joe DiMaggio, Ted Williams, Stan Musial, and hundreds of lesser players—would be returning home to resume their careers.

Harold Henry (Pee Wee) Reese, so-called because he was a successful marbles champion with a marble of that same name and later immortalized as Jackie Robinson's first public Brooklyn supporter, was born outside of Louisville in Ekron, Kentucky, on July 23, 1918. His father was a detective in the railroad yards in Louisville.

Reese was signed by the Boston Red Sox in 1938 and played in their organization for two seasons. He was ready for a big league chance in 1940 but the player-manager of the team, Joe Cronin, was also a shortstop as Reese was and so allowed the smallish infielder to be claimed in a minor league deal by the Brooklyn Dodgers. Reese became their shortstop in 1940 when the Brooklyn player-manager Leo Durocher moved away from the position. Reese was the anchor shortstop on the Dodgers in 1941 when Brooklyn won its first pennant in twenty-one years. Dixie Walker batted .311 for that pennant-winning Brooklyn team.

After the Dodgers lost the 1942 pennant to the St. Louis Cardinals, Reese joined the navy. He was stationed on Guam when the *Enola Gay* dropped the first atomic bomb on Hiroshima on August 9, 1945.

"I was on a ship in the South Pacific coming back from my navy service," Reese once related when asked about the first time he had ever heard the name of Jackie Robinson. "It was late in October 1945. They had dropped the big one at Hiroshima, and I was finally on my way home after two years in the Pacific. I hadn't seen my daughter, Barbara, since I left home when she was eleven days old. I was thinking about that when a sailor came up to me on the ship. He was all excited. He had heard something on the radio he thought might be of interest to me. 'Hey, Pee Wee, the Dodgers just signed a nigger ball player.' I didn't think too much about it. I knew my father wouldn't be overly fond of the idea. The Dodgers were signing a lot of players, and all I was really interested in was getting back home, seeing my wife, Dot, and my family again and resuming my career. A few minutes later the same guy came back. He had heard more about it on the ship's radio. 'The guy's name is Jackie Robinson, and they say he played at UCLA.' It still didn't mean a thing to me. I had never heard of him. Then the sailor said, 'Not only is he a nigger, but he's a shortstop.' Now *that* was different. 'No kidding,' I said. That was the first time I thought of Jackie Robinson. I'll never *stop* thinking about him."

The U.S. Navy was one of the most segregated areas of American life in 1945. Blacks were on board the ship Reese was on as he sailed home. They worked as cooks, hospital attendants, and orderlies for officers. It was a different America.

Reese returned to stardom with the Brooklyn Dodgers, played on pennant winners as a teammate of Robinson in 1947, 1949, 1952, 1953, and on that exalted world championship team in 1955. They would share another pennant with the Dodgers in Robinson's final playing season of 1956.

Later on, Reese would be immortalized as a friend of Robinson's. A magnificent statue of Reese and Robinson with the Dodger captain's arm over the shoulder of his African American teammate sits now outside of KeySpan Stadium in Brooklyn, a minor league home for one of the farm clubs of the New York Mets.

Susan Walker was barely two and a half years old when her baseball-playing father was asked his opinion of the signing by Mr. Rickey. She was born February 16, 1943, spent part of the year in the family's Birmingham home and part of it in the Rockville Centre home.

"The Birmingham home is the one I remember from my childhood," she says. "It was a pink limestone home on an acre of property with a huge stone fireplace and plenty of bedrooms for all of us kids. My mother had this habit of fixing up the house or expanding it every year when my father went off to spring training. I remember one year he came home from baseball and asked my mother, 'Where did this room come from?' She had expanded out front and built a library and a screened in porch."

Susan chased after her older brother, Fred (also called Dixie as her grandfather and father were) and after her sister, Mary Ann. "I guess I was more of a tomboy, climbing trees, catching curve balls from my pitching brother, hitting fungoes to the family pet, never one for the dainty things little girls are supposed to like," she says.

There were two younger brothers, Sean, born in 1949, and Stephen, born in 1954, who kept Susan busy and involved in games as she grew older. She played baseball in the front yard and first base on the school softball team. "I was so good in baseball my father once said I would have easily been a big league player," she says. "He wanted me to take up golf. He said I would be another Babe Didrikson." She took up tennis instead.

There were also two other women in the house that Susan remembers from her early childhood. "Mom always had help with us kids. That was one consolation she had raising a large family. We had two black nannies. They were part of our family. My mother was grateful for their help and demanded respect for them from her children. My dad was businesslike, a southern gentleman, and left the running of the house to my mother," she says.

Susan recalls the two black women as completely different types. "Ophelia helped with the children. She changed them and fed them and dressed them. She was a big woman with a booming voice. She was like a second mother to us. Her word was law when she was left in charge of us during the times that Mom traveled to be with Dixie. I think we were a little frightened of her. Dad built a room and bath for her so she could live with us. She mentioned having a husband but I don't ever remember seeing any man come to the house for her. I don't think I ever knew her last name. I can't recall it ever being mentioned," she says.

Clara was a birdlike figure, very small, very quiet, but a very loving person, who helped with the chores, did the laundry, and worked with Susan's mother, cooking, polishing the furniture, or ironing the girls' dresses so they could stand up by themselves. "She was good company for my Mom when Dad was on the road," Susan says.

"I remember one time she was doing the laundry," Susan recalls, "and there was a pile of dad's undershorts in the basket. 'Should I iron

Mr. Walker's shorts?' she asked. I don't remember what my mother said but it just made me laugh," Susan recalls.

Late each afternoon Estelle Walker would drive Clara, loaded down with food and clothing for her family, back to her home in the black section of Birmingham, drop her off, run some errands, and rush home in time for dinner with Dixie and the children.

That was the daily ritual. The Walkers ate dinner at 6:30. Nobody could miss it. Dixie Walker was in control of the dining room table. Dinner was served family style. "There wasn't a lot of talk at the table except by the adults," Susan remembers. "Children were to be seen but not heard. Mom would put a roast in front of my Dad, a bowl of potatoes, and some vegetables and he would do the serving. Grace was always said at every meal. He would cut the slices of meat, put a potato on the plate, serve up the vegetables and pass the dish down to the farthest end. We always had to ask to be excused from the table after finishing everything on our plates. He would serve us all like that until he was finished. Then he would make his own plate. It was all very formal. When he wasn't home in the summertime we would grab what we could off the table, sort of eat on the run and then rush out to the yard to play, to climb trees, to wrestle around with each other."

There was conflict in the house, Susan remembers her Mom relating, between Dixie's mother, Flossie, and Dixie's wife and the mother of his children, Estelle. "Flossie was very disappointed in her husband. His drinking was a problem," Susan says. "He was unable to support his family, although when Susan was a teenager she remembers him as a loving father who overcame the disease of alcoholism."

His son Dixie was forced to leave school early and went out in the world to support his mother and father. He gave his mother every paycheck to pay the family bills. At a very early age he felt responsible for the welfare of the family. He never had a normal childhood. As a grown man Dixie looked forward to the holidays, especially Christmas. Estelle made sure every holiday was special, with big family meals and lots of presents. When Christmas came along, he wanted to be as surprised as his children and insisted on being the first to see the brightly lit Christmas tree the children had decorated the night before, surrounded with beautifully wrapped gifts. He never experienced anything like that as a child and looked forward to it each year. Dixie believed he had a talent and this talent would get him out of the steel mills. He listened to his heart and this ability led him to be the provider and protector of the family. His father's problems had forced him to forgo his childhood and take a chance on this new life in Birmingham. With his intense work ethic, he was determined to succeed.

"My dad had built this family house of pink limestone from the Alabama mountains during the Depression days of the early 1930s in Colonial Hills," Susan says. "When he married Estelle Mary Shea of New York City he brought her to this home in Birmingham. His mom, dad, and brother Harry were all living in the house with him when Estelle joined them. Flossie was getting the monthly checks to run the house; she immediately resented Estelle for being a northerner and a Roman Catholic. Flossie continued to run the house as if it was completely her own. One day Estelle told Dixie to bring her trunk up from the basement. She was returning to New York City. Dixie could not understand. What was the problem? Estelle laid down the law and demanded her rights as his wife. She would run the household or return to New York. Flossie was shocked when Dixie gave in and told her that Estelle was now in charge. It created years of tension, only resolved after Dixie's dad, Ewart, died in 1965. Estelle was patient and kind with Flossie for the remaining years of her life."

Susan says the last years of Ewart's and Flossie's lives with their son and daughter-in-law were relatively peaceful. "Dixie wanted to lead his father to a sober life so he figured the best thing to do was keep him busy and close by," Susan says. "He and his brother, Harry, built them a ranch house in Hueytown and purchased the hardware store in the same small town. That gave his father a job and the opportunity to build back his self-esteem. It also gave him a reason to be proud of himself as a husband and father. That was just the way it worked out for his final years."

Susan continued her athletic ways through her early teen years. "I just liked to play outside with my brothers as much as I could. With my dad's baseball connections and all that, we didn't have many friends over to the house. We just had fun together. I must have been five or six when I let the brake off our car and it rolled down a hill and hit a tree as I hid below the seat. That was the end of the Studebaker. It was also the end of my driving for a while," she says.

Susan's mother was a devout Roman Catholic and Susan was soon enrolled at Our Lady of Sorrow Catholic School. "The nuns knew who Dad was. Many of them were baseball fans, Brooklyn fans, but they didn't make much of it. I didn't get away with anything," she says.

On special days, holidays, Christmas, New Year's, somebody's birthday, Dixie would go hunting and bring back turkey, quail, or deer for a big family celebration. "There would be wonderful quail with gravy over biscuits that my father made and we would share a great meal. After it was over I would play the piano and sing operatic numbers. Dad loved that. He had a fine voice and enjoyed singing. The house was full of music. My mother just loved music from her days in New York City," Susan says.

Susan was soon enrolled at John Carroll High School in Birmingham, growing into a young beauty, meeting boys besides her brothers, and thinking of college.

"My brother Fred knew I would probably have a date soon, I was thirteen or fourteen, and he wanted to make sure I knew how to act. One day he took me to a movie and we sat up in the balcony. He suddenly moved his arm around my shoulder and then he grabbed my hand and made me slap his arm. 'Now that's what you do when the guys get fresh.' he told me. It was a good lesson learned," she says. Susan recalls her first serious date was with a neighbor. That was all right with her mother who was Catholic as the boy was—but not with her father.

"The boy and I were just sitting in the car talking and he suddenly says out of nowhere, 'Why didn't your father serve in the army in the war?'

I really didn't understand. We had never talked about that at home. I just got out of the car and raced to my own car. I drove home as fast as I could. I saw the lights of a police car but I think they let me go when I raced into our driveway," she says.

As a high school senior Susan sang in the school chorus and had developed into one of the school beauties. No more tomboy. "One of the teachers, the voice coach, came up to me and said she thought I should compete in the Miss Alabama contest. She said I was pretty enough to win it and I had that wonderful singing talent. She gave me some papers that I had to have signed and I took everything home. I was pretty excited about it. I told my mother about it and she seemed supportive. She said, 'We'll talk it over with dad.' When he got home he had his sherry and a nice dinner and then we went into his sitting room. I told him what my voice teacher had suggested.

"No daughter of mine will walk around some stage in a bathing suit," said Dixie Walker.

"I guess that was the end of my chances at a show business career," laughs Susan.

Dixie Walker had dropped out of school and didn't think much of his daughter's ambitions about college and a career. "He was very old-fashioned in that way," she says. "He wanted me to dress well, speak well, have good manners, and meet a young man who could take care of me. 'I don't want you marrying any of those rednecks,' he said one day. He respected my mother for her intelligence, her sophistication, her worldliness from working in New York City, living alone, caring for herself, and helping out with her own family. That's what he wanted for me."

Susan loved singing. She had a beautiful operatic voice and aimed to improve in that area even though her beauty was not to be paraded on a stage.

"I found out there was a wonderful Catholic School up north in Terre Haute, Indiana. I sent them a tape of me singing classical music in Italian. They had a marvelous music program. I applied to the school—St.

Mary's of the Woods—and was accepted with a half scholarship. It was just a few thousand dollars in those days of the late 1950s and early 1960s. My mother encouraged me and said she would pay the rest of my tuition from the family food money. It was amazing how much she could get out of that food money."

Before her senior year at high school, Susan Walker traveled north alone for the first time to a summer music class on the campus of Notre Dame University at South Bend. She was walking across campus to a class one day when she was knocked over by a passing bicycle. "I don't know if it was an accident or not," laughs her husband, Ed, the bike rider. He was an engineering graduate student after having finished his undergraduate work at the famed football university.

He helped her up, asked her why she was on campus, chatted for a few minutes, and asked for her address. He asked if he could write a note to her after the summer ended so they could stay in touch. When he did and Dixie saw her reading the letter, he asked who it was from. She told him it was from a graduate student at Notre Dame who had accidentally run into her.

"Too old for you," Dixie said to his high school senior daughter.

Estelle took the letter and put it in a top drawer of her dresser.

When she prepared to go to school at Terre Haute that fall, her mother suddenly said, "Why don't you write a letter to that nice fellow you met at Notre Dame."

"I was Irish, I was from Notre Dame, and I was a Catholic," says Ed. "That seemed to be enough for her mother even though I had never met her. Dixie didn't like me because he thought I was too old, and because I was Catholic and I was Irish. I think he also didn't like that I was from Notre Dame because he rooted so hard for the University of Alabama."

"My dad was very friendly with Bear Bryant," remembers Susan. "He couldn't shift his loyalties."

Paul "Bear" Bryant, the legendary Alabama football coach who made his fedora hats de rigueur, coached at Alabama. He died in 1983 and is buried in Elmwood Cemetery in Birmingham.

When Susan told her mother she didn't have the address of that nice fellow from Notre Dame, the situation was quickly resolved. Estelle went to her dresser and pulled out the letter Ed had originally sent to Susan.

"I never knew why she saved it, but she did," says Susan.

Susan wrote Ed that she was matriculating at St. Mary's of the Woods in Terre Haute, not to be confused with St. Mary's of the Lake in nearby South Bend, and would be glad to see him again.

"I got off the train from Birmingham and he met me at the station with his friend, Joe Miller [who would later be Ed's best man] in Joe's black convertible Ford. That was fun. They drove me out to school with my steamer trunk hanging over the rear of the car."

Susan was seventeen years old when they met and Ed was twenty-two.

"I was five years and five days older than she was and five years later we were married," Ed recalls. "It was on June 12, 1965."

Dixie Walker was coaching in Milwaukee for an old Brooklyn Dodgers teammate, Bobby Bragan, that summer of 1965. Bragan said Walker could take off with his blessing and attend his daughter's wedding.

"I bought a ring for Susan," recalls Ed, "and somehow it got lost in the mail when I shipped it to Birmingham for Susan to try on. The day before the ceremony I arrived in Milwaukee to drive with Dixie to Alabama. I told him what happened to the ring. I was very upset. He picked up the phone, dialed the postmaster at Birmingham and had him search for the ring. In a little while the package was discovered. The postmaster said it would be delivered immediately to the Walker home at 3415 Montevallo Road in Mountain Brook, a suburb of Birmingham. "That made me breathe easier," says Ed. "Then we got in the car together and started driving south."

They spent about a dozen hours together in the new car, a Chevy Nova convertible similar to Joe Miller's Ford, as they journeyed south. Ed did all the driving. Dixie maintained control of the map. They talked a little bit about Dixie's baseball career; they talked some about hunting and fishing, Dixie's passions; mostly they talked about Susan.

There was one conversation with Dixie that day that Ed remembered many years later. "As we got into Indiana I noticed the route passed very close to the house I had rented for Sue and me for after we were married," Ed says. "It was in Munster, Indiana, about a mile from the toll road we were taking. I asked Dixie as we neared Munster if he would like to take a short detour to see where his daughter would be living. I mentioned that I had picked it out myself and Susan hadn't seen it yet. I clearly recall his response. 'Thanks,' Dixie said, 'but I don't think it would be right for me to see the house before Susan did.' I was a bit embarrassed for suggesting something which he saw as not quite proper. I think he visited us some six months later and seemed very pleased that his daughter lived in such a nice place."

The other memorable conversation of more than forty years ago pertained to the car. "I kept pumping the brakes a lot while we were driving, especially down hills. I was an engineer and knew how cars worked. I knew a new car with new brakes needs to be broken in without overheating. Dixie hadn't said much as we neared the Walker home, except for giving directions. Then we arrived after that long trip. When we finally got inside the house he took me aside and said, 'Ed, you better get those brakes fixed.' I just smiled," he says.

The preparations for the large wedding were moving forward under Estelle's direction. The location at "The Club" in Birmingham had been arranged; the guest list of friends and family had been confirmed; and Susan's dress, a sparkling, gorgeous white gown, had been purchased.

"My mother and father had been married before a justice of the peace in Westchester, New York, while my dad was playing with the Yankees," Susan recalls. "My mother never really had a wedding. I think she really looked at my wedding as her own wedding."

Dixie Walker walked his beautiful daughter down the aisle at the Church of Our Lady of Sorrows, as proud that day as he had ever been on a baseball field, even when his clutch hit beat the hated Giants.

Dixie had one more thing to say to Ed after the wedding. "I think she'll be a wonderful asset in your work," Dixie said.

"I was an engineer," says Ed. "I wasn't sure what he meant. She certainly didn't know anything about engineering. I guess he just meant she was very pretty, people would enjoy meeting her, and she would make a great wife."

Ed and Susan soon were on their way to a romantic honeymoon in New Orleans. They dined together in the finest restaurants and enjoyed their first trip as newlyweds to the Deep South, listened to jazz at every corner, and attended many of the famous shows. "We went to this one club and heard a wonderful revue," Ed recalled. "Then when it ended all these beautiful girls who had sung took off their wigs and revealed they were men. That was a little shocking for two kids like us."

Ed had a job in Whiting, Indiana by then and they settled into a beautiful home in Munster, Indiana. As his skills increased, Ed moved around to other locations and then on to Hammond, Indiana, where he worked for a large international oil firm. "When I was a child I always missed my father when he went on all those baseball trips around the country," Susan says. "Now I was a married woman and I was missing my husband when he went on all those business trips to Europe."

Early in 1969 Ed received some sad family news. His father, Arthur, had suffered a massive heart attack and was gone before Ed could make it home from Indiana. "Just a short time later, maybe a month or so, my mother became ill. She suffered a stroke and when I visited her I knew I had to come back and take care of her," he says.

Elizabeth Cahill needed help from her son. Ed and Susan talked it over. They were a young married couple and had just had their third child, Monica Shea, three days prior to the death of Ed's father. Ed was an accomplished engineer. He could get a job almost anywhere.

"He signed up with a headhunter," says Susan. "We told him we wanted a new position in the New York area. In a short time Ed had a good job offer. We packed up and drove to New York City," Susan says.

Susan had been born in Rockville Centre, her mother had been born and raised in New York City and she had often visited as her father's baseball duties demanded, so the move was not traumatic. "The first thing we did was take a New York area map and draw some circles around Ed's Manhattan office," she says. "Before long we knew that New Jersey was the best place for us, for location, for the community, and for the area's wonderful schools and environment."

They settled in the New Jersey town, enjoyed the growth of their family, entertained an occasional visit from Dixie Walker when his baseball chores brought him east, and established a comfortable suburban life. "Every so often somebody would find out I was Dixie Walker's daughter. Maybe Ed told them. I didn't think much of it. We had never made a big deal of it. When I was a teenager and my father was managing at Toronto we were sitting in the stands and some fan started getting on my dad about what a lousy manager he was. This guy didn't like the way he changed pitchers and he didn't like the pinch hitters dad sent up. He was screaming terrible things at him when my father came out to the mound. I finally shouted at him. 'Shut up. That's my father you're talking about.' This guy had a very strange look on his face. My mom just said, 'Susan, just remember you are a lady. Act like one. They are paying fans.' I sat down," she says.

In 1966 the Yankees invited all of the members of the 1941 Brooklyn Dodgers to Yankee Stadium for a twenty-fifth anniversary reunion of the 1941 World Series. The Yankees beat the Dodgers in five games that year. Mickey Owen lost Hugh Casey's breaking ball in the ninth inning of the fourth game with Tommy Henrich swinging and missing it. Dodgers fans never let Owen forget it. Some forty years later Dixie confided to his son-in-law, "I believe we'd have won that Series if Mickey hadn't lost the ball."

"We had been married a little over a year by then," Ed recalls, "and Dixie invited us from our home in Indiana to be guests with him in New York City. We stayed at a fancy hotel in Manhattan, I think it was the Plaza, and rode a limousine to the ball park. I'll never forget it."

Dixie wore his old Brooklyn uniform, number 11, for the first time in about eighteen years and fans shouted at him from the stands. "The People's Choice, the People's Choice," as he waved and signed autographs.

"Dad always signed autographs when he was asked," Susan says. "He had only one rule. He wrote his name but he would always say to us, 'keep walking.' We got to the car as fast as we could."

"I was with Dixie one time and we parked in the players' parking lot at the stadium. The fans rushed up to me and insisted I sign. 'Who do you think I am?' One fan said I was Fritz Peterson of the Yankees. I just signed 'Fritz Peterson' and kept walking," Ed says.

Dixie got Ed on the field with him as the old-timers were being introduced. The current Yankees were sitting on the bench and Dixie knew most of them from his scouting and coaching days even some fifteen years after he had stopped playing.

"He would walk up to a player and tell them I was his son-in-law and he would introduce me, 'This is Mr. Mantle, Mr. Tresh, Mr. Pepitone, Mr. Clarke.' I would say, 'It's so nice to meet you, Mickey, Tommy, Joe, Horace.' I read the sports pages. I knew their names. I think it embarrassed him a little."

After Susan and Ed moved to New Jersey, they built a social life as well as a professional life. Ed worked for an engineering firm in New York and Susan decided when the children were old enough that she would go into sales.

"I was in my thirties by then and the kids were in school. I needed an outside activity. I decided it was time to explore a professional career," she says. "When my dad found out about it he was pretty upset. 'You're supposed to stay home and take care of the family, as any southern woman would.'"

The social activities, the barbecues, the family picnics, the PTA events soon had a common thread. The word had gotten around that Dixie Walker's daughter lived in town. There were enough old Brooklyn fans who remembered him well.

"By what people would say I started realizing he was a pretty popular player around here, pretty well known, pretty important to a lot of old fans. That never seemed to happen at home in Birmingham. There he was just Dixie, the local boy who made good. There was something else that would come up often, surprisingly sometimes, in the middle of a conversation about kids or sales or vacations or whatever. They would say, 'I know the name, Dixie Walker, wasn't he the guy who . . . ?' Then they would stop in midconversation, almost afraid to continue, certain they had crossed some mysterious line. 'Yeah, Dixie Walker,' somebody would say. 'He tried to keep Jackie Robinson out of Brooklyn.' My face would flush. I knew I showed embarrassment. Why? I wasn't sure. I didn't even know for sure what they were referring to. I didn't know much about my father's baseball history. I was too young when he played and when I was older that was all gone, in the past, never discussed."

One evening Susan and Ed hosted a party in their home. One of their friends asked if he could bring his father along. The father was visiting in town and he had heard that his son knew the daughter of the famed baseball player Dixie Walker.

"It was ironic that my dad was in town on one of his scouting trips and he was staying with us. I thought that would work fine. The man came over, a big man, sort of loud, and I introduced him to my father. He told my dad that he was retired, lived in Manhatten, and had worked in the Greenwich Village area. He said he knew a lot of baseball players in the 1950s and 1960s who hung out in some of the bars in the Village. I guess he was explaining to my dad how much he knew about baseball," Susan says.

Then it started.

"He began questioning my father about trying to keep from playing on the same team as Jackie Robinson. My father's face grew red. He never really answered. He was a southern gentleman, remember, and he always acted with calm and dignity."

When dinner was over, Susan still felt extremely embarrassed and bade an early good night to her friend's father.

Susan knew none of her father's history with the Brooklyn Dodgers. She had never heard of any petition that was supposedly organized by Walker in 1947 to keep Robinson off the Dodgers and knew nothing about a letter he had sent to Branch Rickey asking to be traded that year.

All she knew was that her mother and father loved each other, that they provided a loving home for her and her siblings, that her life was a joyous adventure from her earliest memories, that baseball was the biggest part of her father's life away from home. She knew nothing about her father's connection to Jackie Robinson. She knew nothing of that famous, tumultuous baseball season of 1947.

Her father died in 1982. Her mother died in 2002. Now Susan was determined to take on that mission. She would find out what really happened in 1947. What was her father's true place in baseball history?

4
The Walker Family Baseball Dynasty

Dixie Walker discovered his English roots on a vacation trip with Estelle after his retirement. "My grandfather was a bobby in England," Dixie told Bill Lumpkin, the *Birmingham Post-Herald* sportswriter in an extensive 1981 interview conducted in the den of his comfortable Birmingham home at Old Leeds Lane.

"My dad found out the Walker family was from Stanhope, England," recalls Susan Walker. "He was very proud of the family history."

They visited Stanhope, and Dixie and Estelle searched through church records, talked to local people, chatted with town officials, and walked through local graveyards. They found the names of other Walkers on the headstones and they also learned about Dixie's famous and successful nineteenth-century relative Dr. William Robinson, ironically the last name that would connect with Dixie's baseball career in so significant a way.

"Dr. Robinson discovered a very important way of transmitting electrical impulses," says Susan's husband, Ed, an engineer. "It made for the cheaper transmission of electrical power and helped England become the master of industrial growth in the nineteenth and early twentieth century."

"My father was very proud of that," Susan says. "He hadn't had much formal education but when he came back from that trip he got many books out of the library, studied the career of Dr. Robinson, and was thrilled that he was related to such an important English historic figure."

Dixie's grandfather Frederick Walker and his wife, Katherine, had three small children in Stanhope when Frederick decided it was too much of a financial struggle to raise a family in that small English village. They had heard tales from other relatives, from letters to friends, and from articles in the local journals that a hundred years after the end of the Revolutionary War, there was a financial spurt in the Colonies, now the United States of America, that took in all sorts of people. The language spoken there, if strangely accented, was still understandable. The U.S. economy was growing. Land was plentiful and affordable. It would be an adjustment but they could try it for a few years. The boats sailed both ways across the Atlantic if things didn't work out.

Frederick purchased two third-class tickets for himself and his wife and three more tickets for the children. They sailed from England to New York City in the late fall of 1886, gained entrance at the newly opened Ellis Island center for immigrants, and stared at the recently completed gift from France, the Statue of Liberty, in New York harbor. Designed by French sculptor Frederic Auguste Bartholdi, the monument was a gift from the government of France to the people of the United States in commemoration of the hundredth anniversary of the Declaration of Independence and opened ten years after that 1876 date. France had done so much to help the new colonies gain their freedom from the British crown and now Frenchmen, Germans, Italians, Swedes, Norwegians, Poles, Danes, Russians, Finns, Lithuanians, and even Englishmen were pouring into the booming United States.

On October 26, 1886, President Grover Cleveland addressed the crowd of over a thousand people on the Ellis Island home of the 305-foot-tall statue, and said, "We will not forget that Liberty has here made her home, nor shall her chosen altar be neglected."

Frederick, Katherine, and the children were soon on a train to Pittsburgh, Pennsylvania. They had relatives there working in the coal mines. Jobs were plentiful. Frederick was strong enough to change his career from police work to mining, earning eleven dollars a week as he labored to support his family.

The first American Walker, Ewart Gladstone Walker, named by Katherine for a famed British political leader William Ewart Gladstone, was born in Brownsville, Pennsylvania, on June 1, 1887. Her fifth and last child, Ernest Robert Walker, was born September 17, 1890, in Blossburg, Alabama, after the family had moved south for warmer weather and higher-paying jobs. They moved from one coal mining center to another.

By the early 1900s, as Frederick and Katherine purchased their first small home in Blossburg, the boys soon connected with school friends in the growing American game of baseball. Ewart Walker played in the nearby lots, throwing around a tattered tennis ball at first, then obtaining a used baseball, and finally earning enough money by newspaper deliveries to purchase a clean, new baseball for thirty cents.

Like his sturdy father, Ewart was growing tall and strong. He reached six feet by the time he was sixteen years old and was one of the heaviest boys in the sandlot games at close to two hundred pounds. He liked to throw the ball hard. He was almost always the pitcher in those sandlot games. The games began in summer shortly after daylight and continued deep into dusk. Different kids came and went during the days as lineups were changed and arguments raged as to whose turn it was for an at bat. Ewart didn't care as much for the at bats as he cared about firing the ball past his pals.

In 1907 Ewart was discovered by a scout for the Washington Senators. He was signed to a contract, assigned to a D league team in Georgia, where he was to meet his wife, Flossie. He pitched eight scoreless innings in his debut. He lost the game 2–1 on two errors in the ninth inning and said some angry words to his bumbling shortstop.

Ewart continued to improve at the age of nineteen, moved up to a

C league team at the age of twenty where he was 14–7 for the season, and joined the Washington Senators in 1909 at the age of twenty-one.

The first big league player from the state of Alabama, he was joined by his brother Ernie in the big leagues in 1913. Dixie Walker would make his big league debut with the Yankees in 1931, and his brother Harry, Ewart's second son, would make his big league entry with the Cardinals in 1940. Quite a Walker family big league dynasty, perhaps rivaled only by the Alou family, the DiMaggio family, the Boone family, and the Bell family.

Ewart—soon called Dixie by his Washington teammates for his southern heritage despite a Pennsylvania birth—joined a terrible Washington team led by a hard-throwing kid from Humboldt, Kansas, named Walter Johnson. Johnson would win thirteen games that year of 1909 but lost twenty-five as he struggled to find home plate, a rather common ailment for speedball throwers. The next year Johnson would reverse his fortunes and win twenty-five games as he started a streak of ten straight years with twenty or more wins. His reputation grew throughout baseball and many experts consider him the greatest pitcher of all time. Despite Johnson, Washington would lose regularly, mostly finishing at the bottom of the American League, and earning one of the game's most famous denouncements, "First in war, first in peace, and last in the American League."

Ewart Walker was 3–1 in his first season with the Senators and improved to 11–11 in his second year, 1910, with twenty-six starts and sixteen complete games, a figure that would lead the big leagues in endurance in today's game.

Ewart sent Flossie home from the boarding house in Washington where they lived in the summer of 1910. She was expecting her first child and the lonely days when her husband was away for road games was no place for the expectant mother.

Frederick Ewart Walker, blond and gray-eyed, was born in the home of his grandparents in Villa Rica, Georgia, on September 24, 1910. "Dad was in Washington and mother went to stay with my grandparents in Villa Rica until I was born," Dixie Walker once recalled. "She stayed with them until I was old enough to travel. We joined my father the next season in Washington when I was six months old."

And so began an odyssey of travel for Dixie Walker that would include just about every state in the union as he played eighteen years in the big leagues, four years in the minor leagues, managed, coached, scouted, and worked as a batting instructor in a career that would span some fifty-two years.

"Scouting was the one part of his baseball life he never really liked," says Susan Walker. "When you are a scout you are by yourself all the time and always traveling. It did make my father a great letter-writer to my mom. Every letter ended the same way, 'Yours alone, Dixie.' That always touched me."

Ewart Walker was out of the big leagues with a sore arm and a 25–31 lifetime mark in 1913 as his brother Ernie started his major league time with three lackluster seasons with the St. Louis Browns. He averaged .256 over 1913, 1914, and 1915. Ewart was soon coaching and managing minor league teams, working in the nearby mines during the off season. He battled constantly with Flossie.

Dixie grew older and taller and showed some signs of interest in a professional baseball career as his father had. There was encouragement from Ewart Walker until Flossie put her foot down. "No baseball," she announced. "There's no money in it and there's no time to be at home."

Ewart worked in the TCI mines near their new home in Birmingham and young Dixie joined him there under loose child labor laws of the early twentieth century before he was thirteen years old. "My dad never really had a normal childhood," Susan says. "They needed the money so he always worked after school. He was out of school at an early age and was in the mines. Flossie used to tell him the mines would always be steady work, not like that baseball."

"I played football but not baseball while I was still in Minor High School," Dixie recalled. "I guess I got it in my head that I wanted to play baseball. My father had played, he had managed, and I was always around the game. I remember throwing a ball to other kids in the small clubhouses where they played those D or C league games."

One of the managers at the TCI mine told Dixie he would give him a job so he would be eligible to play on the open-hearth team in the next season. "It's a mystery to me why he thought I could play on that team. I had only played sandlot baseball and never really played on an organized team before that," he said. "I was fifteen, a skinny, scrawny kid. I bet I didn't weigh more than 140 pounds, but I played two seasons with the TCI team."

If a kid can throw hard, coaches want him to pitch. If he also can hit hard, he has to play shortstop—the infield glamour position—or center field, the outfield glamour position.

Tall, rangy, standing six feet, one inch tall and weighing about 170 pounds at the age of fifteen, Dixie started on the TCI team at shortstop. He could throw the ball from the hole, he had range, and he was able to stand tough around second base for the double play when some of those burly miners came in to bowl him over. "You played on those teams," said Dixie, "you had to take your licks."

In his second season with the TCI team, while he still worked a full day in the mines, he played a game almost every day through the early spring, throughout the summer, and into the early chill of fall. He developed a unique batting stance, one that would be lionized in Brooklyn some fifteen years later. He batted left-handed though he threw right-handed and stood deep in the batter's box. He crouched a little at the plate, which allowed him to catch the outside pitch, move his bat quickly forward, and line the ball over the second baseman's head for a hit or past the right fielder into the open spaces of the fenceless sandlot fields.

"I always had more fun pulling the ball," he said. "I could hit an outside pitch to left field but I tried to pull that, too. The inside pitches were always good for pulling for me. The idea was to make contact and hit it as hard as you could, not necessarily as far as you could."

In all his playing years and especially in the years when he was a batting coach, Walker was one of the brainiest students of the game. He was a learned hitter but not a guess hitter. He never decided where to hit the ball until he saw the ball. A .306 lifetime big league average indicated he had made the correct decision.

In his second season with TCI, at the age of sixteen, he played in an all-star pickup game in Birmingham against a team from Mobile. There were hundreds of people in the school stands where the game was played, including his father, Ewart, who was able that day to sit in a corner bench near the right field foul line.

"It was the first time I remember Father being at any of my games," he recalled. "It was pretty scary for me, my father being a big leaguer and all that, and I was pretty nervous."

There was one other problem for Dixie during that late September game in 1926. A better shortstop, a better hitter, and an older guy was also on that team. His name was Ben Chapman. Dixie would have to move to center field that day because Chapman, eighteen, was the best shortstop around town.

Dixie later played with Ben Chapman on the Yankees in the early 1930s and again during the war years of 1944 and 1945 when the forty-four-year-old Chapman returned to Brooklyn as a pitcher, pinch hitter, and outfielder during the years when there was such a great absence of talent. The bottom was probably reached in baseball when a one-armed outfielder named Pete Gray hit .218 in 1945 for the defending American League champion St. Louis Browns.

While Dixie was a mild man off the field, soft spoken, gentle in his ways, charming around his elders and women, Chapman was loud, tough, aggressive, and opinionated. He played the game hard, in a fashion identified with Ty Cobb in the earlier part of the twentieth century, drawing blood when he had to on the bases, asking no favors, and being pals with no one, neither teammates nor opponents.

"We were all competitive. That's how we made our living," Chapman said in a 1987 interview.

He was a Nashville, Tennessee, native who had moved to Birmingham with his family as a youngster, signed with the Yankees in 1927, and joined the team of Babe Ruth and Lou Gehrig in 1930. He had a lifetime batting mark of .302 over fifteen seasons. Dixie and Ben Chapman would become close friends and connect in later years in personal and professional ways.

On that September day in 1926, Dixie moved to center field for the first time and Chapman played shortstop. "We kidded about that day later on when we were teammates. Ben always said he made my career by pushing me to center field. I think he was suggesting I couldn't make it as a big league shortstop. I hope he was kidding," Dixie said. "If you could hit—and I could hit—you could make it at any position."

Dixie must have known the nonfielding position of designated hitter was coming years before it arrived in 1973. All a DH has to do is hit.

Walker's performances for the TCI team, even after Chapman pushed him off his position, began to gain notice. Dixie played for several other teams, a game here, a game there, pickup sandlot games mostly, just with the other kids who never could get enough baseball.

A bird dog came to see Dixie after a TCI game. Bird dogs are the lightly paid or in those days often unpaid scouts for big league teams or minor league organizations. They sit in the stands and jot down facts for the team's office about a young kid: can he run, can he throw, is he big enough, does he have any power, is he aggressive or lazy on the field, does he have the potential to become a full-time big league baseball player?

Lee MacPhail, a lifetime baseball executive and son of Larry Mac-Phail, the general manager who brought the Brooklyn Dodgers to prominence in the 1940s, once told a writer about his experience with scouting. "On any summer day in America some 6 or 7 million kids, ages six, seven, or eight, pick up a baseball for the first time. In ten years or so you might sign a hundred of them. How many do you think make the big leagues of that group? One, maybe two if your scouting system is the best in the game," he said.

A bird dog saw young Frederick Ewart Walker play several games on local sandlots. He liked what he saw. That left-handed swing was quick and level. He played with intensity. His arm was good from the outfield. He could throw. He covered ground easily, not as fast as some, but adequate for a big league level. He knew a ball from a strike, rarely chasing another kid's pitch over his head or down at his shoe tops. He was tall, good looking, trim, athletic looking.

"The hardest part of baseball," Lee MacPhail said in a conversation, "is looking at a kid of sixteen or seventeen and projecting what he might be, what he might look like at twenty-two or twenty-three. Try that with your own kids. See how many times you are wrong."

So many factors take a youngster away from maximizing his athletic potential, girls in lots of cases, drinking, drug use, lack of desire, outside interests, different career possibilities, family pressures, or dozens of other factors.

The bird dog asked Fred Walker if he was interested in coming down to the stadium of the independent Birmingham Barons baseball team for a tryout. No promises. "Sure," Walker said, knowing the ways of the game from his dad's experiences. "Why not?"

His father was pleased but not excited. He knew the ways of the game, too. Flossie was aggravated. "They'll just break your heart," she said. "Go back to the mines."

The scout told Dixie Walker that they wanted to give him a good look, a full tryout over two weeks with lots of instruction from their coaches, hitting drills, fielding, running, throwing, the works. When could he do it?

"TCI wouldn't give me the time off," Dixie told Bill Lumpkin for his *Birmingham Post-Herald* series in 1981. "I was operating an overhead crane at the time. I decided if they wouldn't let me off, I'd get laid off. I was moving a vat of hot steel and jerked it on purpose. The handle on the vat snapped and the metal spilled out on the floor below."

Dixie wasn't hurt in the incident but the floor foreman thought the seventeen-year-old boy was a danger to others in the mine. He decided to send the youngster away, hoping he would mend his ways and come back as a more careful worker. Eighteen dollars a week for a kid that age wasn't to be sneezed at. "They laid me off without pay for two weeks," Walker remembered. "The next day I went to work out with the Barons."

Fred Walker saw his name on a chalk board when he arrived at eight o'clock at the Birmingham ball park that early spring morning in 1928. He was listed among the youngsters who would move to the deepest part of the outfield and show the grizzled old coaches, some chewing tobacco, some smoking cigarettes on the field, few seemingly interested, if he could run. If a kid can't run he will never hit, field, or throw in a baseball tryout camp. That's just the way it was. Now the DH has changed all that. If he can hit he might be able to play. Someone else would run for him when it mattered.

So he ran. Good enough to get into the field for some fly balls. He caught all of them easily. He was asked to throw. He did that, accurately, hard enough, intelligently, to the right spot where an infielder could make a play on it. Then he hit. That stance. The bat back, the small crouch, the quick bat, the fast follow-through. The sounds of the baseball jumping off the bat. Whack, whack, whack. There is no sound like it. No music, no parade, no artificial ball park entertainment in the twenty-first century. The scouts listen for it. The experienced ones never even have to turn around to watch. Good hitters make that perfect contact. Mickey Mantle used to stop practice with the Yankees in his first spring training camp in Phoenix, Arizona, with them in 1951. Whack. The scouts knew. The other players knew. Even the fans knew. Stop eating that hot dog. Just listen. Whack.

At the end of the two weeks, with his mining job probably behind him, with no education to speak of, with no skills to call on for a career, young Fred Walker was called into the small office of the Barons. He was offered $500 for his signature on a contract. He was too young to make it official so he was told to take the papers home and get his father to sign it.

Ewart Walker agreed. Flossie was angry.

"Don't do it," she said.

He signed the document on the small table in the living room. His little brother, Harry, watched as he wrote out his entire name for the first time anybody could remember, Frederick Ewart Walker, in the spot where the team executive had told him to sign.

"Me, too," said the little brother who would later sign a contract with the Cardinals and become known in baseball as Harry (the Hat) Walker, 1947 batting champion, three-time World Series player with the Cardinals, longtime manager, and to many, Walker the Talker.

"Harry did love to talk," says Susan. "But he was always interesting and entertaining."

"I remember going to a reunion with him of his World War II unit," recalls Susan's husband, Ed. "He sure did talk a lot but they all enjoyed him. Oh yeah, one other thing. They all confirmed his story when he told of killing three Nazi soldiers on a bridge in Germany with just a pistol."

Dixie also got even with old pal Ben Chapman for pushing him off shortstop with that signing.

"I once asked Ben how much he got when he signed with the Yankees around that time. He said he didn't get anything. I just laughed at that," Dixie said.

Walker worked out with the Birmingham club, but while chasing a fly ball in spring practice, he turned his ankle and broke a bone. Six weeks later, when he was still not able to run well, Birmingham assigned the youngster to Greensboro, North Carolina. He batted .167 in six games and was assigned to a lower league team in Albany, Georgia. He batted .273 there in sixteen games with his first professional home run and was moved up to Gulfport, Mississippi, near Pascagoula, where he had lived as a child while his father was managing there. His brother Harry was born there on October 22, 1916.

Fred Walker, still a couple of years from earning the nickname Dixie as his father had, played well at Gulfport, Mississippi, in the Cotton State League. He batted .293 in eighty-two games there, hit another homer, and brought his last salary check for the season, $130, back home to Flossie. Not much had changed.

"You'll never make any money," she said. "Your father never did."

Young Fred spent the winter hunting around home, working in the family garden, putting in part-time hours at local stores for some small income, exercising daily, working on housing crews, dreaming of the next baseball season.

He was off to spring training in early March of 1930 with the Vicks-burg, Mississippi, club where he batted .318 in sixty-one games. It earned him a promotion to Greenville, South Carolina, in the old Sally (South Atlantic) League where he batted a whopping .401 in seventy-three games.

One other thing happened. He gave up those leathery small-fingered gloves. He was no longer a shortstop or a third baseman. He was now a full-time outfielder as his body had filled out to a trim, muscular 175 pounds.

"I had heard by then that the Yankees were looking at me. That stuff always gets around in the minor leagues. People talk. But nothing happened and I had no contact with anybody from the Yankees," he remembered.

The Yankees of Ruth and Gehrig were also the Yankees of enormous resources. They spent more money on scouting than any other team and their scouting director, George Weiss, was as renowned for spotting talent as he was for his parsimonious ways. In later years Weiss also had another claim to fame after he sat out the 1961 season and then was hired to build a new team in New York—the New York Mets.

"I later was told," Dixie Walker would one day reveal, "that the Yankees had been interested in me for some time but had heard I had a real drinking problem. Heck, I didn't ever drink. I didn't even know what the stuff tasted like." The Yankees probably had *this* Dixie Walker—though he was still called Fred in newspaper articles—mixed up with the *other* Dixie Walker, his father and by now clearly identified as a serious drinker.

Drinking to excess has ravaged many careers. But sometimes it doesn't matter. Maybe Babe Ruth was an alcoholic. He still hit 714 homers. Mickey Mantle drank excessively from the time he joined the Yankees at eighteen until just before he died at the age of sixty-three in 1995. "If I knew I would feel this good," he said at a press conference in his New York City restaurant, Mickey Mantle's, shortly after he took the cure, "I never would have started." Legendary pitcher Grover Cleveland Alexander came on to close out the 1926 Series win for the St. Louis Cardinals despite being thirty-nine years old and a confirmed alcoholic. Go figure.

The Yankees purchased Walker's contract from Greenville. They assigned him to their best and nearest farm club in Jersey City, New Jersey, so he could play against the toughest minor league opposition and also so they could see if he was ready for the Yankees.

"The day the Yankees signed me the fans in Greenville took up a collection in the stands and gave me a warm send-off and a few hundred bucks," Walker said.

He would leave Greenville for Jersey City, New Jersey, by train in early July. He played in eighty-three games, batted .335, hit seven homers, and knocked in forty-one runs for the Jersey Yankees.

Was he popular in Greenville? You bet. When fans take up a collection for a player they are showing how much they care. All Dixie had to do now was wait a few years until he got to Brooklyn if he really wanted to see affection between a player and the populace.

He was twenty years old at the end of that 1930 season. He learned to find his way around New York City, met up with a few of the players he had known in his two professional seasons, and quickly established himself as a guy who stood up for his baseball rights.

"I was making $275 a month in Greenville and when I got promoted the Yankees offered me $300 a month. That was a pretty good salary in those days. Remember the stock market had crashed and the Depression was growing deeper. I remember walking in the streets of New York City. I saw guys standing on street corners with nice suits selling apples. It made me cry," he said.

Susan Walker said her father was always tight with a buck, a throwback to his days in the Depression. "My mother was a spender and my father was frugal. He often mentioned the Depression and how tough times were then. She grew up at the same time but she knew how to make a fine home. She made good use of her seven family inheritances and his pay," she says.

"One of the other players had told me that big league prospects got $500 a month. I knew I was a good big league prospect. That's what I wanted," Dixie said. "I got to Jersey City and insisted on that amount." The general manager of the Jersey City club called the Yankees and told them about this reluctant rookie. They told him not to budge. The price was $300. Walker didn't budge, either.

He stayed away from the ball park the next day. He threatened to get back on the train and return home to Alabama. He got a call, finally, from the general manager who had arranged for the hotel room. He was told to be at the park early the next morning. Everything would be worked out. He was given the $500 a month salary for the last three months of the 1930 season. Again, he signed his name to a contract.

This is the same player, Dixie Walker, who less than fifteen years later, would be instrumental, along with Yankee pitcher Johnny Murphy, in obtaining a pension from the tight-fisted owners, for the first time, for players after retirement. It would be more than a two-year battle but finally, in 1947, the pension was established based on time in the game. There would also be a plan that carried over to the widows of former players. When Estelle Shea Walker, Dixie's wife of forty-six years, died in 2002, she was receiving a pension of $38,000 a year as a player's widow.

"With that and social security and my father's careful investments and savings," says Susan Walker, "she was able to live out her life comfortably after my dad died."

Walker batted .335 in eighty-three games and clearly was marked as a prospect.

Walker played his first game for that team on a Sunday, got a couple of hits, and played center field. One other thing happened that day. Jim Ogle, a longtime sportswriter for the *Newark Ledger,* always did his homework. He knew that the new outfielder was the son of Dixie Walker, the pitcher who had been on the Washington Senators with Walter Johnson, and that this new kid, Fred Walker, hailed from Alabama.

"Young Dixie Walker was in center field yesterday for the Jersey City Yankees," Ogle wrote in Monday's paper. "I never heard my mom call him anything but Dixie," says Susan Walker. "Once in a while Flossie used to call him Fred. Nobody else. I guess from that time on he was always Dixie."

Maybe Red Barber would remind the fans in Brooklyn once in a while that he was named Fred or maybe a fan, derisively after a bad strikeout, would yell out, 'Hey, Fred,' or maybe a kidding opponent would singsong Fred. But to one and all, through all those years of baseball and beyond, he was always Dixie.

Now it was time for Dixie Walker to make it across the Hudson River and up to the Bronx. Now it was time for Dixie Walker to join the New York Yankees. Now it was time for his first shot in the exalted big leagues.

Oh yeah. Babe Ruth better watch out. Dixie Walker was on his way to Yankee Stadium.

Watch Out, Babe, Dixie Is Coming

Joe McCarthy won a pennant with the Chicago Cubs as manager of the Windy City team in 1929. He lost the World Series in five games to Connie Mack's powerful Philadelphia A's, a team that had shattered the Yankees with an eighteen-game pennant lead. It had been 21 years since the Cubs had last won a Series, a drought that would be at 102 years old and counting by 2010.

The Yankees under gregarious former pitcher Bob Shawkey had a third place finish in 1930, this time sixteen games behind the impressive A's. McCarthy, meanwhile, lost his hold on his Chicago job to a fading .400 hitter, Rogers Hornsby, who undermined McCarthy as a player, defied him openly, and won over Cubs management for the top field position.

Colonel Jacob Ruppert, the beer baron and Yankees owner, decided that the gabby Shawkey was not the man to lead his team back to the greatness of 1927 and 1928. He went after McCarthy and signed him to a one-year contract for the 1931 season. It enraged Babe Ruth, the game's greatest star, who was still a powerhouse and the most popular player in the game at age thirty-six. He wanted the job as field boss of the Yankees as player-manager, an arrangement that was not uncommon in the 1920s and 1930s.

Ruth visited Ruppert and requested the field boss job after the 1930 season; Ruppert wouldn't even give him a serious interview. "He can't manage the team if he can't manage himself," the staid German bachelor boss of the Yankees said of the high-living outfielder.

It was a sour Babe who hit .373 and a league-leading forty-six home runs in his last all-round exceptional season for the Yankees in 1931 under McCarthy. Babe would never get over the sting of being ignored by the Yankee brass for a managerial position and it was with a wounded heart over that slight that he took his last breath of life in 1948.

The Yankees finished second that 1931 season, thirteen and a half games behind the rampaging Philadelphia A's. With sportswriters suggesting the team was suffering from the common baseball ailment of aging, new opportunities for young players appeared.

Dixie Walker, coming off his .335 finish with Jersey City in 1930, earned a spot on the Yankees roster for spring training in 1931. He was twenty years old. He rode the train from Birmingham, Alabama, to St. Petersburg, Florida, checked into the team's headquarters on the beach at the Soreno Hotel, got his uniform from clubhouse man Pete Sheehy, and shagged fly balls in the outfield near the Babe.

He was soon dispatched to the training camp of the Toledo Mud Hens. The Yankees were loaded with talented outfielders including the Babe; future Hall of Famer Earle Combs; Ben Chapman; Dixie's pal Sam Byrd, who also lived in Birmingham; and Dusty Cooke. No use keeping a promising kid like Dixie around just to shag flies and relieve the Babe on hot days. He was sent to Toledo where he could play every day and hone his skills.

In July, Dusty Cooke injured his shoulder, and the Babe, fighting off that aging process, came down with a serious viral infection. The Yankees needed a substitute outfielder. Toledo manager Casey Stengel called Walker into his office. "You're going up to New York," he told the twenty-year-old outfielder. "The Babe needs some rest."

Stengel and the Babe had collided many times throughout their careers, starting with the Babe's pitching performance against Brooklyn in the 1916 World Series. Stengel batted .364 in four games to lead the

Dodgers at bat in the Series but was benched by manager Wilbert Robinson against the young Boston lefthander, Ruth, in a game won by Ruth and the Red Sox 2–1 in fourteen innings. It angered Stengel for the rest of his career that he was "platooned" by Uncle Robbie against the Babe. "Maybe I wouldna hit him or maybe I woulda," Stengel said some forty years later, "but nobody else did much, either."

Walker was instructed to join the Yankees in Washington, D.C. "When they called me up they were playing a series in Washington," Walker recalled in his 1981 interview with Bill Lumpkin. "My father had played there. Gosh. That was a great pleasure for me, starting in the major leagues where my father had played."

Walker's adjustment to big league play was made easier by two teammates, old pal Ben Chapman and new pal Sammy Byrd, both young, flashy Yankee outfielders on the Babe and Lou Gehrig's Yankees under McCarthy. "It may be the first and only time in the big leagues that three players from the same town [Birmingham] started in the same outfield in the majors," Walker said. "We played together numerous times."

Joe Sewell, a diminutive shortstop, was also a member of that 1931 Yankees team. Sewell, who set a big league record for fewest strikeouts in a season, with only three in 1932, and was elected to the Hall of Fame in 1977, was born in Titus, Alabama, in 1898. He died in Mobile in 1990. Sewell stood maybe five feet, seven inches in his playing days and weighed possibly 155 pounds. "I can't remember if all four of us were ever in the same lineup," Walker told Lumpkin. "But it is very possible we could have been there at the same time."

Box scores from 1933 reveal that the four players from Alabama, Walker, Chapman, Byrd, and Sewell were in many games together that year, a far cry from the original big league arrival of Ewart (Dixie) Walker, Fred's dad, with the Washington Senators as the first representative from the state in 1909.

Walker's 1931 debut with the Yankees was auspicious for the youngster who had hit .401 at Greenville and .335 after his call-up to Jersey City in midseason. Walker broke in against one of the league's best pitchers, big Washington right-hander Firpo Marberry, who had won nineteen games for the Washington Senators in 1929 under skipper Walter Johnson, the Big Train, who had succeeded player-manager Bucky Harris. He repeated another strong season in 1930 with a 15–5 mark and would go on to a 16–4 record in that 1931 season.

Ruth was out of the lineup with a virus; Dixie replaced him in manager Joe McCarthy's starting lineup in left field. With only day games played then, Ruth alternated between right and left field depending on the intensity of the sun. In New York's new Yankee Stadium, the House That Ruth Built (fifty-four and fifty-nine homers in his first two Yankee seasons after coming over from Boston), he played mostly in right field. Left field was the tough sun field in the Bronx. "It gets late early out there," wordsmith Yogi Berra would say after teammate Norm Siebern botched a couple of World Series fly balls in left against the Brooklyn Dodgers.

So Walker was in left field for the Babe; Marberry, who would win 147 games in fourteen years, was on the mound; and McCarthy was studying the promising kid from Birmingham. Walker got a double on the first pitch from Marberry in his big league debut. He hit another double, knocked in a run with a single, and caught three fly balls effortlessly in a 6–2 Yankee win.

"Not a bad debut, eh?" he reminisced years later. "I wasn't nervous, either. I had been in professional four years by then, I had been in spring training with the team, and I was comfortable with the guys, especially the other boys from Birmingham."

In the days of eight team leagues and four hundred big league ball players, jobs were scarce and hard to come by. Tradition kept youngsters away from batting practice a good part of the time lest they show off and beat a regular out of a job. Dixie never recalled any of that trauma.

"When it was my turn to hit I hit," he recalled. "Ben [Chapman] always stood near by and he was a pretty outspoken guy. Not too many guys would stand in my way." Walker also recalled that Lou Gehrig, soon to be the Yankees captain, also helped him get his batting practice time in the cage. "Lou was quite a big fellow and pretty important on that team," Dixie recalled. "He just waved me in there and nobody argued."

Walker had one more start for the Yankees that July week, went hitless, and sat on the bench as Ruth returned to the lineup after he felt better. "Babe got back in the lineup by the end of the week and was bustin' homers [he led the league again with forty-six that year] as soon as he got back in the lineup. Me? I was back in the International League," Walker said.

Walker went home to Birmingham over the winter, did some part-time work in the steel mills, tried to fatten up on Flossie's food (she was still against her son's baseball career), and looked forward to the 1932 season.

He would be twenty-one years old the next spring and Ruth would be thirty-seven. All the baseball signs were there that the blond-haired, gray-eyed, soft-spoken youngster from Birmingham would be the successor to the Babe. When would it happen?

Ruth had a virus in 1931, injured his foot in a slide at third base, and ripped open a finger on the outfield chicken wire fence. "It's hell to get older," Ruth biographer Robert Creamer quoted him as saying that year in Creamer's brilliant study of the Babe, *Babe: The Legend Comes to Life*.

Ruth had his last big year for the Yankees in 1932. He was thirty-seven years old. He batted .341, hit forty-one homers, and knocked in 137 runs. The Yankees won the pennant and the highlight of the Series win against the Cubs in a four-game sweep was Ruth's third game home run off Cubs pitcher Charlie Root. That was the famous pointed shot in Wrigley Field.

This was an era when bench jockeys, so called because they were good at needling the other team's players, often kept their jobs with their sharp tongues rather than their quick bats. The Yankees had traded a well-liked shortstop named Mark Koenig to the Detroit Tigers in 1930 and the Tigers had sent him to the Cubs in 1932. Koenig, who backed up starter Billy Jurges after being called up from the minors, had hit

.353 in thirty-three games. Since he was not with the team all season, Koenig had to be voted a part of the Series money by his teammates. They voted him a share of six hundred dollars; a full share was worth more than twelve hundred.

The Yankees, almost always generous in Series shares with part-time players, began needling the Cubs for being cheapskates with the opening game. Ruth, who loved to howl sarcastically at opponents, was one of the most vocal of the bench jockeys. Likewise, the Cubs, with pitcher Guy Bush, Charlie Grimm, Gabby Hartnett, Billy Herman, and Jurges leading the howling, verbally attacked the Yankees, especially the center of the storm, the Bambino. "They got on him because he was getting fat and couldn't run anymore," *New York Times* sportswriter John Drebinger once said. "The Babe told me he heard the worst curse from the Cubs dugout when one of the players called him 'nigger lips.'"

Writer Bob Creamer reported, "The Cubs dragged out the old 'nigger' cry. Guy Bush, a dark-haired, swarthy Mississippian, was Chicago's starting pitcher in the first game and some of the Yankees answered back, 'Who are you calling a nigger? Look at your pitcher.'"

The Babe answered all of this back by hitting .333 in the Series with two homers (Lou Gehrig hit .529 with three homers) and saving his best show for the third game. He hit a two out, two strike pitch into the bleachers after purportedly pointing out to center field. Legend has it that Ruth was pointing to the spot where he soon homered but Root insisted throughout his lifetime that no such a thing happened. "I would have knocked him down if he did that," he said.

The Yankees won the game 7–5, clinched the Series the next day with a 13–6 victory, and Ruth entertained sportswriters for years with various versions of the called shot.

Dixie Walker, meanwhile, put together an incredible minor league season. He batted .350 at Newark, smacked fifteen homers, and knocked in 105 runs. There was no way the Yankees could keep him off the big club in 1933.

Walker made the Yankees in 1933, got into ninety-eight games as a rookie backup for Ruth in right field, especially in the late afternoon of sunny days, hit .274, showed his left-handed power with fifteen homers, and knocked in 51 runs. His short, quick, left-handed swing was perfect for Yankee Stadium with its 295 feet to the right field foul pole and a three-foot-high wall.

Ruth, heavier, slower afoot, and less interested in his performance, struggled through the 1933 and 1934 seasons before being dispatched for his final days as the game's greatest player and celebrity to the Boston Braves. He ended his career in Boston shortly after hitting three homers in one game.

As Ruth slipped with the Yankees in 1933 and 1934 and moved on in 1935, Walker lost his chance to take over the Babe's vacated spot. He had a series of injuries to his knee and to his shoulder. He also suffered from stomach pains during and after most baseball seasons. "He had stomach discomfort throughout his life," recalls Susan Walker. "He was always careful about what he ate."

A shoulder injury suffered with the Yankees really had an impact on Walker's early career. He couldn't throw well enough to play regularly with the Yankees. "We were playing the White Sox," Walker once recalled, "and I was knocked down twice on successive pitches. The catcher was Charlie Berry, a former pro football player, and I got up after the second knockdown and told him I would be coming home hard some day."

Walker had what seemed like his chance later that year. He was on second base when George Selkirk lined a single to right field. Walker ran hard around third and came home standing up as the ball was thrown to Berry, protecting the plate, at home. He crashed into Berry with the full force of his muscular body. The bulky Berry held firm and Dixie went flying. "I was called out and what was worse I dislocated my shoulder," he said.

"Joe McCarthy was the Yankee manager," Walker told Bill Lumpkin. "He hated to see a ball player on the rubbing table. He made me go to bat twice with the bad shoulder. That didn't help."

Doc Painter was the longtime Yankees trainer, and his primary job was pulling and tugging and rubbing the arms and shoulders of pitchers. Any other treatment on players by Painter was frowned upon by McCarthy. In an exhibition game in spring training in 1934 Walker slid hard into second base and reinjured the shoulder. He got to bat only seventeen times during the season of 1934 with only two hits, a miserable summer for the twenty-three-year-old who had hoped to replace the Babe.

Dixie went on the voluntary retired list so the Yankees could replace him on the roster. He went home to Birmingham, had a doctor place his shoulder in a cast, and waited for a natural recovery. The shoulder still pained him when the cast was removed.

"I read an article in a local paper that winter that said tonsils and appendix could keep injuries from healing," Walker remembered. "I went to another doctor and he took x-rays of the shoulder. He saw no problem. He asked me to open my mouth so he could see my tonsils. I told him they had been removed but he said they sometimes grew back. He looked again and said that was my problem so I had the tonsils removed a second time."

Walker played in only seventeen games in the 1934 season and eight more in 1935 before he was sent back to the minor leagues in Newark. Despite the shoulder and knee problems, he still had a .293 average in eighty-nine games.

He was back with the Yankees in New York at the end of the 1935 season. Babe Ruth was gone now and the openings in the Yankees outfield were there for the taking. Walker could not take one of them earlier because of his physical problems. In September he seemed to believe that would finally all change. "I was in New York with [fellow Yankees outfielder] Sam Byrd and his wife and walked past a fruit stand. I picked up an apple and threw it across the street," Dixie recalled. "I knew then my arm was better."

He looked optimistically toward the start of spring training in 1936. He was now twenty-five years old, had certainly adjusted to the Yankees and the big leagues with parts of four seasons at the stadium, and felt he could make it to the rebuilt Yankees outfield.

In November 1934 the Yankees purchased Joe DiMaggio, the Pacific Coast League hotshot who had once hit in sixty-one straight games for the San Francisco Seals, for delivery after the 1935 season. DiMaggio, who had scared off a lot of baseball suitors with a knee problem, was obtained for twenty-five thousand dollars and five journeyman players, third baseman Ed Farrell, pitchers Jim Densmore and Floyd Newkirk, first baseman Les Powers, and outfielder Ted Norbert.

"I was a big star football player at Boston College and had scored a touchdown the day the DiMaggio deal was announced," remembered Til Ferdenzi, later a *New York Journal-American* sportswriter covering the Yankees. "I had the clipping from the *Boston Globe*. It said in big letters, 'Ferdenzi Scores Key TD.' Then under that story, in much smaller type, there was another story. 'Yankees Obtain DiMaggio.' I always carried it in my wallet and when DiMaggio would do something big like the '41 streak [he hit in fifty-six consecutive games] or win a game with a homer, I would pull the clipping out and let the other sportswriters see it while DiMaggio talked to us. It always upset him."

DiMaggio hit .398 in his final minor league season with the San Francisco Seals, led the league with 154 RBIs, and hit thirty-four home runs. DiMaggio had no doubts about his ultimate big league success. "I was cocky, confident, call it what you want," he said years later. "I knew I could play. But I kept it inside myself, inside the shell."

DiMaggio drove to St. Petersburg, Florida, from his San Francisco home with new teammates Frank Crosetti and future Hall of Famer Tony Lazzeri. "I knew Joe's older brother, Vince," recalled Crosetti. "He asked me to watch out for the kid. Lazzeri lived in the same Italian section of San Francisco in North Beach. He called the kid up and arranged the drive south to Florida. You could see DiMaggio was really excited being around Lazzeri."

Crosetti and Lazzeri were both pretty silent fellows. DiMaggio, a twenty-one-year-old old rookie, was even more withdrawn on that car ride than he was normally. "He didn't say a word on the trip for the first few hours," said Crosetti. "His eyes were open wide and he just watched the country roll by. We sat in the front and after two or three hours I would look at Tony or he would look at me and ask, 'Wanna drive?' We'd shift places and that was all the conversation there that went on in the car. Around the third day I turned to Tony and said we ought to ask the kid to drive. Tony turned to DiMaggio in the backseat and asked, 'Wanna drive, kid?'"

"I don't know how," DiMaggio said.

"That was it," Crosetti said years later. "I don't think DiMag said another thing the rest of the trip."

When DiMaggio, the highly touted rookie, arrived for manager Joe McCarthy's training camp with the Yankees, the press hounded him from the first day. Nobody wrote any articles about Dixie Walker that spring. His injuries and various ailments seemed to cause an anxious press to write him off as a serious prospect. DiMaggio was the golden boy in the Yankees' 1936 camp. Dixie Walker was the forgotten boy.

George Selkirk had taken over right field for the Yankees in place of Ruth. He wore the Babe's number 3 on his back, batted in the Babe's third spot in the order, and was expected to supply much of the team's lost power. Journeyman Roy Johnson was in left field; Birmingham pal Ben Chapman was in center field as DiMaggio nursed a foot injury until May 3; and Selkirk was in right. Dixie was on the bench next to young DiMaggio. On that May 3 day, DiMaggio was inserted in the lineup in left field; Johnson was benched; Chapman stayed in center; and Selkirk held down right.

DiMaggio had three hits in his first big league game. A week later he hit the first of his 29 homers for that year and the first of his 361 career homers. The pitcher was left-hander George Turbeville of Turbeville, South Carolina. DiMaggio was on his way to his brilliant Hall of Fame career. Dixie was on his way to Chicago.

With DiMaggio ready to play in early May and Chapman and Selkirk settling in as regular Yankee outfielders, there was no need to keep the sore-shouldered Walker around any more. On May 2, 1936, McCarthy called Walker into his office and informed him he had been traded to the Chicago White Sox for the waiver price of $3,500. "I was hitting about .350 in the early games," Walker recalled. "We were playing the White Sox that day and McCarthy called me just before the game to tell me I was going to Chicago. I wasn't upset. I thought with DiMaggio around now I wouldn't have much chance to play regularly in the Yankee outfield. I thought I could be an everyday player with Chicago."

Chicago manager Jimmy Dykes was excited about getting Walker for his ball club. Dixie had proven that he could hit big league pitching, he could field, he could run, and he hustled. The only question was that damaged right shoulder. Could he throw? Walker started off well with the White Sox. Then he injured his shoulder again when he dove back to first base on a close pickoff play. The White Sox decided that the shoulder should be surgically repaired.

Bob Phillips, a sportswriter for the *Birmingham Post-Herald*, wrote an article in 1937 describing the repairs to Walker's shoulder. "The arm which kept him out of the Yankee lineup for years has been fixed once and for all," Phillips wrote. "Dixie is rather confident. It gave him trouble for the umpteenth time just after joining the White Sox in 1936. An operation had been put off but Walker made up his mind this time to let the doctors do some carving and he hasn't a regret for his decision. He played every game in the 1937 season and that's something he hasn't done in years."

Phillips continued, "Dr. Phil Kreucher of Chicago is the surgeon that did the job. Technical descriptions of his methods would be uninteresting to the layman but suffice it to say the job was a revolutionary one. Kreucher himself had not tried it before but since has performed the same operation successfully on several other persons. As far as he knows, Dixie Walker is the only big league baseball player to have undergone it."

Walker made an off-season trip to Chicago after the 1936 season to attend a lecture by Dr. Kreucher on that particular type of shoulder operation. In 1974 Tommy John became famous for elbow surgery by Dr. Frank Jobe, in which elbow ligament was replaced by a tendon in a procedure called ulnar collateral ligament reconstruction. Commonly known as Tommy John surgery, it has become standard procedure for injured pitchers. Almost forty years earlier, Walker had made baseball history with this procedure.

In an article in the *Chicago Tribune* by a staff correspondent shortly after the surgery had been completed, White Sox manager Jimmy Dykes indicated he thought Walker would be a great ball player if he wasn't so brittle. "If what the doctors say about Dixie after the surgery is true, the White Sox made a bargain when they got him from the Yankees. . . . There was a piece chipped from Dixie's shoulder socket," said Dykes. "Every time he fell on the shoulder the arm would work loose. But by grafting a new socket in place of the old, he now has an arm just as good as ever. Once it heals—and it should be about six more weeks now."

Walker was still walking around the White Sox clubhouse with his arm strapped to his side. He was at Comiskey Park for treatment every day the White Sox were at home, showing an interest in the game and his new teammates, and doing a little assistant broadcasting from the glass-enclosed radio coop.

He had his first full year in the big leagues in 1937 by playing all 154 games, batting .302, leading the league in triples with 16, collecting 179 hits, knocking in 95 runs, and scoring 105 runs. The White Sox finished in third place behind the Yankees, who won with DiMaggio for the second year in a row, and Detroit with slugger Hank Greenberg.

Surprisingly, Walker was traded to the Tigers on December 2, 1937, after his strong White Sox season because he refused an attendance clause in his contract rather than a guaranteed salary raise. He went along with pitcher Vern Kennedy and second baseman Tony Piet to Detroit for catcher Mike Tresh, father of future Yankee Tom Tresh, third baseman Marvin Owen, and outfielder Gerald (Gee) Walker.

Detroit fans were upset when the popular Gee Walker was moved out and replaced by the often-injured Fred "Dixie" Walker. All of that seemed to end when Walker appeared as a guest speaker at the All-American sports banquet at the Detroit Yacht Club. "Dixie Walker Bats 1.000 at D.Y.C. in Detroit Debut," read a headline in the *Detroit News*. The story by sportswriter Charles P. Ward was headlined "New Tiger Outfielder Steals Show at Dinner." It went on to say, "He was given as warm a reception as any ever accorded the popular Gerald Walker. He was the hit of the banquet."

In another article about the premier off-season event in Detroit sports, reporter Bob Murphy wrote, "At the end of the talk Walker had the crowd cheering him just as enthusiastically as they have ever cheered Gee Walker after a home run clout." Harry Kipke, the deposed Michigan football coach, was also one of the honored guests and he was credited by the newspapers covering the event as "rivaling Dixie Walker as the hit of the evening." Quite a boost for the young outfielder to be considered in the same league as a Michigan football coach, even an ousted one.

Susan Walker said she was not surprised to hear about her father entertaining guests warmly at any event where he was scheduled to speak. "A lot of times," she laughed, "he would also break into song at a public event when least expected. He had a beautiful voice and loved any excuse to sing."

Walker spent that winter of 1937 before his 1938 debut with his third big league club at famed pitcher Dazzy Vance's Homosassa Springs, Florida, resort on a fishing expedition with several players, at Chicago as a courtesy to Dr. Kreucher who held a seminar for surgeons about his highly touted procedure on Walker's shoulder, and at Detroit for several banquets and a meeting with Detroit owner Walter O. Briggs, who signed Walker to a $9,000 contract, a $2,500 raise over his last Chicago deal.

"Dixie's looking forward to putting on the uniform of his third big league club," wrote one sportswriter, "with a fatter contract than ever and a rosier outlook than ever." Not only had Dixie's shoulder finally been repaired, his salary increased, and his status as a regular outfielder in Detroit solidified, he was beginning his new life as a married man.

Through teammate and Birmingham pal Ben Chapman, he had met a beautiful young New Yorker, Estelle Shea, while he was with the Yankees early in 1936.

"I had been supporting Mom and Dad and Harry. I had planned to get married that year if I survived the May 15 cut down date," he told Birmingham writer Bill Lumpkin. "The day I was traded I called Estelle Shea and asked if she would marry me that night. We had been going together for some time."

Walker bought a ring for his intended bride and visited several judges before one Westchester County New York judge, Julius A. Raven, the justice of the peace in Armonk, New York, agreed to marry the Irish Catholic girl from New York and the English Protestant boy from Alabama. Teammate George Selkirk served as Walker's best man. "Earlier that evening we had gone to the hotel where the Yankees were staying and had run into Lefty Gomez walking his dogs," Walker recalled. "I introduced Estelle to him as Miss Shea. The next morning when we came out of the hotel we ran into Lefty walking his dogs again. He said, 'Good morning, Miss Shea.' I said, 'No Lefty, it's Mrs. Walker.'"

The new Mrs. Walker followed her husband to Chicago in May 1936, moved to Birmingham with him over that winter, went to spring training with the White Sox in California early in 1937, moved back to Chicago that year, and prepared to look for another apartment in Detroit as Dixie's career changed once again.

This time the apartment would have to be a little larger. There was a third Dixie Walker on the way.

Dixie Walker. Courtesy of National Baseball Library and Archive.

Authors Maury Allen and Susan Walker in 2008 with a photo of her father, Dixie Walker. Collection of Maury Allen.

Jackie Robinson. Courtesy of National Baseball Library and Archive.

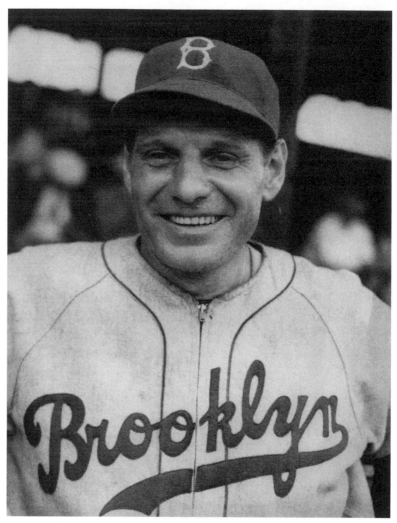

Leo Durocher. Courtesy of National Baseball Library and Archive.

Bobby Bragan. Courtesy of National Baseball Library and Archive.

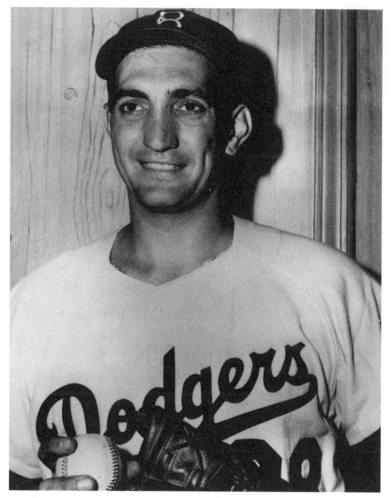
Ralph Branca. Courtesy of National Baseball Library and Archive.

Gene Hermanski. Courtesy of National Baseball Library and
Archive.

Carl Furillo. Courtesy of National Baseball Library and Archive.

Kirby Higbe. Courtesy of National Baseball Library and Archive.

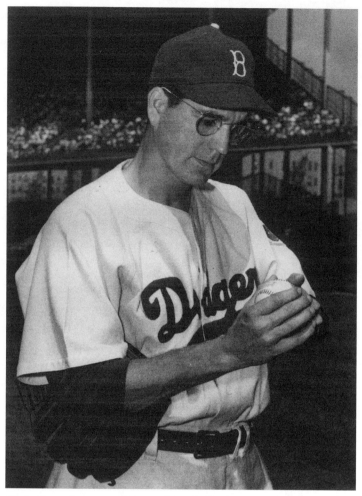

Clyde King. Courtesy of National Baseball Library and Archive.

Pee Wee Reese. Courtesy of National Baseball Library and Archive.

The 1947 Brooklyn Dodgers. Courtesy of National Baseball Library and Archive.

6

Estelle Shea Walker

David A. "Sonny" Werblin started his career as a show business agent in the late 1920s after graduating from Brooklyn's James Madison High School and Rutgers University in Piscataway, New Jersey. He got a position with the huge Music Corporation of America, handled some of the biggest entertainers in the 1930s, and represented dozens of Hollywood stars and the big bands of Benny Goodman, Harry James, and Tommy Dorsey.

He soon worked his way up to a vice presidency in the corporation, traveled in New York's high society circles, dined frequently at the city's finest restaurants, hung out at nightclubs such as the Copacabana, Leon and Eddie's, and the renowned Toot Shor's, where he met many famous athletes—young Joe DiMaggio, boxing champ Joe Louis, and football stars Ken Strong and Ace Parker among them.

Werblin was a big sports fan and frequently could be spotted at games at Yankee Stadium or the Polo Grounds, at championship fights in New York's Madison Square Garden, or at Brooklyn's Ebbets Field, where his hometown team played.

In 1963 he hit the big time in sports when he purchased the New York Titans of the American Football League for a piddling $1 million after the league took over the team from former broadcaster Harry Wismer, the bankrupt owner. Wismer had gained fame with the team as a blowhard owner who walked through the press box announcing exaggerated attendance at Titans games.

After one of these ridiculous counts with clearly less than a thousand people in the dilapidated Polo Grounds stands, George Vecsey of *Newsday* and later a *New York Times* sports columnist, wrote, "Wismer announced the attendance as 19,701, of which 19,000 came disguised as empty seats."

Werblin changed the name of the team to the Jets, signed University of Alabama quarterback Joe Namath for $400,000 in 1965 and built the team that was to win Super Bowl III in 1969. Werblin was gone from the team by then after disagreements with his partners; he moved on to Madison Square Garden as president in the late 1970s.

He entertained the press lavishly during his years as boss of the football team. One of the highlights was a yearly outing at Monmouth Race Track and a magnificent shore dinner at his private club.

Werblin was fond of repeating a line he admitted he had either heard from entertainer Joe E. Lewis or singer-comedian Fanny Bryce. "I've been rich and I've been poor," Werblin would say as he studied the trays of lobster, steaks, and shrimp at his club, "rich is better."

He made a lot of big and important decisions in his professional career. Certainly the best—as far as Dixie Walker was concerned—was to hire Estelle Shea as a secretary in his office.

Estelle Mary Casey Shea was born in New York City on October 11, 1909, the third of the ten children of Patrick and Catherine Casey Shea, Irish immigrants from County Cork, who came to the United States at the turn of the century and settled on the Upper West Side of Manhattan.

In the new country, Patrick opened a horse-drawn moving company in the early 1900s. The business succeeded well enough for the family to live in a modest Manhattan apartment and enjoy the benefits of New York's rapidly expanding economy. Patrick Shea soon expanded his business to include the first commercial horse-drawn buggy rides through Central Park, a practice that still exists more than a century later.

Estelle Shea graduated from high school in Manhattan, took courses at a local nursing school, and soon gravitated into the business community as her father had. She enjoyed music, sang beautifully along with records, and dressed stylishly. She often attended Broadway musical shows with her lucky dates and sang many of the songs she heard. At the age of twenty-one, she had developed into a beautiful young woman with short red hair, dark eyes, a winsome smile, and a trim appearance similar to that of the Norwegian skating star and actress Sonja Heinie.

She decided that show business was for her. She saw an advertisement in the *New York Times* for an assistant to one of the most successful agents in show business, David A. Sonny Werblin. She sat down and wrote Werblin a letter and was called to his Forty-second Street office for an interview.

Her stylish appearance, outstanding looks, incredible self-confidence, particularly for such a young woman in those male-dominated days, and conversational ease won Werblin over immediately. He hired her as his executive assistant for forty dollars a week, a salary far in excess of what most working women, or men for that matter, were making in the Depression days of 1930.

While other females sat in the huge MCA offices typing, taking dictation, and answering the phones, Estelle Shea was assigned by Werblin to get out to the Manhattan hotels and movie theaters and interview the leaders of the big bands. Werblin's MCA had created a new radio program called *Your Hit Parade,* later to be repeated on television, with the bands playing the most popular numbers of the week.

"She was on a first name basis with legendary performers—Harry James, George Gershwin, Ira Gershwin, Benny Goodman, Glenn Miller, and many others," Susan Walker recalled years later. "She knew them, she knew their wives, and she knew their families."

Estelle became a popular figure in the lounges where the bands played in Manhattan hotels and fashionable nightclubs. The leaders of these bands all wanted the recognition MCA's new show would give them and treated Estelle with all the respect they could muster.

She zipped around Manhattan, this lovely young woman, alone, well dressed, clearly confident, hailing taxicabs in the late evenings as she moved from one hotel to another to catch the different performances of the big bands of the day, moving from the Astor to the Taft to the Paramount to the Strand, to the Roxy and to Radio City Music Hall to listen to the groups, talk with the musicians, and report back to Werblin on her ideas for popular success. She tabulated the top ten most requested tunes of the week just in time to form the list for that week's Hit Parade Show as all America waited to hear the final song, the top tune of the week, the American Idol performance of the 1930s.

Estelle Shea could easily have changed the lives of dozens of band leaders and thousands of musicians as her role as Werblin's eyes and ears increased over the next half dozen years. All of that changed on May 2, 1936, when the businesswoman with no interest in baseball married the baseball player with no interest in business. She was now Mrs. Walker. Flossie Walker wasn't happy about her son's marriage to the sophisticated northern Catholic. No family member attended the short ceremony in Armonk.

Estelle Walker celebrated her wedding anniversary every May 2 for the rest of her life. "Even after my father died in 1982 she would take one of the children out to dinner in a fine Birmingham restaurant and celebrate her anniversary," Susan Walker said. "That went on for twenty years after he was gone. They would talk about him and recall many memories. That was how much she loved him and missed him."

The day after their marriage, said Susan Walker, "my dad went to the office of Sonny Werblin." The short conversation, according to Susan, went something like this.

"I'm Dixie Walker, the baseball player with the Yankees, and I've just been traded to the Chicago White Sox," Walker said.

"Yes, and I'm Werblin," said the MCA executive.

"Estelle doesn't work here any more," said Walker.

"Why not?" Sonny asked.

"She's my wife and she is going with me to Chicago," Walker said.

"That was all it took," said Susan. "When I heard that story from Mom years later I could see my dad handling it that way. When it came to his family, he made his decisions quickly, and that was the way it was."

Walker had wooed and won his bride despite her hectic schedule of checking out the bands and the songs as possible top tunes on *Your Hit Parade*. "She had always taken cabs around town from one club to another, one hotel to another to listen to these groups," Susan related. "As soon as my father came into the picture he decided they should walk from one club to another. That way she could save the cab fare money she had been allotted by the company. Any time my father could save a dime or a dollar he did. Remember it was the Depression, and he always considered that money was tight. My mother never really thought that way, especially if it had anything to do with clothing, furnishing, parties—anything like that."

They could also spend more time together, Dixie talking in his Birmingham drawl, Estelle chatting with him, using all the phrases and pronunciations of New York City. They looked at the fashionable store windows of Manhattan, talked of places they had visited and people they knew, enjoyed the hustle of the crowds, stopped for quick meals in local restaurants or coin-operated automats, and held hands affectionately.

Estelle and her new husband took off for Chicago, rented an apartment downtown, and enjoyed the highlights of the Second City.

"She stayed out of the ball parks my dad played in for the first five years of her marriage, but she enjoyed entertaining at home during the season, creating their first home in the Colonial Hills section of the Birmingham neighborhood of Mountain Brook, and attending to her duties as wife and mother," Susan said.

There were occasional off-season visits in the 1940s from Brooklyn teammates and their wives. Eddie Stanky, Bobby Bragan, and Whitlow Wyatt all made appearances. After dinner the women would collect in one room, talking about their homes and children, while the men gathered in another, smoking a pipe or a good cigar, talking about baseball, and sharing the camaraderie so unique to professional athletes.

There were major background differences between Estelle and Dixie that were especially apparent in the early years of their marriage. No marriage counselor could have predicted what was to become an extremely successful union of forty-six years. According to Susan's husband, Ed, the marriage survived despite these differences. She was a northerner from New York and he was a southerner from Birmingham. She was a Catholic and he was a Protestant. She was a skilled businesswoman and he was a skilled athlete with limited business acumen. She didn't get along with most of his family, while he enjoyed most of hers. She had no interest in athletics and his only interest was athletics. She liked the finer things in life (designer clothing, Irish linens, fine furnishings), while he was satisfied with much less. In college sports she rooted for Notre Dame and he rooted for the University of Alabama.

"There was only one real explanation why they made it so well through so many years," explained Susan. "They simply loved each other."

Despite their totally different backgrounds their love thrived, but it was not beyond Estelle to quietly take a hand in directing fate if she disagreed with Dixie. Ed recalled how it was Estelle who helped fate along when she brought forth that first letter that Ed had written to Susan. By saving that envelope with Ed's address, squirreling it away, despite Dixie's edict, she created the opportunity that helped Susan choose Ed as her husband. All this behind the scenes drama occurred because Dixie forbade Susan as a seventeen-year-old to write a letter to a man nearly six years older than she was.

Another example of Estelle's quiet strength, and her ability to do what she personally considered the best thing for her children, was her guiding hand in helping Susan choose the right college for herself. "Estelle paid for Susan's tuition to a Catholic university out of her household funds because Dixie didn't want her to go to a Catholic school up north," Ed remembered.

After Susan did well in school, married Ed, and created a wonderful marriage with five children, Dixie relented. "Eventually he told her he had been wrong on both counts," school and marriage, Ed said. "He didn't mind admitting he was wrong and he offered apologies."

Estelle, like much of the United States, avidly followed the story of the English king Edward VIII and his American sweetheart. When the king fell in love and abdicated his throne in 1936 to marry "the woman I love," the twice-divorced Wallis Simpson, Estelle, who was a true romantic, saw certain similarities to her own situation.

After Ed and Susan moved to New Jersey and began their own family, Estelle often drove up from Birmingham alone, helping Susan with the endless chores of early motherhood, yet discreetly managing to stay in the background. "There were times," Ed recalled, "when she would arrive at the house unannounced, spend a few days helping Sue get organized after one of our children was born, and stay just long enough to see that things were going well. Then she would quietly take off in the middle of the night for home. We would wake up to see her bed made, her bags gone, and her room as neat as if no one had ever been there."

When Dixie left for spring training, Estelle allowed the children more freedom in their Birmingham home. Things were always tougher when Estelle drove north with their family to meet Dixie. This was especially true when the children were young—during his playing days in Chicago, Detroit, and later Brooklyn.

"She had that heavy foot on the gas pedal," laughs Susan Walker. "She always arrived in the town where he was playing a lot sooner than expected. I remember when I was little and we were living in Rockville Centre, New York. These were the days before cars had seat belts. We all threw our shoes out the window, and my older brother put his smelly feet out the window."

Estelle and Dixie's first child, Fred (Dixie) Walker, was born in 1937; their second child, Mary Ann Walker, was born early in 1940. "Dad was playing for Brooklyn then and they had taken this small house in Brooklyn, I think in the Bay Ridge section, and he would drive to Ebbets Field which was about fifteen or twenty minutes away for the games," Susan Walker said.

There was a rare night game and Dixie needed to sleep late that day before leaving for the park. Baby Mary Ann, now six months old, was restless and cranky. She cried for a long time in the small house until Dixie woke up. "As my mother told me many years later my dad was very tired that day and he asked my mother to take the baby to another part of the home so he could get his rest before the game," Susan said. "She took the baby downstairs where it was probably damp and let Mary Ann sleep there. By the time my dad left for the park, Mary Ann was coughing and wheezing. There were no antibiotics then for children. That night, after the game, she was in a bad way and they took her to a nearby hospital. She had contracted pneumonia. She was gone in a day or so. My father never really got over that her death."

In 1941 another girl was born to Dixie and Estelle. They named her Mary Ann in memory of their lost child. Susan came along in 1943; Sean Casey was born in 1949; and Stephen Vaughn, their sixth child, was born in 1954. Mary Ann, Susan, and Stephen are the only surviving children of Dixie and Estelle Walker.

As a youngster growing up in the towns where Dixie Walker played, managed and coached—Atlanta, Houston, Rochester, Toronto, and Milwaukee—Susan Walker had two separate lives. "We always lived in the city where my dad was working for the team and then when the season ended we would go back home to Birmingham. He loved to hunt and fish with his brother Harry while my mother really ran the house. He had a farm where my great uncle Ernie lived and they, Harry and my dad, also owned a small construction company. They also operated the hardware store downtown where my grandfather Ewart always worked. When my dad came home things would go back to his formal way of doing things," Susan recalled.

There seems to be so much glamour to the lives of ball players, according to outside observers, especially the press, but it was all rather routine as Susan was growing up. "I went to a lot of different schools as a child but as I got older we usually stayed in Birmingham until the end of the school year," Susan said. "Then my mother would put the pedal to the metal and we would take off for the town where my dad was working."

Estelle enjoyed those drives north, even with a car full of kids. She never complained about the burdens put upon her to keep the family together. It was her efforts that kept the family under the same roof as much as possible. "She was a very independent woman, well ahead of her time, in the way she controlled the family when Dixie was away," Ed said, "the way she set her own rules, the way she was always ready to explore new adventures."

When Dixie Walker died in 1982, after forty-six years of blissful marriage, Estelle traveled extensively throughout the United States, sometimes with friends, often alone. She toured many of the major cities of Europe, researched her family history in Ireland, came home to entertain old friends in the Birmingham area and visited New Jersey frequently.

At the age of eighty-nine, she moved up north to stay with her daughter Susan and Susan's family. "During those years she was with us—we never called it full time because she always expected to return to her Birmingham home—she accompanied us to the weddings of all three of our sons," Ed recalled. "One was in nearby New York, one was in Rochester, New York, and one was even farther in New Orleans. She flew with us on several trips to Florida and came with us on car trips to Cape Cod, Massachusetts, where my sister Mary lived, and to the Delaware shore. She went with us on a whale watch boat ride off Provincetown, on a Hyannis, Massachusetts, harbor cruise, on a Mississippi river boat, and on several cruises off Cape Canaveral in Florida."

Each fall Susan and Ed spent a good part of the time in their condo in South Bend, Indiana, at the edge of the campus of Notre Dame University during the football season of the Fighting Irish. "She helped with the parties when we had guests and she always entertained with her stories and her wit," Ed recalled.

One summer Ed and Susan took Estelle along on their trip to one of New York State's most scenic areas at Lake George. "Nana/Honey or Gram—as our children called her—enjoyed a pleasant day at the historic Saratoga race track. She was pleased as could be when she picked a few winning horses from her grandstand seat," Ed said.

Ed remembered one trip when Estelle became the focus of attention. She was ninety years old that summer. "We were on a trip to Orlando and we visited Sea World," Ed said. "We spent a long day watching Shamu, the famous whale, and many of the other exhibits. Susan and a friend, Pat McDonald, got in line for a ride on the brand-new roller coaster called the Kracken, a terrifying monster of the sea with seven over-the-top loops and speeds exceeding sixty-five miles per hour. I decided my stomach wasn't up to it and I asked Gram if she would mind staying with me while Susan and Pat took on this wild ride. She quickly announced that she wanted to try out this new ride. The attendants heard about it and they moved her to the head of the line. She took off with the next batch of kids and came out of the wild ride with a huge smile on her face. She had taken on the vaunted Kracken and conquered it."

At their New Jersey home, Estelle would rise early, enjoy coffee and jelly doughnuts with Ed and Susan before they went off to work, he with his engineering chores and she as a sales consultant. "Some days we would come downstairs," Ed said, "and see her sitting in the living room with her sweater and gloves on, ready to join Sue on her sales rounds or go to the office where she had been given her own desk. She would often answer the phones when others were busy with her southern-accented professional voice."

One of her other favorite activities after she moved in with Ed and Susan were frequent visits to Atlantic City. "She would stay up all night at the slot machines," Ed said. "She couldn't see the machines very well by then but she enjoyed the hustle and bustle of the casinos and the sounds of the coins and the ringing of the bells. She was a frequent winner."

"Of all her passions, family was always primary," said Ed. "During the last three years of her life when she was with us she often spoke of her beloved Dixie, kept his memory alive, talked of her children, entertained her grandchildren with tales of her younger days, and related adventures of her youth in New York City, the big bands, the famous people she met, the nightlife she remembered."

Estelle kept active and attractive throughout her final years, making sure her hair and makeup were just so, certain that the clothes she wore were appropriate for the event she was attending, participating in family events and visits with friends.

"It wasn't until the final two or three months of her life that we realized things weren't going well for her," Ed said. "We used to chat each morning around the kitchen table as we enjoyed our coffee and jelly doughnuts. I really noticed a change when she no longer showed any interest in that. . . . Gram had joined us on a visit to my sister Mary on Cape Cod," recalled Ed. "I was working in the Boston area then but I was summoned back to New Jersey for the funeral of a friend."

Susan stayed on Cape Cod and Estelle grew weaker over the next few days. She was finally taken to Cape Cod Hospital on a Wednesday afternoon. By Friday morning the family was summoned to her bedside as doctors indicated the end was near.

She received the Sacrament of the Sick twice, and both times, with the grace of the Sacrament, according to Ed, she rallied. She lapsed in and out of a coma. At ninety-two, there wasn't much time left. Ed drove back to Cape Cod.

Estelle's hospital window faced the Kennedy compound in Hyannisport. Estelle had always identified with Rose Kennedy, whom she admired for caring for her family as Estelle did. Both women lived much of their adult lives in the shadows of their husbands' fame, both suffered the loss of children prematurely, and were always striving for the common goals of a good life as devout Irish Catholic mothers.

Susan and Ed understood family tragedy. Ed had suffered the loss of both of his parents unexpectedly. Even with these experiences, Ed said, the hardest thing we have ever experienced was watching Estelle die over that three-day period knowing there was little anyone could do for her."

Ed, his sister Mary, and Susan stayed near Estelle for the final three days of her life, holding her hands, praying aloud, reading from Scripture about everlasting life, singing songs to her, and doing everything they could to distract her from her pain.

"We sang songs of Ireland," Ed said, "and we sang uplifting Negro spirituals and church songs that had meant so much to her throughout her life. But the songs she seemed to respond to the most, if squeezing our hands was a good indicator, were songs of the city of New York where she was born and raised."

One nurse watching the family interact with Estelle was a Native American from the local Wampanoag tribe. "Your ceremonies and the way you related to her at the end were very similar to what I had known in my youth with the tribe," said Nurse Mary St.-Armand. "You did it the right way."

In the morning of June 10, 2002, Estelle Mary Casey Shea Walker breathed her last. "I remember the words I heard often from her at the end of her life," Ed recalled. "She used to say, 'Don't leave me.' She always wanted to be there with all of us even after her time had passed—even if it meant being there only in spirit."

At her eulogy Ed told the assembled crowd, "She was ever the mother, ever the teacher. She taught us how to live, joyously with faith and love, and she taught us how to die, with courage, dignity, and grace. You'll always be with us, Nana, honey, and just as you asked, we will always be with you."

Ed told the assemblage that there was a verse that seemed to express

Estelle's wish in words that might well have been hers. In the silence of Our Lady of Sorrows Church in Birmingham, where Dixie Walker's final services had been held twenty years earlier, Ed read the poem.

> Do not stand at my grave and weep.
> I am not there, I do not sleep.
> I am the thousand winds that blow,
> I am the diamond glints of snow,
> I am the sunlight of ripened grain.
> I am the gentle autumn rain.
> When you awaken in the morning's hush,
> I am the swift uplifting rush
> Of quiet birds in circling flight.
> I am the soft star that shines at night,
> Do not stand at my grave and cry.
> I am not there; I did not die.

7
Arrival in Brooklyn

There are some baseball seasons that become memorable for thrilling pennant races—the Boston Braves coming back from last place for a miracle pennant in 1914, the 1946 St. Louis Cardinals beating the Brooklyn Dodgers in two games in the first pennant playoff, the 1948 Cleveland Indians beating the Boston Red Sox in a one-game playoff, the 1951 New York Giants winning the third playoff game on Bobby Thomson's shot heard 'round the world, the 1962 San Francisco Giants beating the Dodgers in a playoff, and the historic Bucky Dent homer for the Yankees against the Red Sox for the division title in 1978.

Then there are the individual challenges that light up the baseball sky—the .406 of Ted Williams and the 56 game consecutive batting streak of Joe DiMaggio in 1941, the 1956 World Series perfect game by Don Larsen, the 1961 home run chase of Babe Ruth by Roger Maris (61 in 162 games) and Mickey Mantle with 54, the 31 games won by Denny McLain in 1968, the tainted Mark McGwire (70) hunt for the Maris home run record, and the Barry Bonds chase of the McGwire mark (73 in 2001) and passing Hank Aaron's 755 in 2007 under a cloud of steroid charges.

That kind of individual excitement was what the 1938 season was all about.

After playing his first injury-free season for the White Sox with a .302 mark in all 154 games, the new Detroit outfielder hit .308 for the Detroit Tigers in 1938 in 127 games. There were some knee problems, some leg problems, and a little bit of the old shoulder pain. Hardly anyone noticed Dixie Walker's fine season.

That was Hank Greenberg's year.

Greenberg was the handsome Jewish slugger from the Bronx who had refused a Yankees contract offer because his hometown team had Lou Gehrig settled in at first base. He signed with Detroit after setting hitting records at James Monroe High School, some of which were later broken by Ed Kranepool, a future star with the New York Mets. He joined the Tigers in 1930 and became a regular in 1933, winning his first of four home run titles in 1935 on his way to a Hall of Fame career.

His road roommate that season was another Jewish kid from Brooklyn, a left-handed pitcher by the name of Harry Eisenstat. In one doubleheader, Greenberg hit home runs in each game to win the games for Detroit with Eisenstat winning one of the games and saving the other. When the games ended manager Mickey Cochrane gathered his Tigers in the clubhouse and announced, "Fellows, lock yourselves in your hotel rooms tonight. The Jews in Detroit are going wild."

Greenberg went after Babe Ruth's home run record of sixty homers, set in 1927, and closed to fifty-eight with five games to go at the end of the 1938 season. He faced Bob Feller in the next to last game of the season. Feller set a new strikeout record with eighteen Tigers, including Greenberg, going down on strikes. Hank failed to hit one out and ended the season the next day two home runs short of the Ruth record.

Eisenstat beat Feller in the game 4–1. His career was cut short by service in World War II. He retired from baseball and went into private business in Cleveland when he returned home in 1946 and lived there the rest of his life. He died in 2003. He was eighty-seven years old. "I remember that year very well," said Evelyn Eisenstat, the ball player's widow and also a native of Brooklyn. Both attended James Madison

High School in Brooklyn, knew each other casually in school, and met again and married in 1938 after Eisenstat had gone from Brooklyn to the Tigers.

"Harry and Hank Greenberg were very close pals," she said. "We spent a lot of time together. That was a nice bunch of people on that team. We were friendly with all of them."

Evelyn Eisenstat said she spent a lot of time with the Walkers, the new Detroit outfielder and his new bride. "I think we were all making an adjustment to a new team in a new town," she said. "A lot of the wives would get together when the team was on the road. We often played bridge at each others homes. I think I spent time with Estelle Walker when she had a barbecue at their rented home. Then I returned the favor at our place. I remember that several times late in the year that we had maybe a dozen or so of the players over for barbecues."

Evelyn Eisenstat said she thought Dixie Walker was a very nice gentleman, soft spoken and very helpful at the group parties. "We were all so young then, so full of hope for the careers of our husbands," she said. "We all pulled for each other. The idea was to win and maybe make a few more dollars."

There was one other thing Evelyn Eisenstat, ninety years old, recalled from her Detroit days with Hank Greenberg and teammate Dixie Walker and wife Estelle. "Dixie and Estelle were a lot like us, Harry and I, young, really starting out in the baseball field, trying to establish ourselves in the community," she said. "You could also see in their eyes and the way they conducted themselves, they were a young couple very much in love."

Greenberg settled for the 58 home runs that year, two less than the Babe had smashed in his record 1927 season, batted .315, and knocked in 146 runs, 37 fewer than he had in 1937 as the Tigers finished in fourth place behind the Yankees, Red Sox, and Indians. Jimmie Foxx won the 1938 RBI title with 175 for the Red Sox.

Greenberg won four RBI titles before retiring after his one season with Pittsburgh in 1947. "The one thing I would do every morning,"

Greenberg once said, "was pick up the paper and see what [Joe] DiMaggio did. If I had a better day than Joe did it made me feel a lot better."

Left-hander Eisenstat was 9–6 that year before being traded to the Cleveland Indians in 1939 for future Hall of Famer Earl Averill.

Dixie Walker had his second solid season in a row with a .308 average in 127 games for Detroit with 43 runs batted in, 6 home runs, 84 runs scored, and 140 hits. Unfortunately the damaged right throwing shoulder gave him some pain and forced him to miss more games than he would have liked.

Walker often said later that his toughest opponent in 1938 was the young Cleveland fireballer Bob Feller. "He threw the hardest of anyone in the game and had that great curve ball," Walker said. "I just couldn't touch him."

Robert William Andrew Feller was born November 3, 1918, in Van Meter, Iowa. He pitched his first game for Cleveland in 1936 at the age of seventeen and returned home after the season to finish his work for high school graduation. He was 266–162 in his Hall of Fame career and missed almost four seasons with navy service in World War II.

"I spent 34 months on the battleship USS *Alabama* as a gun captain," Feller recalled during a visit to Cooperstown, New York, for the 2008 Baseball Hall of Fame induction ceremonies. "We first went to the Soviet Union to deliver supplies and then to the South Pacific. We hit Iwo Jima before the invasion. The ship is now a museum in dry dock in Mobile. I got out late in 1945 in time for a few games."

Feller said he didn't recall facing Walker in 1938 but he did face Jackie Robinson a couple of times in exhibition games against Negro League teams after the war. "I didn't think he would hit," Feller said. "I guess I was wrong. I didn't know much about that Dodger situation with Dixie and Jackie in 1947. I was too busy pitching. I ran into Dixie a couple of times during the pension fights with the owners. He was a fine fellow."

Feller had his first big year in 1938 with 17 wins at the age of nineteen, and Walker had a strong season for Detroit with his .308 average at the age of twenty-seven. "The following year I got hurt again," Walker told Bill Lumpkin. "We were playing in Philadelphia and I hung my spike on a ball in the outfield and tore up the right knee. I had to wear a cast. When they took it off, I started working out. I found I could run straight but not cut. Detroit wanted me to have an operation. I said no. I knew the knee was getting better."

Walker said he was walking a golf course on an off day with friends and the Tigers phoned the club. "They told me not to plan on leaving with the Detroit team that afternoon for a road trip," Walker said. "I had been sold to Brooklyn." For seventy-five hundred, the waiver price, Walker's ten thousand dollar a year contract had been assigned to the Brooklyn Dodgers of bombastic Larry MacPhail, the club president, and feisty Leo Durocher, the player-manager of Dem Bums.

In the *New York Times* of July 25, 1939, the lead story on the sports pages detailed the signing of the phenomenal college football star from Columbia University in New York, who had led his school to a Rose Bowl victory over Stanford. "Sid Luckman signs a 2-year deal with the Chicago Bears," the article reported. "Luckman had said since graduation from Columbia last month that he would pass up professional football to go into the trucking business with a brother."

A sweet contract paying the college graduate twenty-five thousand dollars for two seasons convinced Luckman to give the new professional game a look. He went on to become one of the greatest quarterbacks in professional football history and the man credited with establishing the T-formation as the game's new offensive format after starring as a triple threat back with his passing, running, and kicking for the Columbia Lions.

Off to the side of the first sports page of the *New York Times* on this July day was a small article by baseball writer Louis Effrat. "President Larry MacPhail announced the club had acquired Fred (Dixie) Walker from the Tigers and that Van Lingle Mungo would be lost to the team for six weeks because of a broken ankle suffered in the previous Sunday's game with the Cardinals," Effrat wrote. It was the loss of the handsome right-handed pitcher, Mungo, not the gain of the drawling Birmingham out-fielder that most interested the fans of the Brooklyn Dodgers that day.

"I was hobbling around when I reported to Brooklyn in Chicago that July day in 1939," Walker recalled. "I hobbled all year. The fans didn't know what to expect. They had been told I was all wired together."

"He hit .308 for the Tigers in 1938 but his shoulder was troubling him again and now, in 1939, the Tigers asked for waivers on him," wrote Frank Graham in *The Brooklyn Dodgers: An Informal History,* the best book on Brooklyn's early lore ever written. "All the other American League clubs promptly waived on him. MacPhail, needing help in the outfield and willing to gamble on a fellow who could hit, picked Walker up."

Then Graham captured Dixie's significance and his incredible future standing with the team and the town in the 1945 book published by G. P. Putnam's Sons. "There was something about the guy—big, blond, smiling, affable—that caught the fancy of the mob at Ebbets Field al-most as soon as he went to the plate for the first time," Graham wrote. "They yelled to him when he was in the lineup and yelled for him when he wasn't. A new hero, whose popularity in time would rival that of Nap Rucker, Zack Wheat and Casey Stengel, had arrived on the scene."

Part of Dixie's attraction for Brooklyn fans was his immediate suc-cess against the Giants and part of it was his charismatic appearance, his strong silent demeanor, tall, thin, handsome, a look-a-like for contem-porary film star Gary Cooper, the slow-talking, soft-voiced hero of so many Westerns such as *High Noon* and the baseball classic *The Pride of the Yankees,* the life story of Lou Gehrig, a Walker teammate with the Yankees.

In one wry and significant note, Graham would write a few pages later about the Dodgers' desperate attempt—however frustrating—of catching the eventual pennant-winning Cincinnati Reds of 1940. "The outfield still was one weak spot," Graham wrote of the late season run of the 1940 Brooklyn Dodgers, "the pitching staff another, for [Whitlow] Wyatt, [Hugh] Casey and the aging [Freddie] Fitzsimmons were carrying the burden in the box with little help from the others. Walker, whose popularity (somewhat galling to MacPhail, for some reason or another) had reached such bounds as he was known as The People's Choice, was hitting, but he wasn't in the lineup all the time. [Pete] Reiser was thumping the ball too, and so was [Dolph] Camilli. But the Dodgers needed another fleet, strong-armed outfielder, one who could hit and run and throw, and who had been around long enough to maintain the pace of this fast-traveling club." That would turn out to be another future Hall of Famer, Joe Medwick.

MacPhail's attitude toward Dixie was typical of the times, all times. Owners and senior executives of baseball teams are often in conflict with the stars of the team as the players gain the gold and the glory and their bosses lose the ego wars. Megalomania may be the most common ailment among baseball bosses. George (the Boss) Steinbrenner, who brought the Yankees tradition and dynasty back after his purchase of the team with dozens of other partners in 1973, was constantly at war via the press with stars such as Reggie Jackson, Thurman Munson, Catfish Hunter, Lou Piniella, and managers such as Joe Torre, Billy Martin, Piniella, Yogi Berra, and Gene Michael. Steinbrenner's massive ego, the size of Montana, was hardly soothed when the Yankees training camp in Tampa known as Legends Field was renamed in 2008 as Steinbrenner Field. The new Yankee Stadium, opening in 2009, built across the street from the old one in the Bronx, nicknamed the House That Ruth Built, would again be called Yankee Stadium, not George M. Steinbrenner III Field.

So Dixie Walker was a Dodger, number 11 on your scorecards, and, for more than eight years, number 1 in your hearts. The day he reported to the Dodgers in Chicago he was sent up as a pinch hitter by Durocher and struck out. Durocher was so displeased with Walker's swing that he ordered the team doctor to examine Dixie's knees to see if he was all right.

On July 27, 1939, Dixie made his first start for the Brooklyn Dodgers in the National League in Chicago after four minor league seasons and parts of seven big league seasons in the American League. He batted third in Durocher's lineup behind Johnny Hudson at second and Cookie Lavagetto at third. Walker was in center field and was followed in the lineup by Camilli, journeyman outfielder Art Parks, catcher Babe Phelps, journeyman outfielder Gene Moore, player-manager Durocher at shortstop, and pitcher Tot Pressnell.

Walker was twenty-eight at the time of his Brooklyn debut, the same age Jackie Robinson would be when he played in his first game for the Brooklyn Dodgers eight years later in 1947.

Dixie was hitless in his first starting role and made an error in center field when he fumbled a base hit, allowing the Cubs to score a run in a 3–1 triumph over the Dodgers.

His first hits as a Dodger and his first RBI came the next day as the Dodgers beat the St. Louis Cardinals, their heated rival in several tough pennant races, 5–4.

The Dodgers won again the next day 7–3 as Dixie was one for two and pinch hit for when the Cards brought in a left-handed pitcher.

Now Walker and his new teammates were heading back to historic Ebbets Field, which had opened in 1913 and was showing many signs of strain by 1939. They were to go against the Boston Braves, led by manager Casey Stengel, who had played in the first game at Ebbets Field for the Dodgers and had been one of the most noticed, lovable, and entertaining characters in the history of the game. Stengel had been Dixie's manager at Toledo in 1931.

The Brooklyn Dodgers were only a third place team in 1939 but they were the most colorful of clubs and had gained national attention because so many native Brooklynites lived across the country and because everything the players did seemed to make the national news.

Two additions to the scene at Ebbets Field caused fans across the country to take notice. One was the arrival of broadcaster Red Barber from Cincinnati, with his cultivated southern voice developed in his native Mississippi and later in Florida. Barber followed the team at home and relayed a ticker-tape description from the road for the first time that year. His broadcasts were heard everywhere, especially on the stoops of brick buildings in Brooklyn, homes of many Brooklyn fans, over portable radios.

The other innovation was Ladies' Day, an occasional event where female fans were allowed into the park for fifty or seventy-five cents (the average ticket was $1.20) and encouraged to root, root, root, for the home team in their loudest voices.

"Ladies' Day had been instituted at the Flatbush ball park," wrote Frank Graham, "and the shrill cries of the female rooters pierced the ears of passers-by blocks away." Five years later Homer Bigart of the *New York Herald Tribune* was to quote an American soldier who had just come through a Banzai charge by the Japs on Leyte (in the Philippines): "They make the weirdest sound as they rush at you, screaming. It sounds like Ladies' Day at Ebbets Field."

Dixie Walker, blond, tall, handsome, charming, almost always smiling and waving at them before games, quickly became one of the favorites of the gals, dressed in their finest outfits and delightful hats. It was all part of the Ebbets Field ambiance, and Dixie learned to play it as well as Jascha Heifetz played the violin.

Walker started the first game he saw at Ebbets Field against Stengel's Braves. Durocher sent him up against his former Toledo manager's Boston team. Boston had a left-hander in the game, Joe Sullivan, and Durocher, leaning toward Stengel's platooning experience as a player with John McGraw's New York Giants and later in a high art form with the championship New York Yankees teams, considered removing Walker against the lefty and replacing him with a right-handed hitter, Ernie Koy.

Durocher walked up to Dixie as he started for the on-deck circle from the Brooklyn dugout. "Dixie, you haven't seen too much left-handed pitching," Durocher said. "Do you think I ought to take you out?"

"I said no," Walker later related. "I knew what I was going to see. Curves. If the pitcher threw a fast ball, I was dead. He threw the curve and I singled. The fans mobbed me."

In those days the last play of a winning game was almost always followed by an onslaught of fans charging the players on the field, beseeching them for autographs as they jogged toward the dugout and up the ramp to the Brooklyn clubhouse, discussing the game in great detail.

Players used to leave their gloves on the field in those days and in extra inning games it was the obligation of the home team to bring the mitts of the visitors back into the safety of the dugouts. One story about the gloves on the field was often told by an entertaining sportswriter from the *New York Daily News* named Joe Trimble. He was covering a Yankees game against the St. Louis Browns when a ground ball actually rolled to a dead stop inside the glove of Yankee first baseman Nick Etten. Etten, a strong hitter and powerful slugger, led the league in home runs with 22 in 1944 and RBIs with 111 in 1945. His fielding was not much to write home about. After the ball stuck in Etten's glove Trimble wrote, "Nick Etten's glove fields better without Nick Etten in it." Etten chased Trimble the length of a train the next day, as the Yankees were traveling to their next road game, before holding his head outside the last car.

Walker's first impression of the zaniness of the Brooklyn fans and the intensity they would show after a winning game was not considered unusual in those television-free days.

The Dodgers had beaten the Braves 7–6 in ten innings, topped their old hero Stengel's team, and established Walker as one of the favorites in Dodger blue.

Leo Durocher would later say that coach Charlie Dressen, one of baseball's best needlers, asked, "Where is the wheel chair that goes with this guy?" when an often-injured Dixie joined the team. After his dramatic, winning hit in his first Ebbets Field game as a Dodger, there was no more talk about Brooklyn acquiring damaged property. What they had acquired was a fine player and soon to be as popular a Brooklyn figure as there ever was.

Dixie had the knack of connecting with fans wherever he played. He had been sent off from Greenville, South Carolina, in the Sally League in 1930 with a bag of cash donated by grateful fans. He had love letters written to him in Jersey City and Newark as a Yankee farmhand from girls willing to meet the handsome bachelor kid anytime, anyplace, anywhere. He had fans screaming, "Dixie, we love ya," on his few occasions in the Yankee outfield as a substitute for the ballooning Ruth, and he had legions of fans shouting his name in Chicago and Detroit.

The old horse racing expression "horses for courses" may have easily been applied to Dixie Walker. When he came to Brooklyn and played his first games in Ebbets Field, in front of that famous right field wall of a wooden base and a mesh screen angled top, the fans poured out their affectionate calls for him. When Dixie jogged out to right field after a Brooklyn inning and stood in front of the famed "Hit Sign Win Suit" billboard, he was often greeted with applause and loud calls. A Brooklyn clothier, Abe Stark, later the Brooklyn Borough president, had placed the sign on the bottom of the wall, maybe eighteen inches off the ground for the life of Ebbets Field for six thousand dollars.

One player, Red Schoendienst of the St. Louis Cardinals, later a Hall of Famer, said he was the only big leaguer to hit the sign on a fly and win a suit. "We were playing the Dodgers in a close game at Ebbets Field," recalled Schoendienst. "It was either 1946 or 1947 and Dixie was in right field for the Dodgers. I hit a low line drive that never really got high off the ground, one of those shots with a lot of top spin that kept it from falling before it hit the wall. Dixie was playing me more toward center and the drive just caught the sign at the edge."

Early the next day Schoendienst jumped into a taxi cab in front of the Hotel New Yorker, where the Cardinals stayed, and took off for Stark's Brooklyn factory and warehouse to claim his suit as instructed. "By the time I got there and back the taxi cab ride was eleven dollars," Schoendienst remembered, "and the suit sold for ten dollars."

Walker played in 140 games for Brooklyn in the 1940 season, mostly in center field, batted .308, established himself as a fan favorite, especially because of his solid hitting and clutch blows against hated New York Giants, and returned the affection the Brooklyn fans showed him.

Dixie and Estelle stayed in their Brooklyn apartment for a month after the 1940 season ended, rented a new home in the Rockville Centre area of nearby Long Island for 1941, looked forward to another child after the tragic death of baby Mary Ann (the second daughter, also named Mary Ann, was born early in 1941), and became part of the New York community.

"My mother came from a very large family in the New York area," says Susan Walker, "and there always seemed to be relatives around. My mother was close to her family and my dad really got along well with all of them. About the only thing they didn't like about him was that he wasn't Irish Catholic."

"Those eight and a half years I spent in Brooklyn were my favorite seasons in baseball," Dixie often said. "The people just were so kind to me and I grew so close to them."

Dixie purchased a package liquor store in Rockville Centre. He also made some extra cash, fifty to seventy-five dollars (now it is fifty or seventy five thousand for an equivalent appearance) by talking to club groups, a church, the Kiwanis, the Lions, the Elks, or any kind of assemblage of fans.

"Dad just enjoyed doing that so much," says Susan. "He was friendly with the fans, enjoyed telling baseball stories and often would throw in a song or two for the crowd." The Dodgers finished in second place in 1940 some twelve games behind the powerful Cincinnati Reds. The Reds went on to beat Hank Greenberg's Detroit Tigers four games to three in the World Series, with Bill Werber, the Cincinnati third baseman and a former Yankee, leading his club with a .370 average. Werber, who turned one hundred in 2008, still recalled his outstanding Series performance. He died in 2009, the oldest living former big leaguer. "I also lost a couple of hits to great fielding plays," he said over the phone from his retirement community home in Charlotte, North Carolina. "That was a great Series for me."

While the Reds had won by a big margin in 1940, the Dodgers seemed to be the team to beat for 1941. Leo Durocher had established himself as a smart, gambling manager after his second season at the helm. Larry

MacPhail, the bombastic GM, was ready to make any deal he thought could help his team win. Pete Reiser had proven in 1940 that he could play every day and with his great speed displaced Dixie in center and moved him to his more comfortable position in right where Walker had spent much time subbing for the Babe.

Pee Wee Reese had recovered from a broken bone in his foot, suffered on a slide in 1940, and was ready to claim the shortstop position full time from Durocher. Mickey Owen was solid behind the plate; Dolph Camilli, about as muscular as a guy could get in the era before steroids, was the first baseman; Cookie Lavagetto ("Hey, Cookie," the fans yelled every time the popular third baseman came to bat) held down the hot corner; and the pitching with the addition of Kirby Higbe from the Phillies, was solid with Whitlow Wyatt, a lifelong friend of Dixie's, Curt Davis, Luke (Hot Potato) Hamlin, and Hugh Casey in the bullpen.

Hamlin lost a tough game during the 1941 season, and Durocher, still steaming hours later, walked into a Philadelphia restaurant. There was an old lithograph of President Abraham Lincoln and his first vice president, Hannibal Hamlin, on the wall. Durocher saw the picture and bellowed, "Hamlin, Jesus. They shot the wrong guy."

Higbe was also the subject of a Brooklyn baseball story repeated over and over again by sportswriters in the wee small hours of the night while on the road with the ball club. Higbe, it seems, had a girlfriend on the road in St. Louis. When he returned home to Brooklyn with the Dodgers, his girlfriend decided to mail back his perfume-scented pajamas with a love letter. The package arrived at Ebbets Field, and clubhouse man Babe Hamburger, as efficient as could be, drove the package to Higbe's home. The pitcher was out and his wife tore it open and was annoyed and embarrassed at its contents. When Higbe returned home his wife threw the open package with the pajamas and the note at the Brooklyn pitcher. He read it quietly.

"Ahh, honey," Higbe, a tall, handsome, dark-haired lothario announced. "This isn't for me. This is for some other Kirby Higbe."

The Brooklyn Dodgers of 1941 were not only one of the most colorful teams the borough and baseball had ever seen, they were pretty talented. The addition of Owen, a fine receiver who would later become unhappily identified for missing a World Series strike thrown by Hugh Casey, with Tommy Henrich swinging and Higbe, who appeared in a remarkable 48 games with 39 starts and 22 wins in 1941, filled the final holes.

The only position manager Leo Durocher felt uncomfortable about was second base, a position held by a weak-hitting youngster named Pete Coscarart. That would be resolved in early May 1941 when the Dodgers obtained the veteran Billy Herman, sure-handed at the position and a fine hitter, later a Hall of Fame player.

The Dodgers had finished third in 1939, moved up to second, if twelve games behind the Reds in 1940, and seemed certain to be a contender in 1941.

Brooklyn hadn't seen a World Series since 1920 when the Cleveland Indians defeated the Dodgers five games to two in the old-fashioned best of nine.

The Hot Stove League was flaming in the winter months between the end of the 1940 season and the beginning of the very hopeful 1941 season. For so many years the expression of Brooklyn fans, as they studied the winter baseball stories about potential young stars and maturing older ones, was "Wait 'til next year."

On January 1, 1941, the next year had arrived. With what turned out to be the last war-free celebration of a new year in the United States for four years, the Dodgers were ready to fulfill the dream of so many and make baseball history.

8

The 1941 Pennant and
the 1944 Batting Title

Larry MacPhail, eager to show off his impressive team and spread the aura of the Dodgers as far and wide as he could, actually scheduled fifty exhibition games for the club.

The team would begin training in wide open Havana, Cuba (they would return there in 1947 because of the arrival of Jackie Robinson), and then move to their permanent spring camp in Clearwater, Florida, on April 1.

There would be exhibition games scheduled as far away as Houston and Fort Worth, Texas, later big league sites, and a dozen other cities throughout the South, including Atlanta, Nashville, and Richmond. The squad would be divided into A and B clubs so the travel for each player would be minimized though that hardly soothed the anger most of the players felt about MacPhail's greed. "This trip," sportswriter Jack Miley wrote in the *New York Post* before the team took off on its tour, "will make the Lewis and Clark expedition seem like a short walk."

The Dodgers boarded a chartered plane in Miami, flew forty-five minutes to Havana, were welcomed by shouting fans and a booming band (not the Brooklyn Dodgers Sym-Phony), and studied a huge banner posted above the airport administration building that said, "Bienvenido el club Brooklyn."

President Fulgencio Batista, the Cuban dictator, who oversaw the

Cuban tourist nightlife as his major source of income, sent aides to welcome the team at his palace. The Dodgers were then driven to the team headquarters at the stylish Hotel Nacional. There was no sign that 1941 day of a youngster named Fidel Castro who would show up as a hopeful baseball player when the Dodgers returned to Cuba in 1947.

According to Frank Graham, pitcher Van Lingle Mungo was the only survivor of the hilarious visit of the Dodgers in 1931. "He had a good memory for things like that," Graham wrote, "and showed the players some of the better spots: Prado 86, the Florida, Sloppy Joe's, and all of the others. This time, however, there was no carousing. This was a different kind of ball club. Even Van didn't take as much as a beaker of the famed Tropical brew."

Mungo, a big, handsome right-hander with a notorious high kick, had been a favorite of manager Casey Stengel during Stengel's three years as field boss of the Dodgers from 1934–1936. "I used to drive him home myself after games," Stengel once said, "to keep him out of the Brooklyn joints."

Mickey Owen hadn't signed yet so wasn't in camp to take over the catching job, and backup catcher Babe Phelps, claiming illness, stayed away from Havana. Insiders suggested he liked neither flying nor boats, making a trip to Havana from his Maryland home fairly difficult.

On January 31, MacPhail had signed Paul Waner, one of the game's best hitters and hardest drinkers. He was to be a backup to the set outfield of Joe Medwick in left, young Pete Reiser in right, and Dixie Walker with Charlie Gilbert, a promising youngster, platooning in center.

Waner had fished, golfed, and taken excellent care of himself through the off season, Graham reported, and he not only smacked the ball around Tropical Park, where the Dodgers trained, but covered ground like a "strong-legged kid just up from the bushes."

"I'm playing Waner in right field from now on, with Reiser in center and of course Medwick in left," Durocher announced to the press just before the New York Giants arrived for several exhibition games.

"Where does that leave Walker?" one shocked reporter stammered. "On the bench," Leo snapped.

After half a year in 1939 and one full season with Brooklyn in 1940, the People's Choice had become the center of the eye of another Brooklyn storm. That's just about the way it would be for the next seven Brooklyn years for Dixie.

"What's the matter with Leo?" Graham reported fans asking in Brooklyn bars and grills. "Has he blown his topper?"

Durocher was going with the hot hitter and even at the age of thirty-eight, Waner seemed comfortable with his new Brooklyn role.

Walker kept quiet and worked hard at getting in shape. Then the loyal Brooklyn fans, defending their favorite player, fired off a telegram to Durocher at the team's Clearwater hotel.

"Put Walker back in right field or we will boycott the Dodgers," the telegram read. It was signed by no less than five thousand of Brooklyn's aroused fans of Dixie.

If the Green Bay Packers are the only professional sports team supposedly owned by local fans, Brooklyn fans always claimed the same right. No kid growing up in Brooklyn felt any less possessive of the Dodgers than those Green Bay fans four decades later.

MacPhail was always battling for his status in the game and his independence as a baseball boss. "Keep Waner in there," he bellowed to Durocher after the telegram arrived. "If you play Walker I'll fire you." Durocher, about as independent a character in managing the team as MacPhail was in general managing, disregarded MacPhail's bellowing. He was only interested in putting the best nine out on the field.

"Let them holler," MacPhail shouted about the irate Walker-less Brooklyn fans, "I'll show them who's running this ball club."

Well, the truth was that Durocher, now escalated to his status as manager of the beloved Bums, wrote out his first 1941 lineup with Medwick in left, Reiser in center, and Waner in right. Dixie was on the bench as the Dodgers opened the season.

How bad could the 1941 Dodgers be if they could afford to keep a 1940 hitter who batted .308 riding the pines?

The Dodgers opened the season at Ebbets Field before a full house of some thirty-two thousand with the boycotting fans unaccounted for and the hated Giants on the other side of the field. The Giants were managed by the National League's last .400 hitter, Bill Terry (.401 in 1930) who gained negative immortality in Brooklyn when he maligned the team during a late 1934 season press conference by asking, "Are the Dodgers still in the league?"

Casey Stengel's Dodgers rose up to smite the Giants in a late-season series and kept them from winning their second pennant in a row as the Cardinals snuck by them. Brooklyn was certainly, the Giants now knew, still in the league.

Now the 1941 Brooklyn Dodgers, strengthened with the additions of Owen, Higbe, and the apparently rejuvenated Waner, part of the brother team of future Hall of Famers Paul and Lloyd, were set to blow open the National League pennant race early.

A funny thing happened to the Dodgers on the way to the pennant. They were swept by the Giants in the opening series. Brooklyn fans were restless as the team stumbled at the start of the 1941 season. Durocher, showing a little panic, and even a bit concerned about MacPhail's outrage, kept Walker on the bench and even played a rookie, Tom Tatum, when Reiser became ill. Dixie was edgy about all that.

"No matter what he did in baseball," Susan Walker remembers her mother, Estelle, telling her several times through those years, "my dad was insecure about his job. He had a large family to support, money was always tight, and he often thought the next game would be his last game. Then what?"

The veteran Waner began showing the weight of his age in early May, typical of the burdens of baseball, and Walker, at his peak of health at the age of thirty, was ready. Dixie had started a couple of games, pinch hit in a few more, and finished some others in Waner's place through the first thirty games. Now he was ready again for everyday action. "There came a day when MacPhail could hold out no longer against the demands of the mob," Frank Graham wrote. "Paul was benched and the Peepul's Cherce was in right field."

MacPhail, always looking to make a deal he thought could help the Dodgers, picked up veteran infielder Billy Herman, another future Hall of Famer, from the Cubs for sixty-five thousand dollars in early May. He replaced the light-hitting, unsure fielding Pete Coscarart. Now the Dodgers had their pennant team on the field, with Dixie in right, Herman at second, and all the pitchers lined up for the late-season run.

"Every day, it's like a World Series game around here," Herman told Eddie Murphy of the *Brooklyn Eagle*. "What a town."

After twenty-one years without a winner, Brooklyn fans were in a frenzy as the team battled the Cardinals for first place. Graham described the emotion with a wonderful tale in his book. Toots Shor, the famed restaurateur whose "joint," was the most popular hangout in town for athletes such as Joe DiMaggio, Joe Louis, and Jack Dempsey, show business celebrities such as Jackie Gleason and Frank Sinatra, and writers such as Ernest Hemingway, was at a Brooklyn game with *Journal American* columnist Bill Corum.

Shor was not only a popular New York figure but also a marvelous storyteller. One of his favorite tales pertained to Hemingway and a young New York Yankees player by the name of Yogi Berra. One day the baseball player and the famed writer were in his place at the same time. "I went up to Yogi and told him I wanted him to meet Hemingway," Shor said in *Where Have You Gone, Joe DiMaggio?* "We walked over to Hemingway and told him this was Berra, the new kid catcher with the Yankees," Shor said. Hemingway stuck out his hand for a greeting. Yogi stared at the famous novelist. "Yeah," he said, "and what paper do you write for?"

One day at Ebbets Field, the Dodgers were losing. First baseman Dolph Camilli, fighting a slump, came to bat. A fan sitting in front of Shor and Corum yelled out, "Sit down, you bum."

"Watch me have some fun with this fellow," Shor told Corum.

Shor leaned over and tapped the heckler on the shoulder.

"I wish you wouldn't call Camilli a bum," Shor said. "He's a friend of mine and a very nice fellow. If you knew him you wouldn't call him a bum."

The fan glowered and replied, "All right," he said. "If he's a friend of yours I'll lay off him."

Camilli popped out and the fan restrained himself. The next batter was the People's Choice, Dixie Walker.

"You bum," the fan yelled at Dixie, who heard some catcalls on occasion because no hitter can bat 1.000 and fanatic Brooklyn fans expected nothing less from some hitters. "Put the bat down and let somebody hit that can hit."

Toots tapped the excited fan on the shoulder again and he turned around and asked, "Is Walker your friend, too?"

Toots nodded and the fan asked, "Are all these bums your friends?" He nodded again.

"The fan got up and started across the aisle," Graham wrote. "He was headed for a seat in another section. 'I'm getting the hell away from you. You ain't going to spoil my afternoon.'"

With Dixie in right field every day and pounding the right field screen alongside Bedford Avenue at Ebbets Field with regularity, with young Pete Reiser establishing himself as one of the best young players to come along in years, and with Joe Medwick, the veteran, turning in an exemplary performance, the Dodgers were now solid in the outfield. Herman had put extra zip into the infield; Owen was steady behind the plate; and handsome Higbe and Dixie's Georgia pal Whit Wyatt anchored a strong, tough pitching staff. Hugh Casey was strong out of the bullpen and even the bench contributed, with great efforts from Jimmy Wasdell and Lew Riggs.

The St. Louis Cardinals and the Brooklyn Dodgers were engaged in the titanic pennant races that would so distinguish the National League battleground for the next half dozen years.

Branch Rickey, then running the Cardinals, brought up a fine left-handed pitcher named Howard Pollet in late August but waited until September before he promoted the finest hitter in the St. Louis organization, a youngster from the coal mining country of Donora, Pennsylvania, named Stan Musial.

"I always had a fondness for Ebbets Field and playing in Brooklyn," Musial said several years later. "I had a great day there, six hits in a double header, a couple of homers and we won both games. I walked on the field the next day for batting practice and the fans were yelling, 'Here he comes, here comes the man.' I told [Bob] Broeg of the *St. Louis Post Dispatch* about it and he started calling me 'Stan (the Man) Musial.' I thought that was pretty nice," Musial said.

Musial, who won seven batting titles and was considered the finest National League hitter of his time (Ted Williams was always ranked as the game's greatest hitter), hit a blistering .426 in twelve September games. It proved a little late for the Cardinals in 1941.

The Dodgers came in to St. Louis in mid-September 1941 with a one-game lead. Durocher sent Fat Freddy Fitzsimmons, the chubby, aging knuckleballer, against Ernie White of the Cardinals in the first game.

The game was tied 4–4 into the eleventh inning. Walker faced White, a left-hander with a hard curve who would win seventeen games that season, with the bases loaded and two out. No longer a platoon player, Dixie had learned how to handle the tricky lefties as he handled most of the righties. He walked seventy times that year and only struck out eighteen times.

White threw a curve ball on a 2–2 pitch and Dixie slapped it on a line into center field. Two runs scored and that was the ball game for Brooklyn. They now led the heated pennant race by two games with fifteen games to go.

The Cardinals came back the next day behind the youngster Pollet, with Musial getting two hits, and beat Brooklyn 4–3.

The series, and maybe the entire 1941 season, came down to the final game of the set with Whitlow Wyatt facing Mort Cooper in one of baseball's classic matches, two strong, hard-throwing right-handed pitchers, at the peak of their game, matching up in a contest that just might settle the pennant race.

Whitlow John Wyatt, born in Kensington, Georgia, on September 27, 1907, had the same long, winding baseball trail as Dixie Walker before he landed in Brooklyn. He had signed with the Detroit Tigers out of high school, made it up to the big leagues for four games in 1929, bounced up and down within the organization through 1933, drifted to the White Sox and Indians before winding up in the minor leagues again at Milwaukee, and was purchased by Brooklyn in 1939. He could always throw hard but couldn't win regularly until he picked up a hard-breaking slider after some practice with the pitch in the Brewers bullpen. He was 8–3 in 1939 with the improving Dodgers, won fifteen games as a regular starter in 1940, and anchored the Brooklyn winners, along with Kirby Higbe in 1941 with a 22–10 mark and a 2.34 ERA.

"I think he was my dad's best friend in baseball," says Susan Walker. "They visited often at each other's homes. I remember him coming to Birmingham a lot with his wife. They went hunting and fishing together—often with my uncle Harry. I think they coached together at a couple of places and my dad had him as a coach in Atlanta when my dad managed there."

Wyatt always seemed to be matched against the other team's best pitchers by Durocher in 1941 because he was a more phlegmatic personality against the hyper Higbe. He was constantly going against Cincinnati's Paul Derringer or Bucky Walters, Claude Passeau of the Cubs, Prince Hal Schumacher or King Carl Hubbell of the Giants, and when the Cardinals came along with a new hard thrower, Mort Cooper, with brother Walker Cooper behind the plate, Wyatt was the Dodgers' man.

In *The Brooklyn Dodgers* (in Baseball's Great Teams series), sportswriter Tommy Holmes of the *Brooklyn Eagle* and later with the *Herald Tribune* wrote of the game on September 13, 1941, "Everyone in Sportsman's Park seemed to sense that the pennant hinged on the struggle in the warm sunshine between the Dodgers and the Cardinals. The opposing pitchers were Whitlow Wyatt, the late-blooming Brooklyn right-hander, and the younger but equally skillful Morton Cooper, also right-handed. Both would have checkered careers in the majors but neither would perform better than on this day."

I traveled often with Holmes in his later days as a sportswriter covering the new New York Mets (born in 1962) and the Yankees. Holmes had an accident as a youngster that cost him his left arm, but he could type more rapidly with his right index finger than any other reporter on the beat as he batted out his stories.

There was always much sick humor around Holmes in those days, especially involving his problems in dealing with faucets in rest rooms with one hand or his inability to press an elevator key while carrying his portable typewriter. A dozen of us sportswriters were in the fancy Blue Fox restaurant in San Francisco in the early 1960s for a stylish expense account dinner when one of the writers, Jack Lang of the *Long Island Press,* decided he wanted to walk off with a handsome, very large pepper mill as a souvenir of the evening.

"How can you do that?" he was asked.

"I'll put it up Tommy Holmes' empty sleeve and we'll walk out holding hands," said Lang. "After all, this is San Francisco and nobody will notice." Drunken sportswriters often got carried away with their wild ideas. But that time the huge pepper mill stayed on the table.

On September 13, 1941, with the Dodgers leading the Cardinals by one game, Wyatt and Cooper went after each other in one of the great games of the decade, each holding the other team scoreless into the eighth inning with almost all of the 32,691 St. Louis fans howling on every pitch.

Dixie Walker hit a double off the right field screen with one out in the eighth. Billy Herman, a great addition for Brooklyn, was up next. St. Louis catcher Gus Mancuso signaled for a curve and Walker, always a heady player, caught the sign and relayed it to Herman at the plate. Warren Spahn, the winningest left-handed pitcher in National League history, often said the secret of pitching was to throw the batter's timing off and fool him with speed or trajectory. Knowing what pitch was coming wouldn't guarantee a base hit but it certainly made the batter's job easier.

"Billy's owl eyes bugged out so far," Walker said afterward, "that I was sure the Cardinals would catch on and switch."

Cooper, confident in his curve ball, threw the breaking pitch almost belt high and on the outside of the plate. Herman, a fine contact hitter, moved in on the ball and smacked it in the hole between center fielder Terry Moore and right fielder Enos Slaughter for a run-scoring double.

Dixie raced around third base with the run that would give Wyatt one of his seven shutouts, probably the biggest, in his fine 1941 season.

The Dodgers moved on to Cincinnati, Pittsburgh, and Philadelphia (no West Coast games then) before ending the road trip in Boston. Wyatt shut the Braves out 6–0 on September 25 at Braves Field and the Dodgers had their first pennant since 1920.

Dixie Walker was on a championship club at the age of thirty-one in his fourteenth professional season as a ball player.

The train ride home, in special cars, from Boston to New York City's Grand Central Station, was a wild celebration, with players pounding each other, sportswriters unable to write as everybody tore up their yellow Western Union sheets, champagne being spilled as well as drunk, and Dixie Walker leading his teammates and assorted hangers-on in a wild rendition of old songs.

Red Barber had announced the expected arrival time of the train in New York and the crowd grew in Grand Central as the cars passed through Providence, Rhode Island, then New London, New Haven, Bridgeport, and Stamford, Connecticut, in the five-hour journey. The last stop before midtown Manhattan on the train ride from Boston to New York was 125th Street in the Harlem section of New York City.

Manager Leo Durocher, aware of the fans' excitement and knowing that many of the players would rather have skipped the hoopla for private joys (Dixie Walker would much rather have had a quiet glass of sherry with Estelle at their Rockville Centre home) ordered the conductors to skip the 125th Street stop.

Many fans and one general manager, Larry MacPhail, who had rushed up there by cab from his Manhattan apartment that Sunday, looked on in despair as the special Dodger train roared by the uptown location. It would arrive at Grand Central's Forty-second Street stop in eleven minutes. Red Barber said the train would be in the station at 9:23 p.m.

More than ten thousand people, mostly from Brooklyn, had taken subways to the station, collected near the information booth, gathered outside the platform where the train would disembark on track eleven (Dixie's uniform number), and pounded the players in joy as they marched off in single file.

The cops had to come into the station, push the delirious crowd back, open up pathways to the outside cab stands, and ensure the safety of the Dodgers, who had to meet the Yankees in the World Series in six days.

The one sour note to the day of Brooklyn's greatest joy occurred when MacPhail, angered beyond belief when the train roared past him at 125th Street, made it back downtown to the New Yorker Hotel where Durocher was staying and fired the manager.

Durocher admitted he had ordered the conductors to skip 125th Street, not knowing MacPhail was waiting there and wanting his players to be greeted by happy fans at Grand Central.

"You're through, you're fired," bellowed MacPhail.

He stormed out of Durocher's room and much of the joy of the triumph evaporated under MacPhail's attack.

As often happened around Leo and Larry, all was quiet the next day, sort of a 1941 forerunner of the 1970s explosive relationship between Yankees owner George Steinbrenner and Yankees manager Billy Martin, the fire and oil of baseball partnerships.

The people of the Borough of Brooklyn cared little about the squabble between the general manager and the manager. All they knew was "next year" had finally arrived and the Brooklyn Dodgers were the National League champs.

Borough president John Cashmore proclaimed September 29 Dodger

Day in Brooklyn and some sixty thousand people—cops, firemen, sanitation workers, school kids, office workers, church groups, Kiwanis Clubbers, Knights of Columbus, and the twenty-five players and entire staff of the Brooklyn Dodgers, this time led by a waving, grinning MacPhail with Durocher at his side—rode, walked and hopped down Flatbush Avenue from the Dodger offices to Prospect Park for a rally of congratulations.

More than a million fans and school kids in a borough of some 2 million skipped their day's chores to scream their joy and share the pleasure of the triumph with their Dodgers and friends.

Frank Graham wrote, "Old timers said it was Brooklyn's biggest parade since the Fourteenth Zouaves and the Twenty-third Regiment returned from the Civil War."

The World Series opened on October 1, 1941, at Yankee Stadium with Leo Durocher's surprise starter, Curt Davis, battling future Hall of Famer Red Ruffing.

Ruffing, one of the toughest competitors the game had ever seen, limited the Dodgers to six hits and beat them 3–2. Dixie led off, was hitless in three trips, and felt confident that his pal, Whitlow Wyatt would even things for the Dodgers the next day.

Dixie was hitless again the next day, but Wyatt answered the call of Brooklyn fans by keeping Joe DiMaggio hitless in three tries and tying the Series with a 3–2 victory.

Marius Russo, a Brooklyn native who had somehow escaped the Dodgers, beat Brooklyn 2–1 in the third game. It was Russo's line drive off the left knee of the opposing pitcher, Fat Freddie Fitzsimmons, in the seventh inning that did the Dodgers in. Hugh Casey had to warm up rapidly for the eighth inning and the Yankees quickly collected the two winning runs off him. A double by Dixie for his first Series hit and a single by Pee Wee Reese in the bottom of the eighth accounted for Brooklyn's only run.

The next day, Sunday, October 5, 1941, was one of the most memorable in baseball history. The Dodgers led the Yankees 4–3 with two out and nobody on in the top of the ninth. Hugh Casey was pitching for Brooklyn and Tommy Henrich was batting for the Yankees.

"I saw the ball breaking and I swung and missed," recalled Henrich some 65 years after the play. "I turned around on my follow through and caught [Mickey] Owen pushing off his mask and racing for the ball. I just took off for first as hard as I could."

Henrich was safe on first base as Casey's curve or spitter—the legend has never been fully cleared up—got past the catcher. DiMaggio singled, Charlie (King Kong) Keller doubled, Bill Dickey walked, and Joe Gordon doubled as the Yankees collected four runs for the 7–4 win.

Owen, who went on to a long career as a baseball scout, police officer, farmer, and operator of a baseball school that once had a North Carolina youngster named Michael Jordan as a student, was never traumatized by the passed ball.

"It was a low-breaking ball," he recalled shortly before his death at age eighty-nine in 2005. "I got down as low as I could. It just slid past my glove."

The Yankees closed out the 1941 Series the next day with Ernie (Tiny) Bonham, a bulky 215-pound right-hander, beating Wyatt 3–1. Dixie had a single in three trips and ended the Series with a disappointing .222 average.

Dixie and Estelle with their two children, young Fred and the second daughter, Mary Ann, settled into their home in Rockville Centre for a good part of the winter before returning to Birmingham. Dixie spent a great deal of time at the package liquor store with his partner, Estelle's brother-in-law Nicholas Callan, spoke at local clubs for a few extra dollars, and hunted in the Long Island woods with friends.

On December 7, 1941, Dixie drove to the Polo Grounds with Estelle and the two children for a football game between the Brooklyn Dodgers and the New York Giants. A public address announcement soon called for all members of the military to report to their units. The Japanese had attacked Pearl Harbor. World War II began for the United States the next day when President Franklin Roosevelt declared December 7 "a date which will live in infamy," A few days later the United States declared war against Germany.

Dixie Walker, a thirty-one-year-old father of two, with a long history of shoulder, knee, and stomach troubles, had earlier been classified 4F, physically unfit for service, by his Birmingham draft board. It would keep him out of the military during the war.

With Roosevelt's blessing, baseball continued after the United States entered the war. The Dodgers had another big lead in August 1942, as much as ten games, when they started slipping. The young, aggressive Cardinals, a new edition of the Gashouse Gang of the 1930s, was nipping at Brooklyn's heels.

Walker, who had batted .311 in 1941 in 148 games, was injured again. He played in only 118 games in 1942 and slipped to .290.

Larry MacPhail entered the Dodgers clubhouse one day and warned his team that they might not win. Walker, always careful with his money, offered to bet his boss two hundred dollars, a significant sum in 1942, that the Dodgers would win by eight games. MacPhail refused to take the bet. "That proved he was talking through his hat," wrote Frank Graham. "When Larry was reasonably sure he knew what he was talking about, he'd lay it on the line, like anybody else with any sporting blood in him."

The Cardinals swept a three-game series against the Dodgers in St. Louis in late August with Max Lanier winning the opener, Mort Cooper topping Whit Wyatt 2–1 in fourteen innings in one of their classic matchups, and Johnny Beazley beating Brooklyn 2–1 in the final game of the set.

The Dodgers won 104 games in 1942, the winningest total the team ever claimed. The Cardinals, with Stan (the Man) Musial hitting .315 in his first full season, won 106 games. St. Louis went on to defeat the Yankees four games to one in the 1942 World Series.

Many of the star players on the Dodgers team, Pee Wee Reese, Pete Reiser, Hugh Casey, and even general manager Larry MacPhail, who had been a soldier in World War I and had stolen an ashtray from the palace of the German kaiser, were now off in military service. The Dodgers, under Durocher, finished in third place.

The feudin', fussin', and fightin' typical of any baseball clubhouse led by Durocher continued in 1943.

On one afternoon, with Bobo Newsom pitching and young Bobby Bragan, the kid obtained from the Phillies, now catching, Brooklyn beat Pittsburgh in a wild one, 8–7.

Durocher suggested that Newsom had thrown a spitter and caught Bragan by surprise with the trick pitch. "All Newsom had to do was to tip Bragan that a spitter might be coming and tell him to watch for it," Durocher complained to legendary sportswriter Tim Cohane of the *World Telegram.*

Cohane informed his colleagues in the press about the rhubarb—a Brooklyn baseball term for an argument as created by Red Barber—and they all wrote about the turmoil in the Dodgers' clubhouse. The players saw it as Leo's way of embarrassing the veteran Newsom and placating young Bragan.

Veteran player Arky Vaughan, who had replaced Reese, threw his uniform at Leo's feet the next day and said, "If that's the way you're running this club, you can have my uniform."

"You can have mine, too," said Dixie Walker, by now one of the leaders of the team in his fifth Brooklyn season. Walker made no move to take off his number 11 uniform he already had on as one of the early arrivals at Ebbets Field.

Cohane was called at his Yonkers home and agreed to come to the park on his day off and address the Dodgers about the incident. The veteran reporter, who would later gain journalistic fame by scooping the world on Jackie Robinson's 1956 retirement for an article in *Look Magazine,* repeated what he had heard in the Dodger clubhouse from Durocher about Newsom.

In a few days Newsom was traded away; Bragan would still be with the club for the historic 1947 season; and Durocher would gain baseball immortality with his 1994 Baseball Hall of Fame election.

The Dodgers finished third in 1943 with Walker coming back strong with his third .300 season at .302 in 138 games.

Baseball reached its depth in 1944 with many players away in service, many untried youngsters filling positions, and many used-up veterans getting a chance to hang on to their jobs while the competitive coffers were empty. "They're either too young or too old," as the popular song of the day indicated.

Dixie Walker, at age thirty-three, was healthy that year. He played in 148 games, collected his highest career total of 191 hits, and batted .357. It was good enough to win the National League batting title.

When it was suggested later that Walker had won the crown in a low-level war year, he often replied, "I beat out a pretty fair hitter named Musial." Musial had won his first of seven batting titles in 1943 with a .357 mark, hit .347 in 1944, missed the 1945 season while in the navy, and came back to win another batting title in 1946.

Dixie had nothing to be ashamed of in 1944. He had also grown more important in the Brooklyn scene, especially in the year when the Dodgers, hit harder than most teams by the loss of so many quality young players, were battling to stay out of the bottom.

With many players slipping back into the game in 1945 and the Dodgers climbing back to third place, Walker batted .300, led the league in runs batted in with 124, and played in all of his team's games, 154, for the first time.

The People's Choice was at the top of his game and as well liked as any player could be. Evidence of his popularity was seen during the war by the reception he received when he took USO tours to the Aleutians or to the China-Burma-India theater to address the troops.

In an article for the Society for American Baseball Research journal in 1993, writer Jack Kavanagh pointed out that in a 1943 war bonds auction conducted at the famed Waldorf Astoria Hotel in New York City, more than $123 million was raised in auction bids. "Dixie Walker drew the highest bid, over 11 million dollars. After that every time he got a base hit this translated into bond sales," Kavanagh wrote. "Walker took a war-time job between seasons with the Sperry Gyroscope Company, a vital military supplier. He was in charge of employee recreation programs for thousands of men and women who produced intricate instruments to keep aircraft flying."

The war in Europe ended in May 1945 and Japan surrendered officially in September of that year. The baseball players who served in the military would be streaming home for the 1946 season.

The Dodgers and Cardinals waged another titanic battle for the flag; this time it ended in a tie. Both teams had ninety-six wins and played baseball's first ever pennant playoff, the best two games out of three.

Ralph Branca started the first game, was beaten, and the Dodgers lost their chance at the pennant in the second game when they lost 8–3 and left the bases loaded as Eddie Stanky and Howie Schultz, the 1946 first baseman, soon to be replaced by a historic figure, struck out. "I didn't have good stuff in that first game," recalled Branca some 62 years later. "It wasn't nerves or anything. It was just one of those days when your fast ball isn't very fast and your curve ball won't curve."

The Cardinals went on to beat the Boston Red Sox four games to three in a stirring 1946 World Series. Ted Williams hit only .200 with five singles in the October classic. Dixie's brother, Harry Walker, won the final game when he doubled to left center field with two out in the eighth inning of a 3–3 tied game, sending Enos Slaughter all the way home from first with the winning Series run when Boston shortstop Johnny Pesky hesitated in getting the relay to the plate.

Branca said he wasn't terribly disappointed at the loss to the Cardinals because he would only be twenty-one the next season, was in his fourth year as a Dodger, and knew that Branch Rickey and the Brooklyn organization were adding a lot more talented youngsters for the 1947 pennant run.

Dixie Walker's fame and popularity continued to grow through those seasons of 1944, 1945, and 1946. Kids in Brooklyn and throughout America would imitate his closed stance, practice that left-handed swing, and use his name as they batted in their own games.

In the early spring of 1975, Susan Walker and her husband, Ed, were shopping in the children's department of a local New Jersey mall when they spotted a child's shirt. "It showed a drawing of Dixie just below the Ripley's Believe It or Not logo. It said, 'Dixie Walker hit a home run and caught the ball himself. It lodged in the right field screen until Walker shook it loose and caught it. Ebbets Field 1946.' Isn't that amazing?" Susan said. It showed what a historic figure Dixie was. They were amazed. They bought five shirts, one for each of their children, and have them to this day.

The game was against the Pirates and Walker was the only man to catch his own home run in baseball history. Strange things happened in Ebbets Field, few stranger than this catch.

Stranger things were about to happen as the historic 1947 baseball season approached.

9
Jackie's Early Years

The revolutionary figures in baseball's twentieth-century integration were Jackie Robinson, of course; Branch Rickey, the Brooklyn Dodgers boss who signed him in 1945; Commissioner Albert (Happy) Chandler, who allowed Rickey's move to go through; Brooklyn shortstop Pee Wee Reese, who quickly accepted and aided his black teammate; opposing stars such as Hank Greenberg and Stan Musial, who encouraged Robinson; and dozens of personal and political supporters.

One name is always left out of the integration equation.

Jorge Pasquel was a millionaire businessman who owned several teams in the Mexican Baseball League. He had integrated his league with American Negro League stars as far back as 1938 when he brought the heralded, entertaining, talented pitcher Satchel Paige ("Don't look back. Something may be gaining on you.") to Mexico in 1938 for a salary of two thousand dollars a month, and followed that up with appearances south of the border by other black stars including catcher Josh Gibson, third baseman Ray Dandridge, and future Hall of Famer Monte Irvin.

"I played in Mexico before the war because the pay was good and I had a chance to compete against some of the game's best players," Irvin said at the Hall of Fame inductions in Cooperstown in 2008. "There still weren't any ideas that black Americans like us could make it in the big leagues."

By 1946, Pasquel had "invaded" big league baseball and brought Mickey Owen, Max Lanier, Sal Maglie, Luis Olmo, Jimmy Brown, Vern Stephens, Danny Gardella, and about two dozen more south of the border to play in his league. He offered big contracts to Ted Williams, Stan Musial, and Bob Feller. They refused his lucrative offers, but big league owners were stung by his audacity.

Any player who signed Mexican League contracts was suspended by big league baseball for violating his contract and the cherished reserve clause that bound a player for life until "traded, sold or released" by his team.

Original life suspensions were later changed to three-year suspensions as the players grew tired of Mexican League conditions and returned to the United States. Gardella was the only player to sue baseball for its high-handed ways.

The former outfielder on the wartime New York Giants, who hit eighteen homers with seventy-one RBIs for the 1945 Giants, won a compromise offer of sixty thousand dollars from baseball for dropping his suit. Gardella and his wife, Katherine, raised nine children with that money and the income from his insignificant positions, including work as a hospital orderly near their Yonkers, New York, home. Gardella was out of organized baseball after his 1946 season in Mexico until restored in 1950. He played one game with one at bat for the St. Louis Cardinals, then drifted to minor league play and was out of the game at the age of thirty-five.

"I know my law suit didn't make me rich but I was proud that it helped break open the baseball players' slavery and led to free agency," Gardella once said. "I think somebody had to stand up to the owners and I decided to be the guy."

While Pasquel was chasing after big league players for his Mexican League teams, baseball's owners understood two major changes were occurring as a result of the Mexican owner's actions. The game was integrating. (Jackie Robinson with the Brooklyn Dodgers and Larry Doby with the Cleveland Indians would prove that in 1947.) Second, agitation for a pension plan for big leaguers was gaining momentum.

Throughout the winter between the end of the 1946 season and the start of the 1947 season, Dixie Walker, representing National League players, and Johnny Murphy, the Yankees relief pitcher representing American League players, met often with fellow players and with baseball owners or their representatives. There was much talk about a players union (which didn't come about until 1954) but even more discussion about a pension for big league players.

"Dixie didn't need the pension plan for himself," says Susan Walker's husband, Ed. "He was in a position to capitalize on his fame once his playing days were over. During his career, he posed for pipe tobacco ads, a Wheaties cereal box ad, comic book characters, and many more. He knew he could make a living in or out of the game afterward but so many players, especially ones whose careers were cut short by injuries, certainly couldn't."

Dixie's suggestion that the pension plan money be obtained through All-Star game benefits won the owners over.

The plan began in that 1947 season and conditions remained much the same in the pension package until a historic figure arrived on the baseball scene in 1966. Marvin Miller, now in his nineties, was the executive director of the Major League Baseball Players Association from 1966 to 1983. He was born in the Bronx, moved to Brooklyn, rooted for the Dodgers, graduated from James Madison High School in Brooklyn, and attended Brooklyn College, St. John's University, Miami of Ohio, and New York University before starting his career as a labor union economist. He was representing the United Steelworkers of America when he was selected by the players to lead them.

"I was on an elevator at a meeting at the Fairmont Hotel in San Francisco when George W. Taylor, an economics professor at the University of Pennsylvania's Wharton School of Business, got on. I knew him from work I had done with him some years earlier at the War Labor Relations Board. He asked me if I knew a man named Robin Roberts, the baseball pitcher," Miller said.

Miller was a fan, knew Roberts had pitched many great games against his Brooklyn Dodgers, and was now near the end of his career. "Roberts had asked Taylor if he had the name of anyone who might help the players in their negotiations with the owners over salaries, pensions and conditions. My name came up," Miller said.

Miller later met with Roberts, Harvey Kuenn, Bob Friend, and Jim Bunning, now a U.S. senator from Kentucky. He visited spring training camps in 1966 and was selected by the players to lead their battle. "There were two things in order when I took the job—a pension plan created by Dixie Walker and the others in 1946 that paid a maximum yearly amount of $180,000, and the Murphy money," Miller said.

A lawyer named Robert Murphy (no relation to the pitcher) had helped the players obtain spring training expense money for tips, cabs, newspapers, and incidental expenses. Room and meals were provided by the teams. "This incidental money became known as Murphy money and you would visit spring training and hear players ask each other, 'Did you get your Murphy money?' It didn't amount to much," Miller said.

By using Dixie Walker's plan and connecting pensions to the All-Star games in a 60–40 formula favoring the players, the money would be available for all future players. "We had to shoot down Walter O'Malley's idea in the 1970s that the money would be a fixed amount instead of a percentage deal as the All-Star revenue increased through the years," Miller said.

Miller's major contributions—historic changes that should gain him Hall of Fame immortality—include raising the minimum baseball salary from $6,000 when he entered the negotiating arena to today's $350,000 a year; unlimited negotiated free agency; and arbitration for contracts between owners and players.

"I was at the All-Star game in Pittsburgh in 2006," Miller said. "I was invited because I had spent so many years in Pittsburgh with the United

Steelworkers. At the dinner one of the players, Alex Rodriguez, came up to say hello. He was with his wife and they were telling me about the new house they had just bought," Miller said.

Rodriguez, the game's best player, now makes $26 million dollars a year after several signings as a free agent under conditions originally negotiated by Miller. In 2008 he extended his $26 million a year contract for ten more seasons with the Yankees.

"Honey, I want you to meet Mr. Miller," Rodriguez said to his wife, Cynthia. "He's the guy who just bought us our new big house."

Miller certainly changed the salary structure of baseball players. But before Miller it was Dixie Walker who had the most to do with changing their lifelong security with his negotiated pension plan.

In that winter of 1946, he worked long hours on the pension plan. He traveled home to Birmingham often to see how his father and the hardware store were doing. He got himself physically ready for another strong season at the age of thirty-six with the Dodgers. He didn't spend much time thinking about Jackie Robinson.

By 1947, Dixie Walker had clearly become the most popular player in Brooklyn baseball history. The 1941 pennant, the 1944 batting title, and the 1945 RBI crown had all helped. But even more important was his emotional connection with Brooklyn fans.

His newspaper photographs filled baseball scrapbooks of Brooklyn youngsters and his batting stance was imitated in street games throughout the borough. He appeared more often than any other Dodger at public functions and often represented the club at civic events. Brooklyn kids addressed each other often as "Dixie," hardly a common New York City name before the 1940s and the arrival of the outfielder from Birmingham.

A retired New York businessman recalled a story in 2008 that typified the affection so many had for Dixie Walker. "I grew up in the Williamsburg section of Brooklyn, a Jewish neighborhood," said Norm Lev. "On the same floor in my apartment building was a young boy who was a Brooklyn Dodger fan, but even more so, a Dixie Walker fan. He just idolized Dixie. The youngster, named Heshy [a Jewish name for Harry] was also a Yeshiva boy and attended the local Jewish religious school. I was a little older and one day I offered to take him to a game at Ebbets Field. His mother reluctantly gave him permission to go with me. He wanted to sit in right field where he could gaze at Dixie Walker.

"While we sat at the game I noticed that he wasn't paying attention to the events in the game. He just continued to stare at wherever Dixie was positioning himself. Long about the fifth inning of the ball game, he couldn't contain himself any longer and blurted out to me, 'I wish Dixie was my rabbi.' There could be no higher compliment from Heshy," said Lev.

Lev continued, "Such was the love and adoration for Dixie. A stranger compliment for a southern bigot I couldn't imagine."

Until 1947 Dixie Walker's image was clearly that of the most popular player in the history of the Brooklyn Dodgers. After 1947 he was unfairly locked into the negative, racist image the press, the public, and maybe Branch Rickey portrayed in him, a negative portrait that has lasted to this day.

On October 23, 1945, Jack Roosevelt Robinson signed a contract with the Montreal Royals, the top farm club of the Brooklyn Dodgers. An announcement was made in the offices of the ball club at Delormier Downs on Ontario Street in the picturesque, cosmopolitan city of Montreal.

President Hector Racine of the Royals made the announcement, with Robinson sitting nearby at an afternoon news conference. Branch Rickey Jr., son of the Brooklyn boss, represented his father at the event. Jacques Beauchamp of the *Montreal Matin* covered the event for his newspaper and recalled his emotions forty-two years after the signing in an interview with me for the book *Jackie Robinson: A Life Remembered*.

"I was just nineteen years old and I was beginning my career," Beauchamp recalled. "Nobody knew what the announcement would be, but we were told it would be big. We thought it might be a new manager, a big name manager for the ball club.

"Jackie Robinson was there and it was announced that he had signed a contract to play for the Royals. He was a big fellow and certainly looked like an athlete. Black players had played in Montreal before. The previous season there had been a game between the Josh Gibson All-Stars with Satchel Paige and a local semiprofessional club. There were many blacks in Montreal. Nobody made a fuss over them. I'll tell you how big Jackie Robinson became in Montreal. Some people thought he was an athletic hero equal to Maurice Richard, the hockey star. *Nobody* was ever a bigger sports hero in Montreal than Richard."

Beauchamp covered the club all season, became friendly with Robinson, admired his play, respected his skills and even got to know Rachel Robinson. "She was a warm and wonderful person," Beauchamp said. "Everybody loved her around the ball club, and I think she helped make things easier for Jackie."

Beauchamp said that more than forty years after Robinson's arrival in Canada he still could recall significant memories of the historic baseball event. "A few days after Robinson reported for spring training in 1946, I asked Clay Hopper, the manager from Mississippi, how his family was taking it. He said, 'My father is dead. If he were alive he would probably kill me for managing a black player.' I never wrote anything like that because Clay was a nice man, and we all expected he would judge Robinson on his baseball ability. I think he did. Jackie had a great year, of course, won the batting title and led the team to the pennant and the Little World Series over Louisville. I think Jackie's name is still popular around Montreal. He may not be the equal as a hero to Maurice Richard, but he is certainly remembered by older people in Montreal. As for youngsters knowing who Jackie is, I'm not so sure. They may not know him." Montreal baseball fans were more interested in the modern Expos before their move to Washington than they were in the Triple A Montreal Royals.

While Dixie Walker, busy painting his house in Birmingham that October day in 1945, told a reporter he wasn't concerned about the signing of a colored man as long as he didn't join the Brooklyn team, other players hardly noticed.

"I was in school at NYU," recalled Ralph Branca, who had completed two seasons with Brooklyn by the time the Dodgers signed Robinson. "It didn't really register as something special. I was more concerned with getting my arm strong for the 1946 season."

Branca had grown up in an integrated neighborhood of a Westchester, New York, suburb called Mount Vernon, just north of New York City. "I played baseball against players from every race," he said. "Mount Vernon was a very mixed community. Two houses down from our home in Mount Vernon, there was another house rented by a black family. They had kids about our age and we played in the streets with them. You really didn't notice race. You noticed who could hit the ball." Many years after Branca achieved baseball success, he sold his family home to a black family. One of the youngsters in the family, Ken Singleton, went on to become one of the finest outfielders in big league baseball during his time.

"I was on a fishing trip with some friends when I heard the news that the Dodgers had signed a colored player," recalled George Shuba, a 1946 teammate of Robinson's with the Montreal Royals and later with the Brooklyn Dodgers. "It wasn't something I thought much about. I was too busy trying to make my own way in baseball. We started our training that spring of 1946 in Sanford, Florida, and then went on to Daytona. It didn't take long to see Jackie was a fine athlete. He was pretty quiet at first, but by the end of spring training he was warming up to the guys and they were warming up to him. He used to come out to the park each morning in a cab from where he was staying. The other players stayed in a hotel in town. Those kind of things just weren't discussed. We talked about what went on in the ball park, not what went on before or after the workout or the game."

The Royals crushed the Jersey City Giants 14–1 on the opening day of the 1946 International League season. Robinson had four hits, including a home run, in five at bats, knocked in three runs, scored four runs, and drove the Jersey City pitchers wacky with his daring base running.

"The blacks in the stands wanted him to hit every ball out of the park," Shuba recalled, "and maybe some of the southern boys on our team didn't want him to hit at all. I remember the home run he hit because I was the next batter. The ball cleared the fence by a lot and Jackie bounced around the bases. When he got to third base, our manager, Clay Hopper, the Mississippi man, patted Jackie on the back as he would any player and I shook his hand firmly at the plate."

A photograph of the handshake at home plate appeared in most area newspapers the next day. To this day Shuba autographs copies of this picture at all his speaking engagements. "It was the first picture of a black player being congratulated by a white player for a home run," said Shuba. "I have the photo on the wall at my home. It is a significant piece of baseball history."

Al Campanis was a twenty-nine-year-old journeyman infielder with the Montreal Royals in 1946. He played shortstop next to second baseman Jackie Robinson. "Jackie hadn't played a lot of baseball," recalled Campanis in 1987. "You could see that. He was a bit awkward around second base, but he was such a good athlete he seemed to pick things up easily. He got cut a couple of times but he wouldn't budge. The blood ran through his socks once, and I came up to him after the game and said to him 'I think I can help on the double play.' He said he would appreciate that. I told him to come out early the next day and we would work on that together."

Campanis recalled another aspect of being a teammate of Jackie Robinson with the Royals in 1946. "There was some name-calling from the opposing side," remembered Campanis. "When it got real bad we would just holler back for him. Jackie never said a word, but a few of our guys, Herman Franks, Lew Riggs, Johnny Jorgensen, Dixie Howell—we raised some hell with the opposition. I used to let them yell a little, and then I would yell back, 'You wanna pick on somebody, pick on me.' They would yell, 'We don't have anything against you.' It was all ridiculous."

Campanis was born in Kos, Greece, and arrived with his family as a small child in New York City. He starred as a football player for New

York University and also played on the Violets baseball team. The Dodgers signed him in 1943. He was already thinking of a baseball career off the field by the time he teamed up with Robinson in 1946.

He was a Brooklyn scout in 1955 when he discovered a kid pitcher from Brooklyn named Sandy Koufax. He signed him for fourteen thousand dollars. Campanis was soon the farm director of the Dodgers and became the team's general manager from 1968 through 1987.

Campanis is identified as a player who helped Robinson adjust to professional baseball. He often spoke of their close friendship. "We always feel that Jackie is part of the Dodgers organization," Campanis said in March 1987 during an interview at the team spring headquarters at Vero Beach, Florida. "His memory is with us, and there are photos of him all over Dodgertown in Vero Beach. We don't want anyone to forget Jackie Robinson. There is a Jackie Robinson Drive in Vero Beach along with the streets named for Sandy Koufax and Pee Wee Reese and Don Drysdale and all of our great players."

On April 6, 1987, Campanis sat down for an interview with Ted Koppel for *Nightline*. He was in the Los Angeles team offices while Koppel sat in ABC's New York City studio. The program marked the fortieth anniversary of Robinson's arrival in Brooklyn on April 15, 1947.

Koppel asked Campanis why there were so few black managers in baseball and no black general managers. (Frank Robinson, no relation to Jackie, had been named manager of the Cleveland Indians in 1975 while still a player.) "Blacks may not have some of the necessities to be, let's say, a field manager or perhaps a general manager," Campanis replied. The term "necessities," basically ended Campanis's baseball career after forty-four years in the game. A protest over his comments ensued and he resigned two days later. He died in 1998, bitter and disappointed at the lack of support from the game he loved.

There has never been a school for training managers and general managers in baseball. Sometimes a player's playing career matters. Sometimes it does not. Babe Ruth never got a chance to manage. Walter Alston, with one big league at bat, managed the Dodgers for many years.

Tommy Lasorda was a fringe pitcher and a Hall of Fame manager. Ted Williams was a Hall of Fame hitter and an uncomfortable manager.

After the furor over Campanis's remarks, he never really explained what he meant by "necessities." What most baseball observers believed he meant was the key to managerial and general managerial choices are based on relationships. Teammates usually pick old pals as coaches and the coaches become managers because they have relationships with the management. Baseball is a business. It works the way most businesses do. Friends get promoted faster than enemies.

It seems horribly unfair, despite the pressures of political correctness in the 1980s, that the entire career of Campanis, his support of Robinson as a Montreal player, his technical baseball advice, his total acceptance of Jackie as a teammate, should have been destroyed by the use of the single word "necessities."

Walter Alston was picked as the manager of the Dodgers by GM Buzzie Bavasi in 1954. Bavasi had worked with Alston in the minor leagues in Nashua, New Hampshire. Hall of Famer Alston won Brooklyn's one and only World Series in 1955 and managed the club through 1976.

Los Angeles coach Tommy Lasorda, who had played with Robinson on the 1955 Brooklyn Dodgers and Jim Gilliam, an African American coach who played with Robinson for four seasons in the 1950s, were the leading candidates to succeed Alston. Campanis, with the support of owner Walter O'Malley, selected Lasorda as the new Los Angeles manager. He lasted in the job from 1977 through 1996. He was named to Baseball's Hall of Fame in 1997.

After Robinson's signing with the Montreal Royals in 1945 and Dixie Walker's quick comments to the Associated Press, most of the Brooklyn players seemed unconcerned about the historic move. "If you were an established player you just got ready for the next season," Gene Hermanski recalled in a 2008 interview. "If you were a young player like I was in 1946 and 1947 all you cared about was making the ball club."

Many of the southern players on the Dodgers seemed unconcerned about Jackie Robinson's arrival in Montreal for the 1946 season. Robinson turned twenty-seven in January 1946. That was pretty old for a big league prospect. He was also a shortstop, and the Dodgers had the best in the game, they thought, with Pee Wee Reese. He probably couldn't beat out the Walking Man, Eddie Stanky, for the second base position. There was talk he might be moved to first base when he came up to the Dodgers but the Dodgers had Ed Stevens, Howard Schultz, and a youngster named Gil Hodges getting ready to defend first base.

"One thing you have to remember about playing in those days," said Hermanski. "Not too many guys were willing to pop off about conditions on the club. We made six or seven thousand dollars a year and we were glad to get it."

More than forty years after Robinson's 1945 arrival in Brooklyn and his historic meeting with GM Branch Rickey, Clyde Sukeforth sat down in his Maine home and recalled the events of that day for my book *Jackie Robinson: A Life Remembered*. He was eighty-five at the time, a tall, lean, soft-spoken gentleman with sharp blue eyes, a still firm handshake and exquisite recall. Sukeforth died in 2000 at the age of ninety-eight.

"I remember Mr. Rickey saying how he looked for a great colored player all his life," Sukeforth recalled. "He wanted more than a great player. He wanted a player who could turn the other cheek and fight back by exceptional play. He wanted a guy who could carry the flag of his race with his performance and his conduct. When a guy slides in and cuts you in baseball, you are justified in getting him back. What Mr. Rickey wanted was for Jackie to take it, soft-pedal it, keep his mouth shut, and play good baseball. Helping Brooklyn win was supposed to be satisfaction enough.

"It was very exciting to follow Jack's career after that. I admired him very much. He was one wonderful player and a very fine man. I remember a couple of years before he died in 1972 there was a dinner in New York, at Leone's, I think, honoring Jack, and I was invited to attend. They brought me down from Maine, and it was a wonderful evening. Jackie was already looking bad from the diabetes, and I was saddened to see how he slipped back. He had been so big and strong and fast and now he seemed so tired and old. When he died I felt very sad for his family.

"I didn't think much about the part I played in the situation at the time. I was just doing my job. Mr. Rickey sent me out to see a ball player, and I scouted him, same as I did with dozens of white boys. It wasn't that special to me. Now, forty years later it seems more special. I guess today I'd have to say I was part of history. I was lucky. I was in the right place at the right time."

Sukeforth would be a Brooklyn coach in 1947 when combative manager Leo Durocher was suspended by Commissioner Happy Chandler for "conduct detrimental to the game." He was named the temporary manager and was the field leader of the Dodgers in Robinson's first two big league games in 1947 before Burt Shotton was named the team's manager for 1947.

Sukeforth had one other unfortunate connection with Brooklyn Dodgers baseball history. He was the bullpen coach of the Dodgers under manager Charlie Dressen on October 3, 1951, when Don Newcombe faltered against the Giants in the third game of the National League pennant playoff.

Two Brooklyn pitchers, Ralph Branca and Carl Erskine, were warming up in the Brooklyn bullpen deep in right center field. Dressen phoned the bullpen, got Sukeforth on the line, and asked which of the pitchers was ready.

"Erskine just bounced a curve," Sukeforth replied.

"Give me Branca," said Dressen.

Branca faced Bobby Thomson, threw a strike, and then watched as Thomson drove the next pitch over the short left field fence for a pennant-winning homer as radio announcer Russ Hodges screamed, "The Giants win the pennant, the Giants win the pennant, the Giants win the pennant." The hit became known as "the shot heard 'round the world."

Jackie Robinson had an incredible season with Montreal in 1946. He won the batting title with a .349 mark. He was the defensive leader of the team with a fielding average of .985. He led the league in runs scored with 113. He terrified pitchers and catchers with his antics on the bases. He developed the bunt into a personal art form. He led the Royals to the International League pennant by nineteen and a half games and helped his team to the Little World Series title. The Royals had proven without a doubt that a black man could play on a white professional baseball team.

Dixie Walker hit .319 in 150 games for the Brooklyn Dodgers in 1946, with 116 runs batted in and 80 runs scored. He had 184 hits and batted over .300 for the sixth time in seven seasons, with one batting title, one of the most remarkable measures of hitting consistency in National League history.

In 1986, shortly after his eighty-eighth birthday, Albert B. Chandler, the former governor and U.S. senator from Kentucky, sat down at his Versailles, Kentucky, home and recalled his time as baseball commissioner from 1945 with the death of Commissioner Kenesaw Mountain Landis and his removal in 1951.

"Any time there was a hint of a black player being brought into the game, Landis had a standard answer," Chandler said. "I've read the minutes of many meetings. Landis said, 'I've said everything that's going to be said on the subject. The answer is no.' Then he would move on to other business.

"Robinson had that great year in Montreal, and we all knew he would be moving up to the big leagues. Rickey was a little concerned about the reaction of his fellow owners. There was a secret meeting called by the owners. It was held in New York at the Waldorf-Astoria Hotel. No minutes were taken at the meeting. It was held for the purpose of letting the other owners know what Rickey was planning to do. I remember the meeting as if it was held yesterday. I'm eighty-eight years old, but I happen to be blessed with a very accurate memory. I can't say I can recall the comments of all the owners at the meeting. I *can* say I am very sure of the tone of the meeting. The owners were against Rickey doing this thing, and they implored him to forget the whole idea.

"He talked for a good long while about how bringing a Negro boy into the game was just the right thing to do and how Jackie Robinson earned his chance by the fine year he had at Montreal and how he was going to bring him up that spring. There was a resolution of support proposed by Rickey. He wanted the owners to go on record as saying they endorsed his plan and would go along with it. I don't think he was looking for any help, but he was looking to see that his fellow owners would not get in his way.

"The vote was finally taken after a lot of talk and was 15–1 against Rickey. I was at the head of this big table in one of the large meeting rooms at the hotel. I read the votes one by one and all of them were no votes except that yes vote in Rickey's hand. He was very angry, and he got up and walked out of the room."

Several days after the New York meeting, Rickey called Chandler at his Versailles home. He was very bothered by the vote of his fellow owners and wanted support from Chandler. "I told him to come down to Versailles and we would talk about it some more. We went out to my cabin and discussed it for many hours," Chandler said. "Rickey was as emotional as I had ever seen him. He said he didn't know if he could do this in light of the opposition of his partners. He said, on the other hand, Negro people expected Robinson to be brought up. 'There will be riots in Harlem,' he said if he didn't do it. He also expressed fear there would be fires in Ebbets Field and in the Polo Grounds, and he also said his partners said there would be riots between blacks and whites in their parks if he did it."

Rickey continued to talk about the reaction of his Brooklyn business partners, his baseball partners on the other fifteen teams, and his own players if he brought Robinson to the Dodgers. "He was especially upset about something he had read about Dixie Walker. I think he respected Dixie very much, and he was one of his favorite players. Rickey looked at me with lots of emotion and said, 'I read where Dixie Walker says he will stay home and paint his house if I bring a Negro to camp.' Then he asked me what I would do about all this. I told him he could do what he wanted with his ball players, same as anybody else, and if he brought Jackie Robinson up, he would be treated the same as anybody else. I think that was all he wanted to hear," Chandler said.

While all this was going on, Dixie Walker was actually in New York City, attending meetings with Johnny Murphy, the Yankee relief pitcher who represented his fellow American League players as Dixie represented the National League players. They were putting together the final details on the Major League Baseball Players Pension Plan.

"Yes sir, I'm proud of the part I played in bringing Jackie Robinson into baseball," Chandler said, "and I'm proud of the part I played in establishing the pension plan for ball players. When I face my Maker some day [he died in 1991] I can honestly say I never ran away from anything, no matter how difficult it seemed."

Walker returned home to Birmingham to prepare for the 1947 spring training season. Rickey had announced that the Brooklyn Dodgers, still without a permanent spring training home, would set up their spring camp in Havana, Cuba. (They acquired Vero Beach as their spring headquarters in 1948.)

Robinson worked out daily with his brother, Mack, a 1936 Olympian, at public parks near their Pasadena, California home. In late February Jackie Robinson boarded a train near his Los Angeles home for the Dodgers meeting point in Miami, Florida. He was still on the roster of the Montreal Royals.

Dixie Walker boarded a train from his Birmingham home to Miami. More than sixty members of the Brooklyn Dodgers and their number one farm club, the Montreal Royals, gathered in Miami's Fontainebleau Hotel for travel instructions presented to them by the team's traveling secretary, Harold Parrott. The next day they would board a small cruise ship for the three-hour boat ride to Havana.

Both Dixie Walker and Jackie Robinson were in that traveling party. No words were exchanged. Most of the players hardly noticed Robinson as he hung out with his 1946 Montreal teammates. "It wasn't anything special to play with or against black players for me," Brooklyn's 1947

Opening Day pitcher Joe Hatten once said. (He was born and raised in Bancroft, Iowa.) "I had done that often around home in those semipro leagues. I played against everybody, those black barnstorming teams and those teams from New York like the House of David, the guys with the beards, and just about everybody else who would come through Iowa with nine guys and a few bats and balls. I didn't have any feelings one way or another about Jackie being there. If he could help us win, great. If he couldn't, they would get somebody else. That's the way it was with me and every other player."

Leo Durocher welcomed his 1947 Brooklyn Dodgers to Havana. Dixie Walker was determined to have another good year and hoped to lead the Dodgers to another pennant after the 1946 near miss against the Cardinals.

Jackie Robinson was on a backfield with his Montreal teammates, hopeful the Dodgers would give him a big league chance.

Jackie and Dixie in 1947

On March 1, 1947, Frederick Graham wrote in the *New York Times* that a P-82 twin-engine fighter named *Betty Jo* had flown nonstop 4,978 miles from Hickam Field in Hawaii to LaGuardia Airport in Queens in fourteen hours and thirty-three minutes. "Lt. Col Robert E. Thalker, pilot, and Lt. John Ard, co-pilot, looking none the worse for the trip, climbed out of the cockpit to meet their wives and a crowd of 1,500," wrote Graham.

In other stories on the front page of the *Times* it was reported that in Palestine, two Jews were killed in a bomb explosion in Haifa. "There were clashes aboard ships jammed with unauthorized immigrants with 11 British sailors and 38 refugees being injured in the fighting." Premier T. V. Soong of China resigned, with President Chiang Kai-Shek taking over his duties. In domestic, cultural news, Jose Ferrer received rave reviews for his performance as Cyrano de Bergerac at the Barrymore Theater; *Life with Father* was marking its eighth year on Broadway at the Bijou; and *Oklahoma* continued playing to full houses at the St. James Theater.

On the lead sports page of the *Times,* there was a story about traded Detroit slugger Hank Greenberg arriving in Miami from his New York home on Pittsburgh owner John Galbreath's private plane for his first season as a member of the Pittsburgh Pirates. "I certainly intend to play the best ball I know how," Greenberg told the assembled press.

An announcement from league headquarters said Negro League teams would play several games in 1947 at the Ebbets Field home of the Brooklyn Dodgers. In a lead story about the doings of the New York Yankees at their spring training headquarters in St. Petersburg, it was revealed that oft-injured Joe DiMaggio would soon enter Johns Hopkins Hospital in Baltimore for a second heel operation.

The Brooklyn Dodgers beat the Boston Braves 8—0 that day at Havana's Grand Stadium with Hal Gregg, Vic Lombardi, and Kirby Higbe holding the Braves to three hits. It was also noted that two Brooklyn pitchers, Ed Head and Ralph Branca, were battling charley horses.

"Jewish terrorists killed 16 when a British Officers Club blew up in Haifa," reported Clifton Daniel in his dispatch from Haifa, Palestine.

The next day the Dodgers lost to the Braves 5—2. Dixie Walker, rounding into shape, doubled off Red Barrett, scoring Butch Woyt with Brooklyn's first run. The Dodgers defeated the Panama All-Stars 6—3 with Gene Hermanski and Bruce Edwards hitting home runs for Brooklyn.

Roscoe McGowen reported in the *Times,* "The Dodgers, slightly irked by the cockiness of these dusky Panamanian Stars, showed more signs of bearing down." McGowen added a note at the end of his story on the game, "The Montreal Club is due to arrive in Panama. Local fandom are excited by the expected appearance of Jackie Robinson."

The next day, the *Times* reported, "Margaret Truman makes her professional debut as a singer with the Detroit Symphony. Fifteen million hear it from the Detroit Music Hall over the American Broadcasting Company."

On March 29, an inside sports page of the *Times* had a photo of Brooklyn manager Leo Durocher shaking hands with Jackie Robinson in his Montreal uniform before an exhibition game between the Royals and the Dodgers. Robinson, despite having trouble with his stomach "because he and Cuban food don't agree," according to the *Times* report, performed at first base. "It was the first glimpse of Robinson at that position," the paper reported.

Robinson singled off Hal Gregg and made two errors.

It became clear to the Dodgers and to Brooklyn fans that the 1946 International League star would soon become the Brooklyn first baseman. They had two first basemen, Ed Stevens and Howard Schultz, but Durocher wasn't happy with either one.

"A number of Dodger players were rumored to be very unhappy about Robinson's addition to the roster," wrote Dodger historian Tot Holmes in a 1980 edition of the *Dodgers Blue Book,* an annual sold every season at Dodger Stadium. "A petition was said to have been signed and presented to Rickey by some of them, asking that Robinson not be allowed to play.

"The player mentioned most when the petition was discussed," Holmes wrote, "was Dixie Walker."

"We played some exhibition games in Panama during the spring of 1947," Walker told Holmes in that 1980 interview. "While we were there it was announced that Robinson had been signed to join the big club.

"We all sat around and talked about it," Walker related, "and there was quite a bit of discussion. As I recall, I don't know of anybody who didn't feel like they didn't want him."

Lester Rodney, a sportswriter for the Communist *Daily Worker* in New York, remembers advocating for integrated baseball as far back as 1936 when he began writing for the paper's sports section. Rodney was born in Manhattan on April 17, 1911. He grew up in Brooklyn, attended New Utrecht High School, and was unable to get a college education when the stock market crashed in 1929 and his parents could no longer afford to send him to school.

"I grew up in the Bensonhurst section of Brooklyn," said Rodney over the phone from his home in Walnut Creek, California, a few weeks after his ninety-seventh birthday. "I took the subway to Ebbets Field at the age of nine to watch the Dodgers play Cleveland in the 1920 World

Series. The wall on Bedford Avenue didn't meet the street. If you lay down on your belly you could watch the entire game that way. I saw Stan Coveleski beat Brooklyn for one of his three Series wins."

Rodney pushed left wing causes, including baseball integration, as a writer for the Communist daily. "In those Depression days if you weren't for left wing causes the way the country was going you were considered brain dead," he says.

Rodney covered Negro League games, was an advocate for including blacks in the big leagues, encouraged petitions calling for baseball's integration, and named several Negro players as potential big leaguers. One name he frequently mentioned in 1945 was Jackie Robinson of the Kansas City Monarchs.

"I remember asking many of the players, including Dixie Walker, in 1945, if they would play with a Negro. He said he wouldn't in no uncertain terms. He stimulated the 1947 petition. Carl Furillo, a kid from Pennsylvania, went along with that. The Brooklyn Dodgers won their only World Series in 1955. They had a party at the Hotel Bossert in Brooklyn and when Jackie walked into the room Furillo grabbed him and hugged him. 'We did it. We did it.' I was standing right there. People change. The guys in the press box were just the same. I remember John Drebinger of the *Times* saying, 'Jackie looks flashy. They all do. Then the season goes on and they all die out.' Now we might have a black president. It's beyond my wildest imagination."

"I had permission to leave a day early and take my family from Miami to Havana by boat," Dixie Walker once said. "Then we, along with other wives and children, met the Dodger plane that night when they flew in from Panama. It was then that I was told Rickey was really going to lay it on me about the meeting amongst the players and a petition I was supposed to have gotten the players to sign.

"Frankly I cannot recall a petition of any sort that was signed. The charge was completely false. I was so upset by the accusation that when we got to Cuba I went to the apartment and wrote Rickey a letter. I walked down to the Hotel Nacional to deliver it, but Rickey was in Florida with Durocher and Chandler. I gave the letter to someone [traveling secretary Harold Parrott] going to Florida the next day to join Rickey."

Walker continued in his interview with Holmes. "In that letter I never mentioned Jackie Robinson. I simply stated that for various reasons, and since I had spent so many seasons with the Dodgers, a change would be beneficial for all concerned. Therefore, I would prefer to be traded as soon as possible. That is how the whole thing came about.

"When Rickey returned from Florida he called me to his hotel room and, with Mrs. Rickey present, tried his dead-level best to get me to say that I wanted to be traded because of Jackie Robinson. I would not say it then and I have never said it.

"Now I'm not going to deny that I was a southern boy and I didn't think much of the idea of Robinson joining the club. I'd be a liar if I said I did. There were a lot of players who felt the same way.

"You must remember it was the climate of the times. Many are hypocrites now and say that they didn't feel that way back then, but the truth is, a lot of them did.

"To be perfectly frank, I think baseball is a greatly improved game because of the blacks. There is no question in my mind that they are outstanding athletes, and they have contributed much to the game.

"Hindsight is always better than foresight, and I have worked with many black players over the years and I feel that I have helped many of them.

"I have found that blacks and whites are no different in this respect: There are some of them that are a joy to work with and some of them that will give you a fit," Walker continued.

"Looking back, if I had it all to do over again, I would have felt differently. I didn't know at the time if any of the other Dodgers were violently opposed to Robinson.

"I just felt that they had made me a sitting duck and were firing number 8 shells at me," he concluded.

Whether or not a written petition by the Brooklyn players against Robinson joining the team ever actually existed is not known. What is certain is that Brooklyn players, in Panama, in Havana, and in Florida, often discussed Robinson's arrival.

Branch Rickey had hoped for a racial miracle. He wanted the Dodgers to see just how good a player Robinson was, how much he could help the team win, and how much stronger the Dodgers would be with Robinson at first base instead of Stevens or Schultz.

Howard Schultz, eighty-seven years old in 2009, recalled that March spring training of more than sixty years ago from his winter home in Naples, Florida. "I was playing pro basketball with the Anderson club in the 1946–1947 season," Schultz recalled. "I left the basketball team in Chicago and took a train to Miami for spring training with the Dodgers. I had been with them since 1943. I knew Robinson had that great year at Montreal and would soon be playing with us. They didn't want him playing second base because of the possibilities of high tags, cuts, body contact, all that stuff that happens around second, all that friction. His arm wasn't good enough for short or third so he was going to wind up at first base."

Schultz went to the Miami airport as instructed and boarded a plane for Havana where the Dodgers were training. His seat mate was Brooklyn coach Clyde Sukeforth. "Sukey told me on the plane that the Dodgers were planning to use Robby at first base. He asked if I would help him learn the position when I got to camp. Most of the Brooklyn players were on a Caribbean exhibition tour when I arrived and I worked out with him each morning for about ten days on a backfield," Schultz said.

Schultz, one of the few athletes to make it big in two professional sports—with the Dodgers in baseball and the champion Minneapolis Lakers in basketball—was a famous baseball trivia question: Who hit the first postseason playoff home run for the 1946 Dodgers against the Cardinals? He also struck out to end the playoffs in Brooklyn in an 8–3 loss with the bases loaded.

"I went from a hero to a bum in a hurry," he laughed.

Robinson opened the 1947 season against the Braves at first base, with Schultz relieving him for defense in the final inning. Schultz was soon traded to the Phillies. "I grew up in Saint Paul and one of my best pals in Woodrow Wilson Junior High School was a black kid named John Murphy," Schultz recalled. "He went to Central High and I went to John Marshall and we played against each other a lot. I went on to Hamline University in Saint Paul and Stan Tabor, another black, was a teammate so I didn't have any particular feelings about race when Jackie joined the Dodgers."

Schultz was a Brooklyn teammate of Dixie Walker from 1943 when he joined the Dodgers at the age of twenty through 1947. "Dixie was a real great hitter. He really knew the strike zone. He helped me a lot. He was a friendly fellow but we didn't talk too much. I don't think Dixie was the kind of guy who sat around the clubhouse after games and just chatted with the guys. He just played the game hard, showered after it was over, and went home," Schultz recalled.

Schultz said, "I liked Dixie. I hope he liked me."

Schultz's arrival in the Brooklyn camp in Havana was around March 20. "I can't recall anything about any petition against Robinson," he said. "If there was a petition maybe it was circulated before I got to camp. I do recall Rickey called in Dixie, Higbe, Hugh Casey, and Stanky to talk about the Robinson situation. I don't know what was said. All I remember is that they were all gone from Brooklyn after that season," Schultz said.

Schultz had another theory about the tone of the team in that volatile spring. "I think most athletes are inwardly directed," Schultz said. "I never made more than six thousand dollars a year playing baseball. I got to ten thousand in basketball. I was worried about my own job that spring. I was already married to my wife, Gloria. That's the way Rickey wanted it. He pushed players into marrying early so they could concentrate on playing baseball instead of chasing girls."

Schultz went on to coach basketball at Hamline after he retired from professional sports. He and his wife started a candle manufacturing business out of the basement of their Saint Paul home, which they continue to run. "We never made enough money to hire people to run it for us," he said. "Life's been good. We spend the winters in Naples, Florida. I still play golf. We spend the summers in Minnesota with our children and grandchildren."

Schultz, nicknamed Stretch in his playing days for his seventy-eight-and-a-quarter-inch height, is still a memorable name for old Brooklyn Dodger fans. He was mobbed at an autograph card show in Secaucus, New Jersey, in the spring of 2008. "I guess someone would have to be seventy or eighty years old to remember me," he said.

A lot of the fans at that card show were that age.

Branch Rickey wanted the Brooklyn players, late in March of 1947, to come pounding on his hotel door demanding Robinson be added to the big league roster. Fat chance. First of all, players in the 1940s without contracts spanning more than one season, were much too concerned with their own status. Second of all, they each understood this was a volatile issue and no player would step forward into that kind of political cauldron.

While Rickey waited for the knock on the door that was never to come, the ball players gossiped among themselves. They talked a little around the clubhouse and talked a lot when they gathered in groups of threes, fours, and fives, usually after the exhibition games in local watering holes.

Kirby Higbe had been a Brooklyn favorite ever since he joined the club in 1941. He and Whitlow Wyatt were the aces of that pennant-winning club. Much of the steam had gone out of his thirty-two-year-old arm by 1947, but Durocher still considered him a good backup starter and mop-up reliever.

The big, handsome guy from Columbia, South Carolina, had also been one of the most popular players on the team, especially popular with the gals on Ladies Days for his tall, dark, and handsome dashing good looks. One late March night Higbe found himself alone at one of the late-night spots. He looked down the bar and saw traveling secretary Harold Parrott at the other end. The two began talking after a long night of drinking. Higbe, according to Parrott, was rambling on about some petition or other. Parrott couldn't catch all the details but he did hear the names of Jackie Robinson and Dixie Walker. He later recalled Higbe saying, "Ol' Hig just won't do it. The old man [Branch Rickey] has been fair to Ol' Hig. Ol' Hig ain't going to join any petition to keep anybody off this club."

Parrott relayed his conversation to Durocher as he returned to the hotel shortly before 2:00 a.m. Durocher exploded when he heard that Higbe had referred to the petition in his conversation. Durocher had two major reasons for his conduct, neither of which had to do with Robinson's color.

Durocher, first off, wanted the best team he could put on the field. After all he had won a pennant with Brooklyn in 1941, waited through the war years for the talent to return and mature, and now considered the 1947 season a certain winning year. To Durocher's thinking, a Dodger team with Jackie Robinson at first base was the best he could do.

Second, Durocher was aroused to anger by the idea that anybody— Rickey, reporters, fans, or even his own players, could tell him what to do. Durocher, a man of action, went forth to do battle. He gathered his players together in the hotel kitchen, screamed at them like one might yell at recalcitrant children, warned them of the dire consequences if they kept up this attitude, and sent them back to their rooms.

"Leo's talk didn't change my opinion," recalled Bobby Bragan six decades later, "but it sure as hell put the fear of God in me."

Durocher was interviewed about that 1947 spring forty years after it happened. His memories were sharp and clear. He died in 1991 at the age of eighty-six and was named to the Baseball Hall of Fame in 1994. "If I go to war I want Jackie Robinson on my side," he said. "What a competitor. What a fighter. Sure we had our feuds, because he wanted to win and I wanted to win. It was never racial. That garbage didn't mean anything to me. I had no trouble with him in Brooklyn when we wore the same uniform. I had a lot of trouble when I went over to the Giants and we wore different uniforms.

"About that session in Panama you're talking about, yeah, I got the players together after I heard about that damn petition, and I told them what they could do with the petition, and I don't think I got much back talk on it. I told the players Robinson was going to open the season with us come hell or high water and if they didn't like it they could leave now and we'd trade them or get rid of them some other way. Nobody moved. I just told them nobody could tell me who to play and who not to play, and if any of them thought they could they were in for a hell of a shock."

Before Durocher could write Robinson's name on a big league regular season Brooklyn lineup, he was suspended by Commissioner Chandler for the 1947 season. "I was suspended by Chandler before the season started, so I didn't see Robinson in 1947 except on television. He looked like a hell of a player to me. Then I came back in 1948, and he was much heavier than he had been in 1947, and he wasn't going to run and stay strong with all that weight. He said, 'Leo, I'm 195, 200, the same as I was last year,' and I said, 'The hell you are. Let's get on a scale because the scale don't lie.' And when he did it didn't stop until it got to 215, and then he started losing weight. It took a long time, which is why he wasn't the player early that year he was later on when he got in shape.

"By the time I got over to the Giants we recognized how tough he was. I agitated him a little, and he agitated me back. He said some personal things about my wife [Laraine Day] and the Hollywood crowd and things like that, and we got hot a few times. Managers used to coach at third in those days and I would yell things at him and he would yell back all game long. We didn't like each other because we were competitors on different sides.

"I respected Jackie Robinson, and I never questioned his integrity or dedication to the game. He was one hell of a player and he could play for me any time. As far as his standing in the game he wasn't no Willie Mays. Willie was the best that ever lived. It's hard to judge ball players in different times, but I always liked DiMaggio and Musial and Clemente and Willie, like I said, would be the first guy. Jackie wasn't in their class. Just say he was damn good, and he was a hell of a battler."

Most of the anti-Robinson attention focused around Dixie Walker, the alleged leader of the petition and the writer of the letter requesting a trade. Jack Kavanagh, a distinguished New York sportswriter, penned an article on Walker for the 1993 edition of the *Baseball Research Journal,* the annual publication of the Society for American Baseball Research, a baseball research group dating back to 1971.

"Always an up front man," Kavanagh wrote, "before the 1947 season began Dixie Walker wrote to Branch Rickey and asked to be traded for 'reasons I prefer not to go into.' Rickey was willing to oblige Walker and let him escape the culture shock of integrated baseball. This also fit in with Rickey's established practice of trading an aging star while he still could get value for him.

"Retroactive judgments are made that cast Dixie Walker as the ringleader of the resistance to the breaking of the ban on black players. However he actually preferred to give up his favored status as 'The Peepul's Cherce' and simply complete the few years remaining of his major league career somewhere else. Rickey might have been willing to unload an uncomfortable Dixie Walker, but the fans still held him in high esteem.

"The people of Brooklyn were divided on whether adding Jackie to their team was a baseball value that over-shadowed the social upheaval many feared integration would create. When Rickey could not make a trade that would benefit the team, he kept Walker for the pennant winning season of 1947. Dixie hit .306 while playing 147 games, mostly in right field and tutoring his successor, Carl Furillo. Once Dixie had an opportunity to make a personal value judgment of Robinson, he, as well as other southerners like Eddie Stanky and Pee Wee Reese, rallied to the rookie's aid. Walker gave him batting tips, and when the team arrived back in Brooklyn after winning the 1947 pennant on the road, Dixie Walker and Jackie Robinson were impromptu spokesmen for the ball club at a downtown rally."

Kavanagh's commentary continued. "Obviously the color of a player or a prospect no longer set off atavistic resistance with the gentlemanly Dixie Walker. Yet 'pop art' anthropologists and socially sensitive historians refuse to recognize that the initial resistance to integrating professional baseball was only 'skin deep.' A winning team, regardless of its racial makeup, does more for the cause of comradeship than politically correct rhetoric. Once Jackie Robinson and other black players backed up Leo Durocher's assessment that 'these guys can win pennants and put money in all our pockets,' Walker as a player and later as a manager and coach readily adapted to baseball's changed racial scene."

Kavanagh summed up his study of Walker's 1947 actions and the historic baseball standing of the People's Choice. "Dixie Walker has paid an unfair price for what later day politically correct baseball historians decry as racism. If there were amends to be made, Dixie made them. Yet when the Brooklyn Dodger Hall of Fame began to select heroes of the past to honor, it snubbed Dixie. It would have been a great homecoming for The Peepul's Cherce. However, it wasn't until two years after his death in 1982 that Dixie was included. Walker is rarely mentioned among the greats of Brooklyn's past and usually with a caveat reference to his reluctance to participate in Branch Rickey's great Social Experiment. The ironic hard truth is that what Dixie did by initiating his own departure was exactly what much of the borough's white population was also doing. To stay or leave became the people's choice. Most whites chose to leave . . . and even the franchise skipped town."

The Dodgers worked their way north with their Montreal farm club through the early days of April 1947. They were to open the regular season at home at Ebbets Field on April 15 in Brooklyn with lefty Joe Hatten starting for the Dodgers against Johnny Sain of the Boston Braves.

A few days before the opener, on April 10, 1947, publicity director Arthur Mann walked through the rickety press box. He had a news release in his hand and began handing out the sheet of paper as he had hundreds of times before about a traded player, a released player, a new called-up player from the minors, or any announcement the club wanted the fans to know about. "The Brooklyn Dodgers today purchased the contract of Jack Roosevelt Robinson from the Montreal Royals. He will report immediately."

On July 23, 1962, on the steps of the Baseball Hall of Fame Library in Cooperstown, New York, a plaque was revealed for Jack Roosevelt Robinson. It read:

> Brooklyn N.L. 1947 to 1956
> Leading N.L. Batter in 1949
> Holds Fielding Mark for Second Basemen Playing in 150 or More Games with .992.
> Led N.L. in Stolen Bases in 1947 and 1949.
> Most Valuable Player in 1949.
> Lifetime Batting Average .311.
> Joint Record Holder for Most Double Plays by Second Baseman, 137 in 1951
> Led Second Basemen In Double Plays 1949–50–51–52.

The essence of his life was missed in those two announcements, the most important announcements of his professional career: he was a black man. Finally, in 2008, the Baseball Hall of Fame, revised the wording on Robinson's plaque to include the phrase "integrated baseball."

"It didn't mean much when the call-up announcement was given out," said Jack Lang, a *Long Island Press* sportswriter covering the Dodgers in 1947. He reminisced shortly before his death in 2007. "It was a foregone conclusion. Everyone knew Jackie was going to be with the big club before opening day. So much had been written by all of us before that date about Jackie coming up. I think I had it in my notes column a day or two before."

The announcement was made during the fifth inning of the game between the Royals and the Dodgers. Robinson had just bunted into a double play and when he returned to the Montreal bench his teammates were applauding him.

"I don't think there was a moment of thought about the racial aspect of it," said Spider Jorgensen, a 1946 Montreal teammate of Robinson's and a fellow rookie with the Dodgers in 1947. "We were all there on the minor league club with one purpose and one purpose only—to show the guys on the big club that we were ready to play up there. I think we all cheered any guy who was called up."

On page 20 of the *New York Times* the next day, sportswriter Louis Effrat wrote, "Jackie Robinson, 28-year-old infielder, yesterday became the first Negro to achieve major league status in modern times. His contract was purchased from the Montreal Royals of the International League. A native of Georgia, Robby won fame in basketball, football, baseball, and track at UCLA.

"He was blanked at the plate. Jackie had just popped out on a bunt attempt into a double play. Arthur Mann handed out the press release. The last Negro to play in the Majors was Moses Fleetwood Walker, who caught for Toledo in 1884."

Effrat did not omit the racial aspect of the story as he continued in his coverage of the event. "He may run into antipathy from southerners who form more than 60 percent of the playing strength of the league. It is rumored that a number of Dodgers expressed themselves as unhappy at the possibility of having to play with Jackie. Jackie said he was thrilled and said, 'It is what I've been waiting for.' When he was congratulated by his Montreal teammates and offered good luck on his promotion, Robinson replied, 'Thanks, I'll need it.' Dixie Walker, quoted in 1945 as being opposed to playing with Jackie, was booed in his first at bat after the announcement. He lined a single to right and the fans stood up to cheer him as he rounded first base."

Thousands of Negro fans collected outside the park the next day after the game. Many of them were wearing newly minted buttons reading, "I'm for Robinson."

Montreal beat the Dodgers 4–3 with Walker going one for three and Robinson going oh for three in their first exhibition game as Brooklyn teammates. Rookie Duke Snider was two for four; Bobby Bragan was oh for three; Gene Hermanski was two for five; and pitcher Ralph Branca allowed four hits and two runs over seven innings.

"With just a couple of days before opening day all you wanted to do was get your work in, get sharp, and avoid any injuries," recalled Branca about the first game Robinson played in as a Dodger more than sixty years ago. "I don't recall a word about race. All anybody on the club seemed concerned about was whether or not he could play first base for us."

"Did Jackie play in that game?" laughed Gene Hermanski from his Florida retirement home. "I got a couple of hits, I knocked in a run, and I thought it solidified my position with the team and my chance to be in the starting lineup. Maybe the press made a fuss over Jackie playing with us. I don't think any of the players, northerners or southerners, did."

A photograph appeared the next day in the *New York Times* showing Jackie Robinson in his shiny, white Brooklyn uniform with the word "Dodgers" scrawled across the chest and the large letter B on his blue baseball cap. He was being congratulated by his former Montreal manager Clay Hopper with a warm smile and a firm handshake. Hopper had survived a season with Jackie as his second baseman and now was proud to see him move up to the big club.

Winston Churchill made a speech crediting himself with saving Greece from Communism; Henry Ford was buried in Detroit; 132 people were killed in a Texas-Oklahoma twister; and Brooklyn defeated the Yankees 14–6 in a weekend exhibition game. Walker, batting fourth, was one for two in the game; Robinson, hitting sixth and playing first base, was oh for four.

On April 12, the Yankees won 8–1 with Robinson knocking in the only Brooklyn run, a single scoring Pete Reiser. They also won the next day. "Larry (Yogi) Berra, the colorful right fielder of the Yankees, homered off Kirby Higbe," the *Times* reported, "with Walker hitless in a 10–9 Yankee victory with Robinson's popup in the ninth inning leaving the tying run stranded."

In an Arthur Daley column in the *Times,* Walker made his first comments about Robinson since they had become teammates a few days earlier. "Having Jackie on the team is still a little strange," Walker said. "It's just like anything that is new. We just don't know how to act with him. But he'll be accepted in time. You can be sure of that. Other sports have Negroes, why not baseball? I'm for him if he can win games. That's the test I ask."

On the day before the opener, Leo Durocher was suspended for a year by Commissioner Happy Chandler. Durocher attended a Knothole Club (Brooklyn baseball fans) dinner that evening with his actress wife Laraine Day to say goodbye at the elegant St. George Hotel in downtown Brooklyn.

Dixie Walker spoke for the players as he addressed a crowd of nearly fifteen hundred fans urging the Dodgers on for the 1947 season and saying farewell to their beloved skipper. "The people of Brooklyn and the ball club owe him [Leo] even more than they realize. There was nothing fair about his suspension in any sense of the word," Walker said. He was cheered by a standing ovation as Brooklyn fans rallied to their team's cause and seemed completely uninterested in any talk about the history-making event concerning Robinson.

Walker, Kirby Higbe, Cookie Lavagetto, and pitcher Ed Heusser of the Dodgers attended the event, signed autographs long after the dinner, and prepared for the opening of the 1947 big league season.

On April 15, 1947, temporary manager Clyde Sukeforth posted the

Brooklyn lineup on the clubhouse wall. Ed Stanky was leading off playing second base, Robinson batted second at first base, Reiser was in
center field hitting third, and Walker was in right field batting fourth.
Then came Hermanski in left field, Bruce Edwards catching, Spider
Jorgensen at third, Pee Wee Reese at shortstop, and Joe Hatten on the
mound against the Braves.

Johnny Sain was the Boston starter. Johnny Sain was an outstanding
pitcher and even more outstanding pitching coach in his long, distinguished career. He died at the age of eighty-nine in 2006.

In 1987 he talked about that first game Jackie Robinson played in
Brooklyn. "I'll tell you why I remember that game so well," Sain recalled. "I had been in the naval preflight program down at Chapel Hill,
North Carolina, during the war, and I played on the base baseball team.
One day we had a big event with a fund-raising game for the armed
forces. Our base team, which had a lot of pro players, got to play a Babe
Ruth all-star team. It was somewhere in the middle of 1943. Babe managed that team, and all of a sudden here he comes up to the plate. He
was big then, really overweight, and I didn't want to embarrass him,
so I threw two or three pitches well wide of the plate, and he just took
them. Then I walked him. The crowd was a little upset that he didn't
get a chance to swing, but I knew he couldn't get a real good swing off
me then. Buddy Hassett was our first baseman, and I just watched as
Babe walked down to first base, touched the bag, jumped straight in the
air and clicked his heels. I threw the ball over to Buddy for fun, and he
tagged the Babe, but he was on the base. Then they brought in a pinch
runner. That was the last time Babe Ruth ever appeared in a ball game
in uniform.

"Then in 1947 I was the first pitcher to face Jackie Robinson so I made
history again: the first to face Jackie and the last to face the Babe.

"I don't remember any commotion that first day. It was like any other
opener. I can't say for sure how I pitched him because it was forty years
ago, but I know I almost always threw a lot of curve balls to young hitters. I think he grounded out the first time against me."

Robinson grounded out, flied out, sacrificed, and hit into a double play that first day against the Braves in a 5–3 Brooklyn win. There were 26,623 fans in the stands, a slightly better than average opening day crowd for Brooklyn on a cloudy, chilly April afternoon.

"I don't remember our bench getting on him at all that day," Sain recalled. "We had a good ball club [they would win the pennant in 1948] and thought we had a chance to win and didn't want to start the season with a fuss. Robinson was just another player to us, maybe another Dodger we disliked because we disliked all of them. The Giants and the Dodgers were the big rivalry because of New York, but I think there was a lot of intensity in those games with Brooklyn and Boston.

"I came from a little town in Arkansas called Havana, about five hundred people, and there were a few black families, and we all got along well. I don't remember any incidents in school down there, and I don't remember any incidents in the big leagues with Jackie Robinson. He was a real fine gentleman, and I probably would have liked him even better if he hadn't hit so many balls up the middle."

Tommy Holmes batted for shortstop Dick Culler in the eighth inning of that 1947 opener for the Braves and flied out to left field. He was ninety-one years old and living in a retirement home in Boca Raton, Florida, when he died in 2008. He was a Brooklyn native who grew up as a next-door neighbor and friend of famed opera singer Robert Merrill.

"Billy Southworth [a 2008 Baseball Hall of Famer] was our manager," Holmes recalled, "and he was a very fair man. He just wanted everyone on the ball club to play hard. He didn't think bench jockeying was a big part of the game. I don't think you can have any of the stuff Jackie heard from other clubs without the manager allowing it.

"I only got into that opener as a pinch hitter so I was on the bench all game," said Holmes. "It didn't seem like anything special, just an opener, the same as all the others. We were excited to be starting the season after spring training but I can't remember any discussion about playing against Jackie Robinson, the first black, or anything like that. Much of that stuff seemed to become important years later.

"Our pitchers probably knocked him down a few times that year, but they knocked everybody down. In those days that's the way the game was played. I think he went down once and started out for the pitcher but Campy stepped in.

"I used to go up to Grossinger's [a famous New York hotel] in the wintertime for some skating and some fun in the snow. Jackie was there once and we started talking. We hadn't been good friends on the field. Nobody in a Dodger uniform was ever our friend. But he was nice around the hotel, and we chatted easily. He seemed to be different off the field, not as intense, not as competitive as he was when he put on that Dodger uniform.

"I was traded to Brooklyn in 1952 where I always wanted to be. Jackie was one of the first guys to come over and say hello. He was a leader on that team, and when he welcomed me they all welcomed me. It was an honor playing with Jackie Robinson."

That first game of 1947 went into the record books. The world survived. Dixie Walker and Jackie Robinson were soon to be important players on the 1947 pennant-winning team of the Brooklyn Dodgers.

The Pennant, the World Series, and the Long Farewell

The racial abuse heaped on Jackie Robinson in his early Brooklyn days was legendary.

"Jack went to Brooklyn, and I used to go there every year for a visit," recalled Willa Mae Robinson Walker, Jack's sister, in a 1987 interview. "I went to every World Series he was in except the 1955 World Series and that's the one they finally won. In those early days in Brooklyn, I don't think we ever stopped worrying about him. He got so much hate mail and so many threats on his life that he talked about quitting. We worried all the time about him. We used to read some things in the paper about the hate mail and the people trying to get him out of baseball. The phone would ring and we would be afraid to pick it up. We used to think it was a call from somebody saying Jackie was dead. Jackie's mama was scared all the time, but she wouldn't really let on. She just prayed he would be all right and she trusted in God. He called one time and said he had to sneak out of the ball park in spring training with two Negro sportswriters because a gang was coming after him, and he said, 'I might have been lynched.' We all just sat down and cried. Was it worth it? There were lots of times we just thought he should come home and coach at a black school and be done with it. But that wasn't Jack. He was determined to do it and he did it.

"We always worried about him because he was so quick to anger if somebody said something that was insulting. I don't think Jack ever looked for a fight, but I don't think he ever walked away from one, neither."

The baseball pressures on Robinson were enormous. He was learning his way around the big leagues at the advanced age of twenty-eight. He was learning a new position at first base. He was the focus of enormous affection from the Negro fans in Brooklyn and the focus of much antagonism in other parks. The racial animosity often took on sexual overtones. "I remember sitting in the stands at spring training with the wife of another Brooklyn infielder, Bob Ramazzotti," recalled Joan Hodges, wife of the great Brooklyn star and later New York Mets manager Gil Hodges, in a 2008 interview. "We were real close to the field, maybe a row or two back. Brooklyn was playing the Philadelphia Athletics. Connie Mack was the manager and he was at the end of this long bench with his players. He was wearing a long-sleeved white shirt and a tie. It was one of those hot Florida days, maybe 90 or 95 degrees, and there was this old man in the sun. Anyway, Jackie Robinson came to bat, we applauded and one of the Philadelphia players turned around and started yelling at us, 'Hey, are you going to sleep with him?' My face just got red and my Italian blood boiled. Kathy Ramazzotti was a lot more hot-headed than me. She started screaming back at him, all kinds of ugly things, and it was pretty upsetting. Finally, Connie Mack turned around and he pushed all of his players down the other end of the bench."

Robinson's arrival in Brooklyn was followed by black players on all the teams in baseball. It was clear if Jackie made it with the Dodgers, other black players would be joining other teams. Larry Doby joined the Cleveland Indians as the first black American League player in July. The Boston Red Sox were the final big league team to integrate, with Pumpsie Green joining their team in 1959, a dozen years after Robinson played with Brooklyn.

"That wasn't very surprising to me," said Sam Mele, a 1947 rookie with the Red Sox and later a big league manager in a 2008 interview. "We had heard that the Red Sox had looked at Jackie in 1945. It wasn't much of a tryout. Later on they looked at Willie Mays. They wouldn't sign him. How about an outfield with Dom DiMaggio, Ted Williams, and Willie Mays? It was all about the owner, Tom Yawkey. He just said, 'No niggers on my team.' Anyway they waited as long as they could but the pressures built and they integrated. I'm sure Yawkey [he died in 1976 and was named to Baseball's Hall of Fame in 1980] never got over it."

Robinson survived every kind of vile racial attack. There was even talk of the St. Louis Cardinals refusing to take the field against Brooklyn if Robinson was on the playing field. "I heard some talk like that," Stan Musial said in a 1987 interview. "I was not interested in anything like that. My folks had come from Poland and they got a chance to make it here. Why shouldn't everybody get that chance? I won the batting title in 1946 and we won the World Series. That was what I was interested in doing again in 1947. It didn't work out that way but that was my focus."

National League president Ford Frick got wind of the strike threat of the Cardinals and quickly brought the hammer down on any possibility of that.

Ben Chapman of Birmingham, Dixie Walker's boyhood pal and later Yankee teammate, became the center of controversy when the Dodgers came into Philadelphia for the first series between the two teams. Bob Carpenter, an heir to the du Ponts of Delaware chemical fortune, owned the team and appointed Herb Pennock, another former Yankee pitcher, as general manager.

Chapman, who died in 1993 at the age of eighty-five, was close to both of them. He led the verbal assault on Robinson, encouraged his players to malign the Brooklyn rookie, and probably echoed the attitude of the team owner and team general manager in the 1947 world.

"I didn't like the idea he was pushed in the game," Chapman said in a 1987 interview. "There were other players more qualified to be in the big leagues that year. Rickey wanted Robinson. That wasn't right. He should have been made to earn his place.

"Sure, we rode him. We rode everybody. They rode Babe Ruth and

Lou Gehrig when I went to the Yankees. Nobody said anything about that. Everybody in baseball understood that was part of the game. We knocked him down. We knocked everybody down. I didn't tell my Phillies ball club to ride him more than anybody else. I just told them to treat him like they would treat any other rookie. We got on every new player to see if he could take it.

"I'd been around colored people before I saw Robinson. We saw colored people in Birmingham. They had their own schools and things, and they would come downtown to shop and nobody thought anything of it. I think a lot of what happened was caused by the newspapers up there looking for a scapegoat for Robinson. I wound up as the bad guy, and they wrote a lot of things about me that caused me a lot of trouble. I don't want to go into detail now because it is so many years ago. Look, I had a good career and played fifteen years and even came back during the war to pitch in Brooklyn. I had a lifetime average of .302 and played on one of the greatest teams of all time, the 1932 Yankees, and I never got mentioned for the Hall of Fame. Do you know why that is? I think it is because of all the bad publicity I got involving that business. I think Jackie Robinson kept me out of the Hall of Fame.

"I got to admire the boy after I saw him play a few times. He was one of the best competitors I ever saw. He could beat you more ways than you could curry a mule.

"I coached a lot of amateur teams around Birmingham and did real well. We turned out a lot of players for the big leagues. I had a good career, helped a lot of young men, and didn't treat Jackie Robinson any different than I treated other rookies. I'm not ashamed of anything. I think the press should be ashamed of making me a scapegoat."

Robinson had decided early on that he would not push himself on his teammates, especially not Dixie Walker, the team leader, nor any of the other southerners. That was the way he operated in Montreal. That was the way he operated in Brooklyn. He spoke to his mates when spoken to. Pee Wee Reese, the Kentuckian, began speaking to him regularly and casually. Eddie Stanky discussed positioning against hitters. Spider

Jorgensen talked with Robinson as easily as any men who had been teammates and winners a year before. One day there was an even more significant breakthrough.

"We were in the trainers room, about six weeks or so into the season," Dixie once recalled. "Jackie was on the rubbing table and I walked by before batting practice and just mentioned that Jackie's stride was pretty long." They were soon at the batting cage before the game and Walker demonstrated to Robinson what he was talking about.

"I think you'd be better able to handle that curve ball if you didn't stride so far," Walker said.

"Like this?" Robinson said, as he shortened his batting stride.

"That's about it. A little shorter. A little quicker."

"I'll try it," Robinson said.

That afternoon Robinson had a line drive double, a bunt single, and a single up the middle.

"Thanks, Dixie," Robinson said quietly later in the clubhouse.

Harry Walker, Dixie's brother, talked about the 1947 season in an interview in 1987. "Dixie and I used to go fishing together at some lakes about three hundred miles from Birmingham. We spent a lot of time together alone in those days. Dixie never brought up Jackie's name. I was playing for the Phillies that year, won the batting title with a .363 mark, and I asked Dixie what it was like batting behind Jackie. He said he didn't like that jumping back and forth Jackie did on the bases. It was very distracting.

"I know there was a lot written then about Dixie and Jackie, and I think you have to understand the times. We didn't have much contact with black folks, and when Dixie said what he did it was like a man seeing a green door and not wanting to open it because you didn't know what was behind it. I think we just didn't know what it would be like when the blacks came into baseball.

"After a while we all got to playing with the colored players, and there was no fuss made about it. The Cardinals and the Dodgers had a great rivalry and so did the Phillies and the Dodgers when I went over there.

Jackie was a great player and you had to be real alert to play against him. He had catlike ability, and he could accelerate so fast. He never shut that motor down.

"Jackie was always fired up in a game. It was great to play against him because he made you play your best. What was interesting from the standpoint of drawing fans was that Jackie drew fans all over the league in those days, but the other colored players didn't. Even when Willie Mays came into the league in 1951, he never drew fans the way Jackie did. Willie wasn't as hungry as Jackie was. He didn't play with the same fire day in and day out.

"I think those days are behind us now. Nobody feels angry about what happened then. It was all so new. How could anybody know how to act? I remember a couple of years ago I was at an old-timers' game in Los Angeles, and I saw Campy [Roy Campanella] on the field in his wheelchair, and I went up to say hello to him, 'Hi, I'm Harry Walker. I used to play . . .' He stopped me. 'I know you. You used to hit a lot of line drives against us.' We had a real nice conversation, talked about some of those great games we had with the Dodgers, and talked a lot about the old players. We had a nice conversation, and before we had to break it up, I was telling Campy about my grandchildren."

Robinson's average dropped to .230 at the start of the 1947 Brooklyn season. The curve ball was eating him up, a common experience for young players. If you can't hit a big league curve ball, you can't hit in the big leagues. After Dixie Walker's suggestions he began handling the curve better. He could always hit the fastball. He was gaining confidence each day as his teammates began rallying around him publicly. Eddie Stanky challenged the Phillies bench to get on him rather than Robinson, who had vowed to Rickey he would not answer back. Pee Wee Reese put his arm on Robinson's shoulder before a game in Cincinnati when fans were bellowing at him. The moment was captured later with a memorial statue of Robinson and Reese at the entrance to Brooklyn's KeySpan stadium, home of the Mets' minor league club.

Gene Hermanski discovered that Robinson could give and take a needle as well as anyone. "Part of the fun of being a ball player is the needling that goes back and forth with the guys. There isn't much of it when you lose but that Brooklyn club was a winning team and we rode each other pretty steadily about everything," Hermanski said. "After a few weeks Jackie was as much a part of it as anybody."

Joe Garagiola, later a famed broadcaster and entertainer, was a backup catcher for the Cardinals in that 1947 season. In 1987 he told an interviewer that Jackie Robinson was simply the most exciting player he had ever seen on the bases in baseball. "In the clubhouse meetings we not only went over how to pitch to him, we went over how to defend against him on the bases. 'If Jackie is on first we do this. If he is on second we do this. If he gets to third, watch out, he'll steal home.' He was the only player we ever went over like that. When he got in a rundown he would have everybody involved, including the vendors. The park would be in an uproar. He was the most daring player I ever saw.

"Jackie had inner conceit as a player. He drove pitchers and catchers crazy. He would actually yell at the pitchers, 'I'm going, I'm going. Do anything you want, pal, you can't stop me.' Then he would go and steal the base. When he got on, it was the Jackie Robinson hour, he would so dominate the play while he was on base. Everybody would be caught up in his antics, the pitcher, the catcher, all the fielders, the bench, the clubhouse boys, everybody in the ballpark. He was the most intimidating player on the bases I have ever seen.

"Jackie was also a tremendous clutch player. In a big game, in a big spot, he seemed able to do whatever had to be done. Jackie Robinson was very tough with or without a bat in his hands. You don't think that way about many players.

"Jackie took an awful lot of heat in those early years. I don't know of another player who could have handled that and not exploded. I mean they called him every name you could imagine and threw at him and cut him and did everything to run him out of the league. There should be a special place in baseball recognizing Jackie for more than his baseball ability. He was a very special man."

Robinson was hitting better as the season progressed and Dixie Walker was hitting steadily as he almost always had. There seemed to be more hits for Dixie on the left side of the diamond than on the right, a sure sign that at the age of thirty-six his bat was slowing down.

"Mr. Rickey was pretty good at spotting that," Walker once recalled. "Even though my average was still up there [he batted an impressive .306 in 1947] most of my big hits were going the other way. Rickey could see better than anyone that I just didn't have the bat speed I had a couple of years earlier."

While there was still some racial anger expressed at Robinson at visiting ball parks, the fans cheered his play at Brooklyn's Ebbets Field, and his teammates became more comfortable around him. "In the first month of the season you didn't hear much from Jackie and after games he often waited to go into the shower until the other guys were out," said Gene Hermanski. "Then it all became routine. We had a lot of laughs after the games and maybe six or eight guys would be in the shower at the same time as Jackie and we would all be kidding around together."

Some of the league's biggest stars gave Jackie encouragement as the season moved along. Hank Greenberg, the great Jewish star from New York, went out of his way to make Robinson feel comfortable. "Hang in there, Jackie, you'll be all right," Greenberg told the Brooklyn rookie after he jogged down to first base after a walk.

"I'm trying," Robinson replied.

"I know what you are going through," Greenberg said.

When Greenberg made his big league debut as one of the rare Jewish players with Detroit in the early 1930s, he heard every anti-Semitic attack he could imagine. He had originally been offered a contract by his hometown New York Yankees but refused their bid because they had a huge superstar first baseman, Hank's position, in Lou Gehrig.

"I even used to hear one of my teammates, Schoolboy Rowe, tell other teammates how Jews were so cheap and controlled the banks and all the money in the country and wouldn't spend a nickel," Greenberg recalled. "I had to laugh to myself. That was from a teammate who used to sit around the hotel lobby all morning waiting for somebody to drop a newspaper so he could pick it up without paying. Do you know what a newspaper cost in the early 1930s? Maybe a penny or two."

Greenberg was a constant newspaper reader. "Joe DiMaggio was my big competition," he said. "I had to read the paper every morning to see what Joe had done so I could keep up with him. Of course, in the late 1930s I had to read the newspaper every day to see what was going on in Europe with Hitler and the Jews."

Ralph Kiner, who won seven home run titles in a row from 1946 through 1952, was a Pittsburgh teammate of Greenberg's in 1947, Hank's only year with the Pirates. "I remember playing softball against Jackie in Pasadena under the lights before the war," Kiner recalled. "It was at Brookside Park and he was the shortstop on his team. Everybody knew Jackie. He had this big reputation for basketball and football and track. Actually I think baseball was his worst sport. His brother was on the 1936 Olympic team, and Jackie got a lot of attention as soon as he started playing college sports at Pasadena Junior College and then later at UCLA.

"I had played against Negro players in California, and I had played against Negro League teams around Pittsburgh after I came to the Pirates in exhibition games. The Homestead Grays were the local Negro League team, and it was a real fine ball club. We had some good games against them.

"I was very close to Hank Greenberg, and I remember talking to him about Jackie. Hank thought Jackie would make it if he remained calm. That was the big thing, not to lose self-control. I think Jackie was a very disciplined player, but he had that fire burning inside.

"Jackie Robinson was a tremendous player, especially on the base paths. You know what I remember now about him, his eyes, those deep, intense eyes that always seemed to be staring at you."

Ralph McPherran Kiner was born October 27, 1922, in Santa Rita, New Mexico. He was four and a half years old when his father, a steam shovel operator, died, and his mother, a working nurse, moved with her only child to Alhambra, California, where a sister was living. "I was still in grammar school when I got interested in baseball and listened to the 1934 World Series on the radio. Hank Greenberg was a star for the Tigers in that Series against the St. Louis Cardinals and he became my favorite player," Kiner said as he sat on the back porch of the Otesaga Hotel in Cooperstown, New York, during the 2008 Baseball Hall of Fame induction weekend.

"In 1939 I was a junior in high school and played in an exhibition game against the Negro League All-Stars. I hit a home run my first time up against Satchel Paige. When I batted again, Paige asked infielder Buck O'Neil who that kid was who had hit that homer. He told him my name was Kiner and I was a high school junior. That time he struck me out," Kiner said.

Kiner remembered the trade that brought Dixie Walker to the Pirates in 1948. "Dixie was a laid-back guy, didn't talk much. We all knew he was THAT MAN from Brooklyn. I don't recall ever talking to him about what happened in Brooklyn in 1947 with Jackie or anyone else over there. I just knew we had given up two pretty good players in Preacher Roe and Billy Cox to get him. He helped us finish fourth and I hit forty home runs that year," Kiner said.

"I knew Dixie had been involved in setting up the pension plan with Marty Marion and Johnny Murphy. I got involved in that later. We kept that same 60–40 split from the All-Star game money for the players, with me and Allie Reynolds making a deal with the owners. The thing I remember most about the 1948 season was the fact that Bing Crosby was one of our owners and when he saw that the team was doing well he rewarded us with a record player in the clubhouse. The song we played over and over again was 'Cigarettes and Whiskey and Wild, Wild Women.' That was the theme of that team," Kiner said.

Kiner said there were no black players on the 1948 Pittsburgh Pirates. "I think the general impression of the players then was that black players weren't good enough and wouldn't make it. Everybody looked on Jackie as an exception. When Branch Rickey came over from Brooklyn to run the Pirates he didn't rush to sign black players. He was always interested more in making money than in integrating baseball," Kiner said.

As the 1947 season moved on, Dixie Walker worked closely with the young Brooklyn outfielder Carl Furillo. He was a tough line drive hitter, a fine fielder, and had an exceptional throwing arm, which had earned him the nickname the Reading Rifle, from his time as a young player in Reading, Pennsylvania, near his hometown of Stony Creek Mills, Pennsylvania. Walker taught Furillo how to play that tricky right field wall in Ebbets Field adjacent to Bedford Avenue.

"I think Dixie knew that Carl was a talented young player and would probably take his job," said Gene Hermanski. "He still gave him plenty of time out there."

Furillo would be a Dodger star until he was unceremoniously released during the 1960 season while recovering from an injury in Los Angeles. He was bitter about that and sued the Dodgers, collecting a small increase on his baseball pension. He claimed he was blackballed from baseball after the suit, a theory later publicly denied by Commissioner Ford Frick.

Furillo had a tough time in retirement, running a Queens delicatessen for a while and even working as a laborer and elevator installer on the World Trade Center in the early 1970s. He died of leukemia in 1989.

In a 1987 interview, Furillo revealed that he did know about a Dodger petition against Robinson in March of 1947. He never mentioned Dixie Walker's name. "I was lying in my bunk in the barracks in Panama in the spring training camp in 1947," Furillo recalled. "Some of the older players, Ed Head, Hugh Casey, Dixie Howell, came over to me and said they had this petition to keep the nigger off the team, and I should sign it. They said if I didn't sign it the niggers would have my job. I signed it. I was an innocent bystander, a kid, the only Italian boy in all this. What the hell did I know? I had watched him play that spring, and it looked like everybody was trying to cut off his legs.

"Rickey took care of the petition thing and it didn't take long to see

[Jackie] was a natural ball player. The other teams screamed all kinds of garbage at him and we would scream back at them, and they would yell at us for protecting the nigger. You know why they didn't like him? Because he could beat them. If he was a bum ball player you would have seen how quick they would have liked him. Nobody could compare with Jackie, and it didn't take me long to realize he was going to help me feed my family. Salaries weren't all that big in those days and I wasn't going to make a big fuss over what color a player was if he was helping me win. You can bet on that.

"I remember Ben Chapman calling him those horrible names, and I remember Enos Slaughter getting all over him, and we gave it right back to them—me and Gilly [Hodges] and Pee Wee and the rest. By the time Jackie could answer back a couple of years later, he didn't need any help. He could take care of himself with his mouth or his fists or anything else they wanted.

"Jackie got a little sassy later on, and some guys didn't like that. He had a tough time getting along with Walter Alston. I think he didn't have much respect for Alston. I didn't have much respect for him myself. Alston was afraid of the players because most of us made more money than he did, and that galled him. He only liked the brownnosers on the team, and the guy he got along with worse than Jackie was Pee Wee. He kept hearing and reading in the papers how Pee Wee was going to take his job. That caused some friction between Alston and Pee Wee.

"Jackie was just a tremendous ball player and he could beat you in so many ways. He was one of us, and I think he did an awful lot to eliminate discrimination just by the way he played and the way he handled himself.

"The best times I ever had with Jackie were just listening to Jackie fight with Leo [Durocher]. When Leo managed Brooklyn in my first year there, he treated me like dirt. Leo was in love with himself. And didn't care about young players. I didn't have much use for Leo and we finally went at it in the Polo Grounds. Jackie was right there. He didn't have much use for Leo, either. Jackie had a real sharp tongue. It was fun playing with him. The guy was good for us, good for baseball. Where the hell would the big leagues be today without Jackie Robinson?"

With Jackie Robinson asserting himself as a big leaguer, with Dixie Walker adding another sparkling season to his resume (.306 average in 148 games, 94 RBIs, 77 runs scored, and 162 hits), with Ralph Branca winning 21 games at the age of twenty-one and with Reese, Bruce Edwards, Pete Reiser, and young Furillo all having outstanding years the Dodgers won the pennant by five games. They would face the New York Yankees again in the World Series as they had six years earlier in 1941.

"I played against Jackie in his first professional game in Jersey City in 1946," recalls Bobby Thomson, the man who hit the most famous home run in baseball history. "I was with Jersey City and Jackie was with Montreal. It was a big game because Jersey City mayor Frank Hague made it so. He would bring out the bands, the municipal workers, all the cops, all the firemen, the school kids, and everybody. It was the biggest holiday of the year for Jersey City. Add all that and Jackie's opener. It was quite memorable."

Bobby Thomson was born October 25, 1923, in Glasgow, Scotland. His father, James, a carpenter and cabinet maker, decided to move the Thomson family to the United States for a better economic opportunity.

"I was the last of our six kids. My mother was pregnant with me when my father decided to leave. He had to choose between leaving the family behind or taking all of us, including his pregnant wife, to America. He went alone and finally got a job before sending for us. I was two years old. We settled in Staten Island. There was one black family in the neighborhood. Every Christmas my father would make up a food basket and bring it to them. I remember their family name, Illridge. There was quite a fuss in the press about Jackie in that first game in Jersey City. I didn't notice much. I was just trying to establish myself as a ball player," Thomson says.

Thomson was brought up to the Polo Grounds in the last month of the 1946 season, hit .315 in 18 games, and played against Jackie and Dixie

Walker and the Dodgers in the second series of the 1947 season in the Polo Grounds. He played second base and hit two home runs.

Thomson hit 29 homers as a Giants rookie in that 1947 season. Johnny Mize hit 51, and the Giants as a team set a record with 221 homers. They finished fourth behind Brooklyn, St. Louis, and Boston.

"Horace Stoneham [the Giants owner] gave us team rings with the orange band in Giants colors and a diamond spelling out the number 221. It was a great season. We were never out of a game," Thomson says.

Thomson says he doesn't remember exchanging words with Jackie Robinson or Dixie Walker in any of the games between the heated rivals in that 1947 season. "I was new to baseball, a very quiet, shy kid. I think the only Dodger I ever talked to was Eddie Stanky because we used to leave our gloves on the field in those days and he kicked my glove way down toward the bullpen," Thomson says. "I told him not to do that again."

Thomson hit his famous home run on October 3, 1951 off Ralph Branca giving the New York Giants the pennant after a three-game playoff. "All I could think of as I rounded the bases," he recalls, "is that the home run beat Brooklyn. That's what really mattered to me."

The Brooklyn Dodgers lined up in the last week of September for the official 1947 team photo. Jackie Robinson is seated in the front row between outfielders Carl Furillo and Al Gionfriddo.

Dixie Walker is in the back row standing on a chair next to Arky Vaughan with his head turned away from the camera toward the right.

"I don't know if that was because he didn't like playing with Jackie or he was mad at Rickey for talking about trading him or what," said Gene Hermanski.

Mark Langill, the official Los Angeles Dodgers historian, said the team photo has been the subject of some controversy around the Dodgers for years. Dixie Walker was never quoted on the subject despite working for the Dodgers for many years. "Long before Jackie's arrival, Dixie turned his head in at least two other team photos. I just checked the 1943 team photo and he's turning his head while in the second row.

There's another version in which he is in the top row and turning his head again in a pre-1947 team photo. So even if he was mad or protesting something in 1947, it wasn't the first time he turned his head in a team photo," Langill said.

Robinson had established himself as a significant Dodger on that team with a .297 average, a league-leading 29 stolen bases, 28 sacrifice hits, 12 homers, 5 triples, 31 doubles, 125 runs scored, and much excitement on the base paths. "Robinson was very tough to control on the bases," said Yogi Berra, a catcher on the 1947 Yankees who would have many battles with Robinson in World Series games through 1956. "We did better with him when we kept him off the bases."

By the time the 1947 World Series approached, the tone of the team had dramatically changed. "The team had become paramount," said Rachel Robinson in 2008.

Susan Walker met Rachel Robinson, Jackie's widow, at a couple of Dodger old-timers' games and at a back-to-Brooklyn reunion. Rachel had always been friendly and courteous to her, despite the alleged aggravations of the past and the reputed Walker antagonism toward Robinson.

"We never really talked about the past," Susan says. "We were just at these events, chatted about our families and things like that, and were introduced on the field."

"I can't hold grudges from the past," said Rachel Robinson, more than sixty years after the controversial 1947 season. "I really don't remember a lot of the things from that year or what was said then."

After Robinson died in 1972 at the age of fifty-three, Rachel Robinson turned her attention to the newly funded Jackie Robinson Foundation. The organization solicits funds from individuals and businesses to pay the costs of college for deserving minority students. "One of our biggest donors is Derek Jeter of the Yankees," Rachel said. "He has given us a great deal of money to send many youngsters through college." More than a thousand youngsters have gained college educations and reached successful life goals through the foundation.

"What I remember most about that 1947 season was the team coming together in the later months, playing well and winning," Rachel said. "That was just such a great thrill. After all it was our first year in the big leagues and here we were playing the famous New York Yankees in the World Series."

Rachel said one of the most memorable events from those days was the arrival of catcher Roy Campanella as the Brooklyn catcher. Campanella would go on to win three Most Valuable Player titles. "Of course, all the pressure was on Jack being the first and all that," said Rachel, "but the arrival of Campy really meant a lot to us. It showed the experiment was working and the door was open. Now players would be judged on their abilities."

Rachel said she would go to almost every game with her small son, Jackie Jr., and really got into the Brooklyn pennant race after the middle of the season. "By then it was really all about baseball and what mattered was winning or losing. It was all so exciting. Even after we got ahead we took nothing for granted. Every game was tough, every at bat was important, and we were all so thrilled and excited when the Dodgers clinched the pennant," she recalled.

Rachel said she felt as if she belonged on the team and the group had become more important than any individual as the wives sat in the stands after the Dodgers clinched the pennant and discussed their outfits for the opening of the World Series. "You know how important that always is to everybody," she said. "We had won and now it was important that we all look the part. You didn't want to be overdressed or underdressed when something that important was coming up and all the reporters and photographers were around. A lot of the other wives really helped me with that."

It was clear that Estelle Walker, who had already gone through a Brooklyn–New York World Series with Dixie in 1941, would set the style for all of the wives of players. Baseball tradition has always been that way. "I think I had more contact with the other wives of the players during that World Series time than at any other time during the season,"

Rachel said. "We all understood that it was about winning and pulling together."

Branca opened the Series for the Dodgers at Yankee Stadium against rookie Frank Shea of the Yankees, who was 14–5 during his first season and won two Series games. Robinson was at first base, batting second, the first black to play in a twentieth-century World Series; Walker was in right field for Brooklyn.

Jackie was hitless in the first game and Walker collected two hits and knocked in a run for Brooklyn.

Branca retired the first twelve Yankees he faced as the Dodgers clung to a 1–0 lead in the opener into the fifth.

"Then DiMaggio got an infield single and I just tightened up," recalled Branca. "I was a kid, twenty-one years old, in my fourth season with Brooklyn, and when I lost the no-hitter I just went to pieces." Branca gave up a couple of hits, hit a batter, walked three Yankees and was out of the game trailing 5–1.

He won a World Series game in relief but never got another start in that Series from manager Burt Shotton. "I had won twenty-one games and I was the guy down the stretch the team counted on," said Branca. "I couldn't believe Shotton would skip my turn when it came around again, especially in a Series like that when we were using up a lot of pitchers."

Six decades later, Branca is still angry about not getting a chance to redeem himself after the first-game loss. "Things might have been different if I started again. I might have won and still have been able to relieve in the seventh game when we lost. I just think the old man [Shotton] had something against me," Branca said.

The Dodgers broke up the Bill Bevens attempt at a no hitter in the fourth game when Cookie Lavagetto hit a pinch hit double scoring Al Gionfriddo and Eddie Miksis with the winning runs in a 3–2 triumph.

Yankee reliever Joe Page pitched five scoreless innings (how about that, Mariano Rivera?) with only one hit in the final game as the Yankees won 5–2 and locked up their second Series in a row against Brooklyn. It would climb to five in a row before the Dodgers finally beat the Yankees in 1955 before 71,548 fans at Yankee Stadium.

Robinson hit .259 in the 1947 Series and Dixie hit .222, including a second game home run against the tough Yankee right-hander Allie Reynolds. Dixie played all seven games in the Series. There was a strong feeling that Dixie's last at bat at Yankee Stadium, where he had broken into the big leagues sixteen years earlier, would be his final at bat for the Brooklyn Dodgers.

There had been rumors throughout the season that Dixie would be traded. A deal was arranged with Pittsburgh before the June trading deadline. It fell through. As the Dodgers drove for the pennant most of the trade talk died down. Now the stories appearing in the New York papers didn't talk much about a trade for Dixie but suggested that he would probably retire at the end of the 1947 season. He was thirty-seven, an advanced age for ball players in the 1940s.

"I stole second and got a big strawberry on my hip," Walker told Bill Lumpkin of the *Birmingham Post-Herald* early in 1982. "Clyde Sukeforth was one of our coaches. Clyde was in the shower after the game. When water hit that place on my hip, it burned like the devil. I said, 'That won't happen to ol' Dixie again.' Clyde took that to mean I was quitting after that year." Dixie simply meant that he wouldn't be sliding without protective pads under his uniform pants in any more World Series games. It was all forgotten as the Series ended.

Walker went back to his temporary Rockville Centre home. He continued attending to the package liquor store business. He appeared at several banquets in Brooklyn celebrating the Brooklyn pennant for a hundred or two hundred dollar fee, a pittance compared to today's players who receive up to twenty thousand dollars for a card show signing appearance. He attended to family business, spent more time with Estelle, wrote letters to friends and teammates, met with other players to discuss baseball pension details, and relaxed during a pleasant New York autumn.

In a few weeks Estelle packed the family clothes, got the children ready for the move home to Birmingham for the winter and prepared for whatever was to come.

They drove home to Birmingham in late October. Dixie worked around the house. He did some quail hunting. He went fishing for several days with brother Harry, who was still celebrating his 1947 batting title, making the Walkers the first brothers to accomplish that difficult feat. He spoke occasionally by phone to officials in the Dodger front office.

"There was an indication that if I retired I might be offered the managerial job at St. Paul," Walker recalled. "It was not put down on paper so I didn't consider it a real offer. Besides, I was making twenty-two thousand as a player and a managerial job at St. Paul would only pay ten or twelve thousand dollars."

Walker believed that he could still play a couple more years in Brooklyn—or elsewhere if it turned out that way. "I know he was very careful about money," says his daughter Susan Walker. "I don't think he would have walked away from a larger salary. He was always the kind of man who turned a nickel over on both sides before he would give it away."

Walker sat tight at home until an announcement was made in New York about a deal. In those days, before Marvin Miller's era of enlightenment began in the 1960s, players had no say over when they were traded or released. They often read about it in local newspapers or received calls from teammates or friends who heard about a deal.

On December 9, 1947, John Drebinger wrote in the *New York Times*, "As the baseball clans descended on New York yesterday for the annual three-day major league conclaves that open at the Waldorf-Astoria today, it remained for the Dodgers to hold their familiar position right in the center of the spotlight.

"Having about run out of reasons for keeping the matter any longer a secret, the Brooks finally broke down and confirmed the oft-repeated and as often denied report that Dixie Walker had been traded to the Pirates. With the popular 'peepul's cherce' of Flatbush, go Vic Lombardi, the pint-sized southpaw pitcher, and Hal Gregg, tall right-hander.

"In exchange the Flock [another nickname for the Dodgers] receives Billy Cox, who was the Bucs regular shortstop last summer; Elwin (Preacher) Roe, a left-hander; and Gene Mauch, a young infielder who was with the Dodgers a year ago and [was] shipped to Pittsburgh in the Kirby Higbe deal.

"At the age of 37, Dixie thus goes to his fifth major league club after nine seasons in Brooklyn where he attained a popularity unmatched by any Dodger since the days of Zack Wheat and Babe Herman. A product of the Yankees, with whom he came up in 1933, he was cast adrift when shoulder, arm and leg injuries were believed to have all but terminated a highly promising career."

Drebinger continued to extol Dixie's play with Brooklyn, pointing to the pennant-winning team of 1941, of which he was a vital member, his batting title in 1944, and his contribution, with the .306 average, to the 1947 pennant winners.

The story dealt with other aspects of the baseball meetings in New York, especially the desire of the St. Louis Browns to play more night games. Current rules prevented any team from scheduling more than two night games with each opposing club.

There was no mention of Jackie Robinson in the story detailing the trade of Walker.

After the trade was announced to the New York press, Dixie received a call at his Birmingham home from Roy Hamey, general manager of the Pirates. The Pirates—with an aging Hank Greenberg playing his final year and a young Ralph Kiner becoming a one-dimensional player with great home run skills and small defensive skills—had finished last in the 1947 season.

Hamey thought Walker could strengthen the Pittsburgh offense and help many of their young players, including another outfield prospect named Wally Westlake. Branch Rickey, in the meantime, had acquired a pitcher in Roe that was to be an anchor on the very successful Boys of Summer, as writer Roger Kahn described the Dodgers of the 1950s, as well as the finest fielding third baseman of his era, laconic Billy Cox.

Dixie Walker said at the time, "Naturally I regret leaving Brooklyn but I cannot say I am unhappy at going over to Pittsburgh. In nine years with the Dodgers I made many close friends. I love those Brooklyn people."

Branch Rickey had actually told Dixie the previous month that he would be traded to Pittsburgh if he didn't want the job as St. Paul manager. Dixie wrote Rickey another letter indicating that he chose to remain in major league ball and he disliked leaving Brooklyn for many reasons. "First of all, my package liquor store in Rockville Centre. In the past, during the baseball season, I have had an opportunity to keep in touch with the store. Then again, for nine years I have played before the finest and most sincere group of people a man could ever hope to play before.

"The newspaper and radio men have been most kind and generous in their treatment of me."

For Brooklyn fans it was a hard blow to take. Dixie Walker was as beloved a figure in Brooklyn baseball history as any man. Now he was gone. Fans could never have guessed that in less than ten years, the franchise itself would be gone.

Former major leaguer Ewart Walker with his wife, Flossie, and son, Fred, in 1915. Collection of Susan Walker.

Fred (Dixie) Walker in 1928, just before he left Birmingham for a professional baseball career. Susan Walker says she never saw her dad with that wavy blond hair. Collection of Susan Walker.

Ewart Walker and his son Dixie proudly display a splendid catch of trout after a fall fishing trip near Tuscaloosa, Alabama, in 1933. Collection of Susan Walker.

Estelle Shea Walker in a 1935 studio portrait when she worked for Music Corporation of America boss David A. (Sonny) Werblin. She scouted for singers and bands to perform on the show *Your Hit Parade* before she married Dixie Walker. Collection of Susan Walker.

Dixie Walker and his bride, Estelle Shea Walker, in front of their home in Mountain Brook, Alabama, after the 1936 season. Dixie and his dad, Ewart, built the residence out of pink limestone from the nearby Alabama hills. Collection of Susan Walker.

Babe Ruth (*top*) with his hands on the shoulders of rookie Dixie Walker in a 1933 Yankees team photo taken in St. Petersburg, Florida. The photo hung on the walls of Golden Rule Bar-B-Q restaurant in Irondale, Alabama. Susan Walker says her dad and his brother often ate there. Dixie claimed it served "the best pork barbecue and sauce I've ever eaten." Collection of Susan Walker.

Estelle Shea Walker with her daughter in a picture taken in Rockville Centre, New York, where the Walkers lived during baseball season. Collection of Susan Walker.

Susan Walker (age six) in one of her dance cos-
tumes. Susan continued dancing through her high
school years. When a voice teacher suggested she
try out for the Miss Alabama contest, her dad ve-
toed the idea. Collection of Susan Walker.

Dixie Walker in spring training with his third big league team, the Detroit Tigers, in 1938, the season teammate Hank Greenberg had a shot at breaking Babe Ruth's home run record. Greenberg fell short with fifty-eight homers. Walker hit six and had a .308 average. Collection of Susan Walker.

Dixie (*left*) and Harry Walker on a duck hunt in Sumiton, Alabama, shortly after their playing days ended in the 1950s. Susan Walker remembers the spectacular Thanksgiving dinners from their catches and how close the brothers were. Collection of Susan Walker.

Dixie Walker's favorite baseball photo of himself, taken during the 1941 pennant-winning season with the Dodgers. He had become a star on the team after an injury-filled career and was Brooklyn's most popular player, the People's Choice. Collection of Susan Walker.

Maury Allen (*left*) with Steve Garvey. Garvey was Dixie's prize pupil during the years Walker worked with Dodger hitters. Over nineteen seasons Garvey hit .294 and was the National League MVP in 1974. Photo by Janet Allen.

The Final Playing Years
and a New Career

Dixie Walker hit .316 in 129 games for the 1948 Pittsburgh Pirates. They moved up from last place to fourth place behind Boston, St. Louis, and Brooklyn.

"He was an important player on that team," said 1948 teammate Ralph Kiner in 2008, on one of his rare broadcasting visits with the New York Mets. "He helped a lot of the young players. I was a right-handed hitter and he was left-handed, of course, but I still got a lot of tips from him. I learned a lot about hitting, especially pitch selection, just watching Dixie work a pitcher at the plate."

Dixie got off to a slow start with the Pirates in 1948—a new team in a new town, different conditions in Forbes Field instead of Ebbets Field, with new management and teammates. All of that added up to a period of adjustment.

He got a big boost in early May when the Pirates came into Ebbets Field for a three-game series against the defending National League champions. Dodger fans arranged to give Walker a day in his honor at his nine year home in Brooklyn. More than thirty thousand fans showed up on a crisp Saturday afternoon. Guests and Brooklyn teammates still with the club, including Jackie Robinson, gave him a standing ovation when he was called to home plate.

Estelle Walker was given a huge bouquet. Dixie's children, Fred (little Dixie) later another big league prospect, Mary Ann, and Susan, dressed in their finery, accepted toys around home plate and stood gawking at the crowd on the field, including Brooklyn borough president John Cashmore.

Suddenly Tex Rickard, the Brooklyn public address announcer, called the attention of the fans to the open gate in center field. Through the gate, with one of the Brooklyn grounds crew members at the wheel, came a shiny, new black Studebaker. "Studebakers were manufactured in South Bend, Indiana," said Susan Walker's husband, Ed. "That was the first thing I think he got from South Bend. The second was me, with the help of Susan's mother, who always pushed my cause."

The car was driven to home plate and Red Barber, in charge of the ceremonies honoring Dixie, urged Dixie into the front seat. He turned the key and wheeled the vehicle around the home plate area as the Brooklyn fans cheered their departed People's Choice lustily.

"That was the car I demolished as a child—it was the Studebaker," recalls Susan Walker. "I know the car I demolished was new and it was the only car my family had at the time. I remember seeing pictures of it. I was about the right age to be allowed to play outside by myself. I got into the car at home in Birmingham, let the brake off and went flying down our driveway. The car didn't make the turn behind our house but kept going. The car hit a tree. I had fallen down under the steering wheel. Pure luck I wasn't killed."

Robin Roberts joined the Philadelphia Phillies on June 17, 1948. His first game in the big leagues was against the Pittsburgh Pirates, with Dixie Walker in right field, Ralph Kiner in left, and Wally Westlake in center. "I don't remember much about the game or facing Dixie," Roberts said as he lounged off the Leatherstocking Golf Course in Cooperstown, New York, during the 2008 Baseball Hall of Fame induction weekend. "I was called up and left Wilmington, Delaware, where I was pitching for the Phillies farm club, arrived at Shibe Park after a train ride at 4:30, and started the game at 8:05. Ben Chapman was the manager and asked if I could pitch. I told him I could. A few weeks later Chapman was fired and Eddie Sawyer took over. Then we won two years later with the Whiz Kids," Roberts said.

Chapman, who had led the assault in 1947 against Robinson, had quieted down by then. "In the few weeks I played under him I don't recall a word about Jackie. Why would he say anything? The Dodgers were beating our brains out. I can't remember anything about facing Dixie. I just knew he was one of the best and most respected hitters in the game. Dick Sisler was our first baseman and when we played Brooklyn they got all over him for his stuttering. He would get back at them with that famous homer winning the pennant in 1950. He wasn't much of a fielder but this one game against Brooklyn he made two or three great plays. After the game he was smiling and stuttering terribly when he finally blurted out, 'I'm hell with the leather.' I think I remember most about Dixie's work with the pension. I got involved in that later on. Dixie was certainly a leader in that department," Roberts said.

Dixie Walker picked up steam with his bat in the second half of the 1948 season with Pittsburgh. He soon had his average over .300 for a .316 finish and proved to be the league's most effective pinch hitter with 13 hits in 40 chances for a .325 average off the bench.

"Age was catching up with me that year," admitted Walker in a 1980 midsummer interview with Tot Holmes. "I had back trouble on and off through my career and it flared up again early in that season." Manager Billy Meyer of the Pirates used Walker carefully, rested him properly, and squeezed out a pretty productive season for the big league veteran.

"What I noticed—what everybody seemed to notice," Walker later said, "was that most of my hits were to left field. I had only two home runs and fifty-four RBIs in over 400 at bats [408]. That was pretty much a signal that I was about through as a big league hitter. Rickey had noticed that in Brooklyn and had mentioned it to me in my last year there of '47. I don't know if he was telling me to retire or what but he was certainly aware that I was no longer the tough Brooklyn pull hitter I had been."

As the year drew to a close, Les Biederman, the veteran newsman for the *Pittsburgh Post-Gazette,* wrote a column suggesting that Walker would not play again after the 1948 season and instead would be offered a managerial or coaching position in the Pirates minor league system. "I don't recall saying anything about quitting but when the newsmen began writing that I was, it seemed close to becoming a fact," Dixie said.

Fred Haney, the general manager of the Pirates, met with Dixie one day toward the end of the 1948 season and asked him if he would consider playing another year at the age of thirty-nine. "I told them that I would be better off not playing because I didn't think I could help the club any more," Walker said.

"Let us worry about that," Haney said. "We think you can help us win."

Walker was offered thirty thousand dollars for the 1949 season, the largest amount he ever made in baseball, and was given another incentive for a last year on the field. "If you play this one last year for us," Haney told Walker, "you can retire and go to our New Orleans team as a field manager or as general manager or coach third in Pittsburgh or be a scout in our system."

Ron Swoboda, a World Series star with the 1969 championship New York Mets, now a broadcaster in New Orleans, once summed up the attitude of baseball players at the end of their careers. "Ball players are the only people who die twice," Swoboda said. "They die when they are released and then they die again at the end like everybody else."

Walker was trying hard to hold off that first death when he agreed to play for one more season in 1949, his twenty-second season as a professional baseball player.

He got into 88 games for the Pirates in 1949, played a little first base as most veteran outfielders do, collected 51 hits to bring his career total to 2,064 and batted .282. After the last game of the 1949 season he walked up to Haney's office at Forbes Field, told the general manager he was now officially retiring as a player and inquired, "Which of the jobs do you want me to have?"

Haney hesitated and Walker, as astute a baseball man as could be, with his years in the game dealing with front office types and extra experience as he dealt with executives and owners over the pension plans, quickly got the message. "To hell with that," he told Haney. "Just give me my pink slip and I'll go home."

Racism existed in baseball long after Dixie Walker moved on to Pittsburgh from Brooklyn, long after he retired, long after black players were allowed to stay in the team hotels, dine in the club hotel dining rooms, ride the team bus, reach the game's higher management positions.

Shortly after President Barack Obama was inaugurated in 2009, former Brooklyn Dodgers great Don Newcombe, an African American pitcher who was Jackie Robinson's teammate from 1949 to 1956, recalled racial conditions in baseball six decades earlier. "I remember when I met with Dr. Martin Luther King Jr. 28 days before he was killed in Memphis in 1968," Newcombe told Peter Vecsey of the *New York Post*. "He said, 'Don, you'll never know how easy you and Jackie and Doby and Campy made it for me to do my job by what you did on the baseball field.' Imagine, here is Martin, getting beaten with billy clubs, bitten by dogs and thrown in jail and he says we made his job easier," Newcombe, eighty-two, recalled.

Newcombe described the racism that existed around the Dodgers six, seven, eight years after Dixie Walker had left the game as a player. "Cal Abrams [a Jewish utility outfielder for Brooklyn] would tell us what the white players were saying behind our backs on the buses we weren't allowed to ride on," said Newcombe. "They'd say to hell with those black players. They wanted to be in the big leagues. Let 'em suffer."

Dixie Walker, the man unfairly accused of spreading racial antagonism in big league baseball, had passed from the major league scene.

Soon he was back in Birmingham, attending to the hardware store with his dad, working in his garden, hunting and fishing with his brother, and not terribly concerned about his future.

"My mother would go fishing with him at times when there was no one else around to get out there in the water with him," recalls Susan

Walker, "but she really hated it. She only did it to please him. She most enjoyed when he had Harry to go with or somebody else. Then she would get up at 3:00 a.m. to fix sandwiches for him for the trip, kiss him goodbye, and go back to bed."

Before many weeks had gone by in that fall of 1949, Dixie Walker received a call from Earl Mann, owner of the Atlanta Crackers minor league team in the Southern Association, one of the premier clubs in minor league baseball.

"How would you like to manage our ball club next season?" Mann asked.

"I think I'd like that fine," Dixie replied.

He was soon named the manager of the Atlanta Crackers, actually played in thirty-nine games for them as a forty-year-old (he batted .273), and won the pennant.

His Atlanta teams finished in sixth and second place in the next two years. He brought old pitching pal Whitlow Wyatt of the Dodgers, who had become a full-time farmer in nearby Kensington, Georgia, back to baseball as his Atlanta pitching coach. Dixie caused a bit of a fuss in mid-summer when he named Wyatt, his forty-three-year-old pitching coach, as his starting pitcher for an exhibition game between the league-leading Crackers and the Southern Association's All-Star team.

Wyatt went seven innings, allowed three hits and one run, and gained credit for Atlanta's 8–2 victory. It enraged George Trautman, the high commissioner of minor league baseball, who instituted a new rule that prevented coaches from playing in All-Star games.

Walker was involved in another rhubarb, as Red Barber described field fights or off-field furors, in 1951. While playing in a game against the Mobile club, Don Nicholas, a Mobile outfielder, crashed into Atlanta's catcher, Leroy Jarvis, in a home plate collision. Nicholas was tagged out after he was jolted at home by the burly catcher. It was ruled by plate umpire Paul Roy that Jarvis had given Nicholas an illegal hip and was guilty of obstruction. He allowed the Mobile run to score.

Walker, usually calm, was outraged by the call. He stormed on to the field defending his catcher and was soon in a heated verbal battle with all of the umpires. He was thrown out of the game as the crowd continued to roar. "Before the storm was done, Jarvis had been stricken by nervous prostration, an Atlanta pitcher had swallowed his chew of cut-plug, and the umpire who charged Walker with insubordination and other nefarious violations," wrote Furman Bisher in a 1952 *Sport Magazine* article describing the event, "forfeited the game to Mobile. The next 30 days were a living hell for the chap who had been the 'Peepul's Cherce,' in Brooklyn, the National League player representative, and all that represented stability on the big-league field."

Walker did not even know he was suspended until informed by the reporter for the *Memphis Commercial Appeal* the next afternoon. "It was a ridiculous decision," Walker told the *Appeal's* Emmett Maum, according to an article in the July 11, 1951, *Sporting News,* baseball's bible at the time. "Our catcher has every right to go up the line which he did," Dixie said. "I would not have a catcher who would not try to make that play. What happened was that the runner hit Jarvis just as he was catching the ball, bounced over him, and missed the plate. I yelled to Jarvis to tag the man. He ran over and tagged him and umpire Roy called the runner out. Then when Paul Chervinko, Mobile manager, ran up and yelled about it, Roy called him safe because of 'obstruction.' Now I don't know what 'obstruction' is but I do know my catcher has every right to go for the ball and I told Roy as much."

Dixie continued, "Naturally, I figured it was the type of play that required argument, particularly since we were being done an injustice. But it would have been impossible to calm my boys down and get them back on the field right at the moment. Roy threatened to forfeit the game."

The only real casualty in the uprising, wrote Maum, was pitcher Joe Reardon of Atlanta, who swallowed his chewing tobacco, a common baseball experience for many through the years. He abruptly lost all interest in the argument as he became violently ill. Catcher Jarvis also took a little beating during the furor, got woozy, and fainted in the clubhouse as the players gathered in the locker room.

League president Charlie Furth had suspended Walker for 90 days after the incident, fined him one hundred dollars, a meaningful sum in 1951, and embarrassed the soft-spoken Alabama gentleman beyond belief.

Whit Wyatt, Dixie's Dodgers pal and now his pitching coach, was named temporary manager of the Atlanta Crackers. "If the ruling by the league president stood," Bisher wrote, "Walker would be out of baseball at the start of the 1952 season."

Owner Earl Mann defended Walker, appealed to Furth, and battled for vindication. "Walker's Atlanta constituents flooded the league president's office and the local newspapers with letters of vilification and threat. It was a severely trying period for Walker, who could not travel or visit with his team in the clubhouse, and in addition, could draw no pay for the period," Bisher wrote.

Mann demanded and received a hearing before Trautman. "Even in criminal court," Mann said, "no man is guilty until [he is] proven guilty and here is one of baseball's finest gentlemen who has been convicted without a hearing."

Trautman, who had been summoned to Washington, D.C., for a congressional hearing about baseball's monopoly status, granted Mann a hearing. With Hughes Spaulding, a revered Atlanta attorney, defending Walker and directing the case, Trautman relented. He based his clearance of Walker on an old baseball rule 4.13(d), which requires a one-minute warning before forfeiture. Home plate umpire Roy had no watch. On that technicality, the forfeiture was disallowed and Walker was reinstated.

The thirty days of penalty and nonplay stood. Trautman said that Walker could not be compensated for the thirty days of play and pay he had already lost when the ruling was reversed. "This really doesn't disturb me," Trautman told the Associated Press, "since Walker had prolonged the fuss and deserved some suspension."

"Walker's managerial embarkation would have occurred sooner," Bisher wrote, "since Branch Rickey had offered Dixie the billet on

Brooklyn's American Association farm at St. Paul, this in spite of the fact that Dixie had been gone a year from the Dodger organization and that he had been unjustly pictured in relation to Negro players."

Hardly an article appeared about Walker in his days as a minor league skipper that did not mention his standing with the Dodgers and his often-confused position regarding Robinson.

Big league baseball in the early 1950s was made up of eight teams in each league, twenty-five players on each team for a total of only four hundred players. Gossip traveled fast and impressions of players, possibly untrue or tarnished, were fixed. Walker's image as the leader of the anti-Robinson southern group was clearly fixed.

After three seasons of minor league baseball, Walker yearned for another chance at the big leagues. He was not unhappy as a minor league manager in Atlanta, especially since he was relatively near his Birmingham home, but he clearly felt he had earned a big league opportunity.

In 1952 a Brooklyn teammate, Eddie Stanky, known as the Brat for his pugnacious personality and play and also as the Walking Man for his great skill at forcing pitchers to walk him despite a modest bat (.269 lifetime average and twenty-nine home runs in eleven seasons) was named the manager of the St. Louis Cardinals.

When Walker's third season in Atlanta ended he called Stanky at his home in Mobile, Alabama. "I've heard that you may be making some changes in your coaching staff," Dixie told Stanky.

"It's possible," he said. "We're still working on our staff."

"Keep me in mind if you decide to make any changes," Dixie said.

If there is an old boy network in any business, it is clearly in the baseball business. Most managers have the right and privilege to name their own coaching staff members and more often than not the jobs are filled with former teammates, pals, and baseball buddies.

Walker played with Stanky in Brooklyn from 1945 through 1947 and they talked often on the bench, in the clubhouse, and at dinner on the road about the way the game should be played, about how to improve, and how each man might someday have an opportunity to hire the other. That was just the way it worked out.

Walker started the 1953 season as Stanky's hitting coach. He enjoyed being back in the big leagues, dealing with the best players in the game, and enjoyed the improved conditions—a single room for coaches in team hotels, meal money increased to $7.50 a day, and improved facilities in every ball park.

On July 31, Dixie was asked to leave the Cardinals big league club and take over the Houston Buffs team in the International League, replacing ousted manager Al Hollingsworth. "I didn't want to go," Dixie recalled, "but the Cardinals insisted. So when I got to Houston and took over the club I signed for the 1954 season as well."

Walker's job was to teach the young Cardinals farm hands in Houston how to play "Stanky baseball," that aggressive heads-up style Stanky had made so popular in his playing days with the Dodgers, the pennant-winning Boston Braves in 1948, and the New York Giants under scrappy Leo Durocher in the dramatic come-from-behind season of 1951.

Minor league managers are often measured by the big league players they turn out. Dixie took a raw, awkward eighteen-year-old left-handed kid named Eddie Mathews in Atlanta, converted him from an outfielder into a third baseman, taught him the strike zone, and sent him on his way to a Hall of Fame career with the Braves.

In Houston he developed two other players who would achieve big league success. Slugger Ken Boyer would hit a 1964 World Series grand slam homer against the Yankees, and Don Blasingame would become a longtime stylish fielder and tough hitter.

In 1955 Walker returned to the big leagues under the leadership of old pal Stanky again. Owner Gussie Busch, the beer baron, finally got tired of Stanky's aggressive ways on and off the field, fired him late in the year, and replaced Stanky with his Rochester Red Wings skipper, none other than Dixie's brother, Harry Walker.

"I didn't want to go to Rochester," Walker once said. "It was far from home, away from the big leagues of course, and in a league I was very unfamiliar with. But someone had to go and I certainly wouldn't embarrass Harry by making a fuss. So I went."

Walker finished out the 1955 season in fourth place in Rochester and climbed to second in the 1956 season. He beat Miami and Toronto in the playoffs and captured the league championship.

A multimillionaire named Jack Kent Cooke ran the Toronto club. He would soon become one of the founders of a new league, the Continental League, which would battle the big leagues for recognition. It never got off the ground but it did lead to baseball expansion into Canada with eventual major league clubs in Toronto and Montreal.

Cooke decided the first step toward improving his franchise and maybe eventual big league status would be the hiring of a popular, experienced, big name skipper. He chose Dixie Walker. Walker won a pennant his first year with Toronto, finished in second place the following season of 1958, and struggled through his third season with Toronto in 1959.

That team was made up mostly of veteran players, many of whom had played in the big leagues and saw their careers now fading away. They were all facing their first "death," and discipline, loyalty to the team, and recognition of Walker's status as leader of the club meant little to them. "I was a teenager by then and on the few occasions I would see my father he seemed distracted, nervous, and unhappy," remembers Susan Walker.

One day, after a tough loss, and a beer-drinking clubhouse, Walker called Estelle at home. He was distraught as he described the difficulties he faced with this team and the pressures he no longer seemed capable of handling.

"I feel terrible, Stell, I just can't stand it any more," he told his wife. "I feel like jumping off a tall building." As always, Estelle Walker was a strong, calming influence on her husband.

"Don't do that, dear," she said. "Just go into the office tomorrow, tell them you are quitting and come home. I'll be waiting here for you."

Walker did just that. A sympathetic Estelle Walker welcomed him with a warm kiss, a fine meal, and his favorite slippers.

"I had some trouble with those players in Toronto," Walker would re-call years later. "I just packed up and came home. I decided I had enough managing and I would never do it again."

Walker, who suffered from ileitis most of his adult life, was in much pain as he returned to Birmingham. "It took him quite a while to get back to himself," recalls Susan Walker. "But I think a few fishing trips with Harry and some hunting outings got him back to normal."

Dixie was soon back in the big leagues with the Milwaukee Braves when John McHale, general manager of the team, called and asked him to coach the club under the direction of his old Brooklyn coaching pal, Charlie Dressen.

Bobby Bragan, one of Dixie's 1947 Brooklyn teammates, became the Braves manager in 1963 and Walker agreed to go out on the road again for the Braves as a scout.

The Braves, who had begun baseball's expansion west with a move from Boston to Milwaukee in 1953, now moved again. This time the Milwaukee franchise shifted to Atlanta and Dixie was home again in the South, back in his native Georgia as a member of that organization, and comfortable with the team as he celebrated his fifty-fifth birthday.

His dreams of becoming a big league skipper seemed now to be fad-ing but he continued to draw a big league salary and liked the freedom of the scouting position. No one could really explain and no one ever said whether Dixie's negative relationship with Robinson in Brooklyn kept him from a big league managerial opportunity despite so much minor league success. But Walker could now clearly be identified as a baseball lifer, one of the men who always seem to have some sort of a job in the game, even if it is not a top job.

He scouted for the Braves for half a dozen years and could be seen fre-quently in press boxes in New York, Chicago, St. Louis, and Pittsburgh. Sportswriters ran into him often in the new Shea Stadium press box in Queens, sitting in a back row, a notebook in front of him, glasses over his eyes or sometimes propped on his head, his stare fixed on the play-ers on the field in front of him.

Conversations with Dixie would begin about some player he liked or a kid he managed, someone like Eddie Mathews, grown into stardom now on his way to a Hall of Fame career or a youngster he had seen in the minor leagues with a quick bat. "Ahh, those teams were always fun to be with," he said one day about his time in Brooklyn. "I think I just loved every minute of it when I played with Pee Wee and Cookie [Lavagetto] and all the rest of the wonderful fellows on the Dodgers. And those fans, my oh my, they were, well, different. They sure did love their Dodgers and we sure did love them—Hilda Chester and Shorty [Laurice] and the Dodger Sym-Phony and all the rest. Those were wonderful days, the best I had in baseball by far."

He made a note on his sheet in that firm handwriting of his, adjusted his glasses over his eyes, and studied the next New York batter. Then he continued. "We didn't win all the time," he said, "but we always gave the fans a good show. I think that is what Mr. Rickey believed in, a competitive team, even if the Dodgers didn't win. And then Mr. O'Malley, when he took over went along with just about the same thing. You can't win every year, that's the way baseball is, but you certainly can spend money and keep the franchise active."

There was never any talk of any controversy around the Dodgers in those meetings during his scouting days. The Shea press box and the back dining room for press, scouts, broadcasters, and assorted old-timers was hardly the place for serious conversation.

Dixie would have animated conversations with Ralph Kiner, the Mets broadcaster in the 1960s, still on the job in 2008, and a former Pittsburgh teammate of Walker's in 1948 and 1949. Mostly they were talking about hitting, when their conversations were overheard, or about some youngster that Dixie had seen in the minor leagues that he was certain would be displaying his skills soon on the big league level.

Other players of his time who were now scouts would sometimes visit the press box at Shea and wind up in a conversation about old times with Walker. Buddy Kerr, a New York Giants shortstop in the middle 1940s and a frequent opponent of Dixie's Dodgers in those heated battles, was a New York Mets scout. He often sat near Dixie in the press box and they laughed about incidents from the past.

"We had this one crazy doubleheader, Dixie," Kerr once said to the former Dodger. "Do you remember it? We beat you something like 26–2 in the first game and you beat us 2–1 in the second game. Baseball can be crazy, can't it?"

"I think that was in 1944," Walker replied. "That was a pretty good year for me. I won the batting title."

Dixie would often get kidded about winning the batting title in 1944, a season when many of the game's great stars were off serving the country in World War II. "I remember one year when Harry [Walker] was managing the Pittsburgh Pirates," Dixie once said. "We had a banquet for him in his hometown of Leeds [Alabama] and a lot of his pals came down to honor him. Joe Brown, the general manager of the Pirates and Harry's boss was there and our pal Eddie Stanky and Stan Musial came to the banquet. It was quite an event."

Musial got up at the banquet, Dixie recalled, and started telling the crowd in his laughing light manner about his career, which had ended in 1963, just a couple of seasons before Harry Walker became the field boss of the Pirates.

Dixie had beaten Musial by ten points for the 1944 title. That was good enough for Dixie to claim the title's legitimacy.

Musial talked about that year, congratulated Dixie on that fine season, and then pointed out that Harry won the coveted batting title in 1947.

"You've got to be real proud of these Walker brothers," Musial told the hometown Leeds crowd. "Between them and me, we had nine years that we led the league in hitting."

Of course, the audience, hip on baseball statistics, knew that Stan led the National League in hitting seven times by himself.

On another scouting occasion at Shea, Walker was greeted by Moe Berg, the mysterious former player with the Red Sox, Indians, White Sox, Senators, and Dodgers. Berg had once gone on a barnstorming trip to Japan in the early 1930s and claimed his photos were used by the army air corps on the famous World War II flight by Jimmy Doolittle over Tokyo. Berg was supposedly a member of the Office of Strategic Services (forerunner to the CIA) during World War II and was involved in secret missions.

Berg played with the Red Sox from 1935 through 1939, was Ted Williams' first roommate there, and was often seen in his black suit and subdued ties freeloading sandwiches and soft drinks in press boxes at Yankee Stadium, the Polo Grounds, and later at Shea in the 1960s. He died in 1972.

"He can speak 13 languages," Casey Stengel once said of the highly educated Berg, "but he can't hit in any of them." He did hit .243 and did last fifteen years in the big leagues. Walker and Berg crossed paths often in the late 1930s when Walker was with the White Sox and Tigers and Berg was the backup catcher at Boston.

"His main job with the Red Sox," manager Joe Cronin once said of Berg, "was protecting the batting practice baseballs."

Berg sidled up to Walker often, talked quietly as Dixie jotted down facts in his notebook, shared a press box lunch with him and reminisced about their time in the American league.

Walker's scouting assignments ranged from studies of the big league operation to examination of the youngsters in the far-flung Braves minor league system. On occasion he would be asked to look at a youngster in high school or college that the Braves might be interested in signing. Walker was considered an expert in sizing up hitting talent.

"He was as good as they come," said former Braves general manager John McHale, shortly before his death in 2008. "He was dedicated to his work and turned in some of the most detailed reports. It was a privilege to have Dixie in our organization for so many years. He was as good a baseball man as you could find."

Dixie felt the same way about McHale. "My association with John McHale was always very enjoyable," Dixie once said. "I consider John and the O'Malleys [Walter and son Peter of the Dodgers] the cream of the crop."

After eight years with the Braves as a coach, scout, and spring batting instructor, Walker was let go at the end of the 1968 season.

Paul Richards, a legendary baseball figure in Atlanta, was put in charge of the Braves after the franchise moved from Milwaukee to the Georgia capital.

Walker and old pal Whitlow Wyatt, the organization's pitching instructor, were released as Richards brought in new people, many of whom had worked for him in Baltimore. That's the way life goes for baseball people.

Dixie Walker was fifty-eight years old in 1968, still energetic, still certain he had a lot to offer to any organization that might need his lifetime of baseball skills and experience. He was at home in Birmingham over that winter, spent time on the farm where his mother now lived alone after his father's death in 1965, worked on the Birmingham house, fished and hunted with Harry, as always, and gave little thought to his baseball future. If there was to be a baseball future, he would happily accept it. If there was not to be a baseball future, he would happily accept that also. As a prudent investor, he had saved enough for his retirement years. He knew he could take care of his Stell, the family home, and all the family obligations without leaving home again. But it would still be nice to get out to a spring training field, swing a few bats for fun, and look at some promising youngsters.

He sat in his office at home one day, picked up his pen, put a piece of paper in front of him, adjusted his glasses, and began to write a letter. "Dear Walter," the letter began. It was for Los Angeles Dodger owner Walter O'Malley at the team headquarters at Dodger Stadium in Los Angeles. "As you may know," the letter read, "I am no longer connected to the Atlanta Braves organization. If you think I might be of any service to the organization of the Los Angeles Dodgers, I would be happy to discuss a possible position with your team."

It had been more than twenty years since Walker had worn a Dodger uniform. He had no connection with the Los Angeles organization except through the O'Malley family, which had been involved with the Dodgers in his Brooklyn days but really had a secondary status at the time under Branch Rickey. Things had changed. Walter O'Malley not only was the owner of the Dodgers, he was considered one of the most powerful men in the game of baseball. He had led the move west after the 1957 season and he had seen his team and the San Francisco Giants prosper as baseball expanded into California. His contributions to the game would be recognized in 2008 when he was inducted into the Baseball Hall of Fame. But in the late 1960s he was riding high on the strength of two Hall of Fame pitchers, Sandy Koufax and Don Drysdale, who had brought much glory to his team, and the excitement of Maury Wills on base, as an equal to Jackie Robinson, in a splendid 1962 Most Valuable Player year.

Dixie waited a few days. Finally, there was a phone call from Dodger general manager Buzzie Bavasi. He wanted to know if Dixie Walker wanted to join the Los Angeles Dodgers as a hitting instructor starting in spring training at Vero Beach.

Dixie Walker was about to prove that you can go home again.

13
The Sweet Dodger Days

In 1948 a Vero Beach, Florida, businessman by the name of Bud Holman contacted Buzzie Bavasi of the Brooklyn Dodgers concerning a new spring training home for the Dodgers. Brooklyn had trained at Havana in 1947 with side trips to Panama, Honduras, and Miami. Walter O'Malley, a co-owner of the Dodgers, had instructed Bavasi to look for a new permanent site for the team.

Holman told Bavasi that the U.S. government had abandoned a naval station at Vero Beach and returned the property to the city. It was a quiet resort area on the east coast of Florida with perfect spring weather, access roads, a nearby airport, and plenty of room for growth. The Dodgers acquired the property and began more than sixty years of spring baseball there.

Sportswriters visited the site of the Dodger spring complex in 2008 for the final time. The Dodgers, under new owner Frank McCourt, had decided to move their spring training facility to Glendale, Arizona, which was closer to Los Angeles.

Farewell ceremonies were held on the day of the last spring game with former manager Tommy Lasorda entering the field under crossed bats, former Brooklyn pitcher Carl Erskine singing the national anthem and playing "Take Me Out to the Ball Game" on his harmonica, and former National League MVP Maury Wills signing autographs as the game was played.

The complex included the stadium named after the local business-man, Bud Holman, who had lured the team there and energized Vero Beach's economy, with residences for all the players and staff, dining halls, several practice fields, swimming pools, golf courses, and tennis courts.

Vero Beach was probably the most famous spring training location of any baseball team. Visitors could walk along the pathways leading to the residential areas or the dining rooms, and cross streets were named after Sandy Koufax, Jackie Robinson, Duke Snider, Gil Hodges, Roy Campanella, Don Drysdale, Pee Wee Reese, and many other Dodger greats.

There was at one time a street named for Dixie Walker.

In the main building of the complex were huge photos of Robinson stealing a base, Snider hitting a home run, Koufax striking out a batter, Reese putting a tag on a sliding runner, and Furillo firing a bullet throw home.

There was one small photograph of Dixie Walker, the team's 1944 National League batting champion and two-time pennant winner, on a side wall. "After Dixie joined us as a batting instructor in the early 1970s we presented him with a silver bat for his 1944 hitting title," said Peter O'Malley, son of longtime Dodger owner Walter O'Malley.

"My father really liked Dixie a lot. He knew him, of course, as a Brooklyn player and he brought him back with us as a hitting instructor in the late 1960s. They used to play golf a lot at Vero Beach and Dixie was always a big favorite during my dad's March 17 St. Patrick's Day parties every year at Vero Beach with the wearing of the green," Peter O'Malley said.

O'Malley showed off an old photo of Dixie and Walter O'Malley at one of their golf outings at the Safari Pines Country Club in Vero Beach. Dixie is congratulating O'Malley, wearing a cardboard king's crown after the Dodgers chairman of the board defeated Walker in the head-to-head match 5 up with 4 to play. Dixie has his left arm draped affec-tionately over the shoulder of his wife, Estelle, as other wives of Dodger executives, Ginny Ozark, Bess Campanis, Alice Hartsfield, and Lela Alston, look on.

Another important person in Dixie Walker's life as he returned to the Dodgers in 1969 after being separated from the organization for over twenty years was Buzzie Bavasi. Emil Joseph Bavasi was born in Astoria, Queens, New York, on December 12, 1914. He died May 1, 2008. He was ninety-three. His father, Joseph, delivered newspapers and his mother, Sue, a native of Jersey City, New Jersey, was a homemaker.

He picked up the lifelong nickname of Buzzie from his older sister, Lola, who said the youngster buzzed around the house as soon as he could walk. "She said I buzzed around like a bee," Bavasi said in an interview early in 2008. "Pretty soon everybody was calling me that. I have lifelong friends who have no idea that 'Buzzie' is not the name on my birth certificate."

Joe Bavasi's newspaper delivery business prospered and the family moved from working-class Queens to the upper-class suburb of Scarsdale, New York, in Westchester County, a few miles north of New York City. "One of our neighbors was Ford Frick, who was a newspaperman then and would later become National League president and baseball commissioner," Bavasi said. He was also named to baseball's Hall of Fame in 1970.

Frick, a good pal of Babe Ruth's during much of Ruth's playing days with the Yankees, was the commissioner in the memorable 1961 season when Roger Maris and Mickey Mantle challenged Ruth's home run record of sixty set in 1927. Frick ruled the record could not be truly recognized unless it was done within 154 games of the new 162 game season. Maris hit the sixty-first homer on the final day of that season amid much controversy involving an asterisk in the record books next to his name.

"My parents were very friendly with Ford and I would sit around our house and listen to him tell great stories about baseball, a lot of them about Babe Ruth I never would hear anywhere else," Bavasi said.

After graduating from DePauw University in Greencastle, Indiana,

Bavasi had an interview with Larry MacPhail, then running the Brooklyn Dodgers, through Frick's efforts. "They offered me a job as the business manager of their lowest farm club in Americus, Georgia. I took it because I wanted to be in baseball," he said.

He moved to Valdosta, Georgia, then to Durham, North Carolina, before serving in the infantry in Sicily and Italy during World War II. "After the war I went back to Brooklyn and Mr. Rickey, who was then running the club, assigned me the position of finding a franchise up north where we could play the two newest Negro players we had just signed, Roy Campanella and Don Newcombe. Rickey had already assigned Jackie Robinson to Montreal for the 1946 season instead of St. Paul where the Dodgers had their best prospects," he said. Rickey had decided the international city of Montreal, with its large French and European population, would be more comfortable for Robinson than the middle-America Minnesota town.

Bavasi said he was a little embarrassed one day in 1946 when he asked his boss why he selected Montreal over St. Paul as Robinson's first professional baseball home.

"I wanted him with the Canadian club," Rickey responded.

"I forgot that Mr. Rickey didn't drink," Bavasi said more than sixty years later. "I thought he was referring to the booze he could get in Canada."

Dixie Walker had another strong season for the Dodgers in 1946 with a .319 average while Bavasi spent most of that year in Nashua, New Hampshire. Campanella and Newcombe played there to much success. Robinson was in Montreal, burning up the International League.

"I got to know Dixie a little bit that season when I made trips back to Brooklyn for organizational meetings. He was a fine player and a real good man around the club," Bavasi said.

Bavasi was promoted to general manager of the Montreal club after Walker was traded away to Pittsburgh in 1947, became the general manager of the Brooklyn Dodgers under new owner Walter O'Malley in 1951, and was the head man when Brooklyn won its one and only World Series in 1955.

Bavasi left the Dodgers after the 1968 season, shortly after he brought Dixie Walker back to the organization, and became president and part owner of the expansion San Diego Padres. Ten years later famed Hollywood cowboy singer-actor Gene Autry, owner of the California Angeles, hired him away from San Diego to run the Angels. He retired after the 1984 season and two California playoff teams.

At the age of ninety-three, he was on the computer almost every day, sending emails across the country to old baseball friends and former players such as Duke Snider, Ralph Branca, Maury Wills, and Steve Garvey. His memory was still sharp and he hadn't forgotten the two most dramatic seasons in his Brooklyn baseball history, 1951 and 1955.

"In 1951 we lost the pennant when Ralph [Branca] gave up that cheap shot homer to Bobby Thomson at the Polo Grounds. It was my mother's birthday," Bavasi said. "We had a big party all set for her that night. After Thomson hit the homer we cancelled the party. How could you have a party after something like that?" But Bavasi and the Dodgers partied well into the night after the October 4, 1955, victory by Johnny Podres over the Yankees for Brooklyn's only World Series triumph.

"That team won because Podres pitched two great games," Bavasi said, "but it wasn't the best Brooklyn team. The 1952 team was better. All of the players, Jackie, Campanella, Pee Wee, Gil Hodges, Snider were really at their peak."

Bavasi said he was very proud of bringing Dixie Walker back to the Dodgers. "He was an incredibly popular player in Brooklyn, and I think a lot of Dixie's aura carried over to the Los Angeles Dodgers," Bavasi said. "He was gone a long time from the organization by then but everybody knew who he was. He had won a batting title and players respect that kind of thing. When he talked about hitting, they listened. You couldn't get hitting instruction from a more knowledgeable guy."

Walker had been traded away from the Brooklyn Dodgers after Jackie Robinson's rookie year with the team in 1947. He had batted .306 with ninety-four runs batted in. He was still, at the age of thirty-seven, a very productive player. "When Dixie was traded I was very upset," said Bavasi. "I thought he could still play and still help us. This is the only time I thought Mr. Rickey was wrong. I don't know if it was because Mr. Rickey thought he was slipping badly or because of the letter he had written asking for the trade or all the fuss involving Dixie over Jackie. It didn't seem like a good move for the ball club."

Bavasi said he recalled talking with Dixie during that famous spring training in Havana, Cuba, in 1947. "Dixie told me in complete confidence that he saw nothing wrong with the Dodgers bringing Jackie to the club. He had watched him and played against him in those games between Montreal and Brooklyn and he knew that this guy was an exceptional athlete," said Bavasi.

Bavasi paused in his conversation and thought back to that time more than six decades ago. "You have to keep in mind that Dixie lived in Birmingham, Alabama, and he knew that his neighbors would have run him out of town if he had taken a different attitude publicly about the first black player in the big leagues," Bavasi said. "This was a different time, different values, different attitudes. We can't put today's morals and ethics and values on a time in the past."

Bavasi said he was back in Brooklyn in midseason in 1947. Dixie had given Jackie some batting tips that helped get the rookie out of a slump. "He didn't like the way Jackie jumped around on the bases," said Bavasi. "Dixie saw that as a distraction. I guess he didn't see it as that much of a distraction because he still was able to hit over .300."

Early one afternoon, before a game, Bavasi noticed Jackie and Dixie walking to the far edge of Ebbets Field. There was a sliding pit there where many of the players would practice their sliding skills. "I remember Dixie working with Jackie on his sliding skills in that pit," said Bavasi. "Dixie was always a good base runner and excellent slider. He knew how to cut a bag, come inside or outside, make the fielder really look for him with the ball for the tag," he said. "He ran and slid three or four times like that in the pits. Then Jackie did it. He picked it up right away. He was that good of an athlete."

Bavasi said none of this was ever described to the press at the time. "This is just the way Dixie wanted it," said Bavasi. "Too bad this wasn't made known at the time. I think it would have made it easier for Dixie. This was just something he didn't let on about because he was always concerned about the reaction of people at home."

Bavasi said in 2008 that his memories of Dixie Walker remain vivid and pleasant to this day. "He was really a good man to have on a club, on the field and off," he said. "It all transferred later on to his relationships with players when he was coaching. He was especially good with young players. Not a lot of coaches are. It takes too much patience to work with kids."

After rejoining the Dodgers in the 1960s, Walker would work with players in spring training and then spend a good part of the rest of the year traveling from town to town where the Dodgers had a farm club. He and Estelle would get into his red van, spend many hours together, talking about the children and the grandchildren, visiting with other baseball friends, and enjoying seeing many other parts of the country.

Almost invariably, as he sat in the press boxes of these small minor league parks, a local reporter, recognizing the People's Choice as an important visitor, would ask for an interview. Walker always obliged. The reporter and Walker would dance around the interview for a few minutes, talking of Dixie's play with the Dodgers, his batting title, the pennants won in Brooklyn in 1941 and 1947, the thrilling Series with the Yankees both times, and his opinions on current stars.

One other subject always surfaced. Jackie Robinson.

In a typical interview with Stanford Chen, sportswriter for the *Bellingham (Wash.) Herald* in 1975, Walker bristled when the reporter asked about Jackie.

"Too much has been said about that," Walker replied. "I just don't want to talk about it any more."

Chen's article, mostly about old-time players, did cover the subject as most articles about Dixie did. "A sore point with Walker, a Georgia native," Chen wrote, "were the innuendoes of racism, especially when Jackie Robinson first broke in with the Dodgers." Chen reported that his newspaper had recently run excerpts from Leo Durocher's autobiography, written with Ed Linn, *Nice Guys Finish Last*. "It said Walker and another player led a petition drive to keep Robinson off the team," the reporter wrote. "Walker denied any involvement with the petition but did say he wrote a letter to Dodger president Branch Rickey asking to be traded," Chen wrote.

Then he quoted Walker on the subject. "Everybody assumed it was because of Robinson," Walker said. Chen's article continues, "He said he gets along with blacks and whites and color has no bearing on judging a player's talents. Walker said black athletes have kept up the quality of baseball."

Chen soon switched the emphasis of his article from Dixie's past to baseball's present. Dixie told him he had been inactive so long (more than twenty-five years by then) that he couldn't compare today's top players to players in his day except to say that the Dodgers' Sandy Koufax, retired some ten years by then, and California's Nolan Ryan, still going strong, would rate well with the all-time best pitchers. On that list would be Lefty Grove, the pitcher Dixie considered the toughest to hit.

"He's the fastest pitcher I ever faced," Dixie told the reporter. "It was like hitting against sheer power. Babe Ruth didn't have any trouble hitting him, though."

"Another toughie was fire balling Bob Feller," Chen reported about Dixie's old-time choices.

"Hitting against him was like a nightmare," Walker said. "It was no fun when he was wild. And it wasn't any fun when he had control."

Walker went on to say that Joe DiMaggio, the youngster from San Francisco who succeeded Dixie as the Yankee center fielder in 1936, was the best all-around player he ever saw, and Ted Williams was the best hitter. Defensively, Dixie liked Marty Marion, Pee Wee Reese, Phil Rizzuto, and the current Cincinnati shortstop Dave Concepcion.

"Several years ago," Chen wrote, "when the Dodgers celebrated the team's centennial, the Los Angeles fans picked Walker, Duke Snider and Zack Wheat as the all time Dodger outfield. Neither Walker [nor] Wheat ever played in Los Angeles.

"His job as a traveling batting instructor means many miles across the country and he and his wife tool the length and breadth of the country in that red van," Chen wrote.

"I think both my mother and dad liked those years together very much," says Susan Walker. "We were all gone from home by then. They were together and they were seeing places and doing things they never could do in the first thirty-five years of their marriage."

Dixie did all the driving and Estelle did all the navigating as they motored across the country on Dixie's scouting assignments, pausing often to enjoy the scenery, shopping in local stores, and dining in the best local restaurants. One weekend in 1975 they were in Waterbury, Connecticut. The Dodgers had a fine minor league team there and Dixie was there to examine a couple of their best prospects to see if they were ready for big league play in Los Angeles. Estelle could enjoy the magnificent New England scenery. Ron Harrison, a reporter for the *Waterbury Sunday Republican,* sat down with Dixie before a game between the Waterbury Dodgers and the Quebec City Cubs.

It was July 25, 1975, Barbershop Night at Municipal Stadium in Waterbury with each male "chronologically advanced enough" to shave receiving a razor from a sponsor and several different barbershop quartets and quintets providing the evening's entertainment for a crowd in excess of thirty-five hundred in the old town park.

Unlike most reporters interviewing Dixie in those days, Harrison jumped right in with the Jackie Robinson questions from the start. He talked about the petition in the Brooklyn spring training camp in Havana, the letter Dixie wrote to Rickey, and what he called a Dodger "rebellion" against the arrival on the team of the Montreal star.

"I never had any trouble with Jackie," Dixie replied calmly to the sportswriter. "The only time we ever had a cross word was at Philadelphia early in the season. He was at second base dancing back and forth—it was bothering me. I shouted for him to stop but he just waved me off. I was born and raised in the South. I owned a business in the South. A great many people would look at me in a light where I had betrayed the South. I learned the South was wrong. I have always gotten along with blacks since. I saw Jackie many times after that at old-timers' games and we always shook hands."

Harrison finished the questioning of Walker about Robinson and moved quickly to tales of other Brooklyn stars of Dixie's time. "Leo Durocher, who managed both Pete Reiser and Willie Mays," Harrison said, "claims that Reiser could have been Mays' equal if he hadn't crashed into so many walls. What do you think of that?"

"Pete was a great ball player, no question about that," Walker said. "I don't want to take anything away from Pete, because he's a friend of mine. The greatest ball player I ever saw was Joe DiMaggio. I didn't see as much of Mays as I did of DiMaggio. Both were outstanding hitters with great power. In base running you had to take Mays over DiMaggio, both were great outfielders but Joe wasn't as spectacular an outfielder as Mays was."

Harrison told Dixie that around 1954 or so, during the Dodgers' final years in Brooklyn, the fans voted Walker the all-time Dodger right fielder ahead of the popular Carl Furillo. He thought that was quite an honor for Dixie. "They had another poll years later in Los Angeles for the fans," Walker said, "and I was chosen again."

Harrison asked Walker what he told young hitters as he worked with them in the far-flung Dodger organization. "I preach this to hitters," Walker said. "Analyze yourself, where your power is. A lot of times the players resent that. I tell the Dodgers players, just take what comes natural for a home run instead of waiting for a home run pitch. It's a hard thing to get over. The present-day ball player should take batting practice with the idea that the pitcher who will be pitching tonight will be warming up in the bullpen with the curve, the change he'll throw to that hitter. They take batting practice and play long ball too much in my book. I remember when Ruth and Gehrig took batting practice—

half of the fans would be sitting out there just to see those fellows hit the long ball. Maybe there are 20 percent who can go for the long ball. The other 80 percent can't."

Harrison soon switched the interview to personal questions and Dixie answered all of them with ease.

"What is the origin of your nickname?" he asked.

"My dad, who pitched for Washington, was called Dixie. When I started playing, the first time I looked in the paper," he said, "I was called Dixie."

Harrison then asked, "Did any of your sons play professionally?"

"We had six children," Walker replied. "We lost two. My oldest son, Fred Dixie Walker, signed with the Cards for a forty thousand dollar bonus. He tried for five years but as high as he got was Memphis of the Southern League. He graduated from Auburn University and became a construction engineer. He was skin diving off the Florida Keys two years ago when I got word he was missing. They never found his body."

Harrison offered his apologies and asked about Dixie's brother, Harry. "He's with the Cardinals now. Bing Devine [St. Louis general manager] has him double checking on ball players recommended by their scouts. He also scouts the big league teams for the Cardinals."

Harrison asked Dixie if he and Harry were ever batting rivals.

"Not really," Dixie said. "I think I helped Harry the year [1947] he led the league in hitting. When he got to the point where he had a crack at it, I said, 'Think about my average being .357 and try to beat it.' He hit .363. Positive thinking is important in hitting."

The barber shop quartets were tuning up now for the final two songs before the game, "Take Me Out to the Ball Game" and then the national anthem. Harrison thanked Dixie for his time, shook hands with the former big league star, and walked away. Dixie opened his notebook and recorded the starting time of the game, 7:38 p.m., and began his evening's work. Estelle sat in her seat in the stands, sipped a cup of coffee, and read a book. The Walkers were just another couple of hours away from another happy journey in the old red van to another baseball city. They were happy just to be together.

In another interview in the *Birmingham News* of February 12, 1971, columnist Alf Van Hoose asked Walker if he had ever returned to Brooklyn after being traded away in 1947. "No," Dixie said. "It's not because I'm mad at anybody or because I didn't want to return. I loved it there. There just hasn't been an occasion for me to go back. Oh, I've been to New York dozens of times since. Several times I've thought I'd go over there. But it just never worked out that I did. Of course since they've torn down the park for a high-rise apartment building I wouldn't know how to locate myself I guess. It wouldn't be the same without the park."

"Paradoxically," Van Hoose wrote, "Brooklyn loved Dix because he was a winner. The borough's affection was more commonly reserved for great losers, including the prince of losing managers before World War II, Casey Stengel."

Van Hoose continued, "Walker, who will be in baseball and his state's Hall of Fame someday, still prefers to discuss baseball today rather than yesterday."

He summed up his profile of Dixie Walker by writing, "Dixie Walker, with his drawl, honesty, folksiness and talent, simply conquered Brooklyn's heart. They loved it, and also the man, in and out of old Ebbets Field. Walker, a Birmingham resident even way back, relaxed all winter except for feeding 21 cows on his 52-acre farm near Leeds, and ship-shaping his barn and fences for the summer."

Walker had only recently returned from New York where he was an honored guest at the Bill Corum (a *New York Journal American* sportswriter) dinner and was with old Brooklyn teammates Pee Wee Reese, Gil Hodges, Eddie Stanky, Frenchy Bordagaray, and Van Lingle Mungo.

"Walker confessed scores of Brooklyn tales surfaced. Some of them," Van Hoose wrote, "Dixie thought might have even been true."

Van Hoose wrote that Dixie took pride in his hitting instruction with the young Los Angeles Dodgers and noted that the team batting average improved from .230 in his first year with the club to .254 and .270 in his next two full seasons.

Van Hoose wrote in his column that Walker would soon be on his way again to the spring training headquarters of the Dodgers at Vero Beach and would spend more than six weeks working with the talented Los Angeles batters. (Estelle would set up their home in a nearby apartment.)

"Brooklyn stories would probably bore them," Van Hoose wrote, "dark ages history, but what an old king-size Brooklyn batter tells them about a swing will go in one ear—and stick."

One player on the Dodgers in those days would not be bored by Brooklyn stories. He was part of them. His name was Steven Patrick Garvey of Tampa, Florida, first baseman of the Los Angeles Dodgers and later San Diego Padres from 1969 through 1987.

Steve Garvey was born in Tampa on December 22, 1948. His father was a Greyhound bus driver and in the spring of 1956 he was assigned to drive the Brooklyn Dodgers to several Florida towns—St. Petersburg, Clearwater, Bradenton, Ft. Myers, and Winter Haven—after the team flew over from Vero Beach on the Dodgers private plane. "I'm working on a book about those early days," said Garvey in a 2008 interview. "It's called 'My Batboy Days,' and it has a lot about my early years with the Brooklyn Dodgers. I was really engrossed in Dodger history from my earliest days."

As Joe Garvey drove the Brooklyn Dodgers to their March games across Florida, Steve Garvey sat on the bus alongside Jackie Robinson, Roy Campanella, Gil Hodges, Duke Snider, Carl Erskine, Carl Furillo, Pee Wee Reese, Clem Labine, Jim Gilliam, and all the rest of the famous Dodgers of Brooklyn. "I wasn't even eight years old then but they were all so nice to me. Sometimes I fell asleep on their laps but they took good care of me," he said. "Then when we got to the ball parks I would suit up in my little uniform with *Dodgers* across the chest and work as an extra batboy. Pretty soon I got to know the difference between all the bats for all the guys and in a year or two, by the time I was ten or so, they trusted me as the official batboy."

Joe Garvey continued driving the Dodgers for the next decade or so, long after the Brooklyn franchise had shifted to Los Angeles and long after most of the Brooklyn stars, Hodges, Reese, Snider, and the rest, had left the organization. "By that time, 1965 or 1966, I was in college, seventeen, eighteen years old, and I was no longer around in spring training. I always knew I wanted to play for the Dodgers," he said.

Garvey starred in baseball and football at Michigan State University and made his debut with the Dodgers as a drafted player on September 1, 1969. He struggled with the bat early in his career but by 1973 he batted .304 in 114 games, the first of his seven seasons over .300 on his way to a brilliant career over nineteen seasons with a .294 average. "Dixie Walker was the most significant person in my career," said Garvey. "He taught me how to hit with authority to all fields."

Garvey had become the anchor of the Los Angeles infield that played together for over eight years, an incredible feat as free agency sent players here, there, and everywhere in the 1970s.

With Garvey at first base, Davey Lopes at second, Bill Russell at shortstop, and Ron Cey at third base, the Dodgers made it to the World Series three times, in 1974, 1977, and 1978, all losing efforts before beating the hated Yankees in 1981.

Garvey played on ten All-Star teams, set a consecutive games mark with 1,207 games played from September 3, 1975, through July 29, 1983 when he broke his thumb in a home plate collision against the Atlanta Braves.

He moved to the Padres for five seasons in 1984, hit a walk-off playoff home run against star relief pitcher Lee Smith of the Cubs (he was always booed in Chicago after that), and led the Padres to their first National League title. The Detroit Tigers beat the Padres in the 1984 World Series in five games.

Besides his playing excellence, Garvey was known for two things during his nineteen years as a big leaguer. One was for his hair, smooth, perfectly combed, dark black, seemingly unaffected by heat, humidity, or a baseball cap. Second, his wife was the perfect match for the handsome Dodger and Padre first baseman, wonderfully attractive, well spoken, incredibly confident, and appealing to any camera. Cyndy Garvey became the representative of all the cheerleader-type wives who connect with professional athletes. They had two daughters and their home life was an open book for years to most Los Angeles media.

Cyndy Garvey became a television correspondent, anchored several shows in Los Angeles and New York, and became a well-known and popular celebrity in her own right. The marriage ended in 1983 as Cyndy Garvey's career continued to escalate and Steve Garvey moved away from the television and movie center of Los Angeles down the California coast to more subdued San Diego.

After his playing days ended in 1987, Garvey used his good looks, his instant identification, and his intelligence to start up a marketing and television production company outside of Los Angeles in Indian Wells. He is also a popular motivational speaker, with more than fifty well-paid appearances a year before major corporations.

Garvey is married to the former Candace Thomas. They have two children, including a fifteen-year-old baseball star with professional ambitions named Ryan. "I would be very happy if he got into baseball," Garvey said, "but I would be just as happy if he got into business. Whatever he does is fine. My father took me on those bus rides with the Dodgers because I wanted to go but he never suggested that the only thing I could do was be a baseball player."

When he looks back on his career and hopes for Baseball Hall of Fame recognition, Garvey credits Dixie Walker with changing his life. "I can't tell you how much Dixie meant to me and how much he changed my life," said Garvey. "We spent all those hours together. He taught me so much about hitting. He really made me into a 'guesstimator,' a batter who guesses on the pitcher's next pitch and seems to know where it is and what speed it is coming at you. If you get that down it isn't difficult to hit the ball hard."

Garvey said Walker had his own ways of teaching and some of the young players, himself, Lopes, Cey, Russell, many others, might give the old Dodger a hard time as they labored under the hot sun in the fields of Vero Beach each March. "You get to the big leagues with certain skills and you think those skills will carry you all the way through," Garvey said. "Dixie always preached that it was a mental game, the batter against the pitcher and you just had to be a little ahead of him to be successful. He would make hitting suggestions, changes in your stance, changes in your approach, maybe a different mental attitude. If you didn't pick it up right away, he might show a little impatience. Sometimes he could get a little crotchety."

Sometimes it would all come together for Garvey. "Dixie would make a suggestion about hitting a 2–2 slider away and I might drive it to right field for a double in the game and we would go out to dinner later that night and talk a lot about hitting. He really appreciated that. It was always fun to be with him and before you know it we would be talking about his old Dodgers and he would be telling great stories about playing with Pee Wee, Jackie, Duke, and the rest," said Garvey.

Walker had a lot to do with instilling a level of confidence at the bat in Garvey that was probably unmatched during his time.

"I just thought I could hit anybody," Garvey said. "I always wanted to be up there against [Tom] Seaver, [Steve] Carlton, [Nolan] Ryan and the rest, you know, two out, the bases loaded, last of the ninth," he said. "That was a challenge, to be the hero, to be the best. That was something Dixie instilled in me early on. He said he loved being at the plate in a tie game, especially against the Giants, with the fans screaming at Ebbets Field."

Garvey does a lot of speaking now before large corporate groups. He sees that as a similar challenge. "I always tell them the toughest thing in my baseball career was facing Nolan Ryan in a big game with two strikes on you," Garvey said. "You knew that hundred-mile-an-hour fastball was coming at you. Speaking is the same thing. You are facing that huge audience with about forty-five minutes in front of you to convince them it was right to bring you in there."

As he nears his sixtieth birthday, Garvey hopes the Baseball Hall of Fame will recognize two old Dodgers in the coming years, himself and Gil Hodges, the longtime Brooklyn first baseman. "Wouldn't that be something if we both got in the same time, me and Gil," Garvey said. "I think we both deserve it. I hope the voters recognize us some day."

He said nothing about the chances of Dixie Walker, a .306 hitter over eighteen seasons, getting into the baseball shrine in Cooperstown, New York. For some reason, Dixie Walker's name never seems to come up with Baseball Hall of Fame voters.

Walker enjoyed those Vero Beach years tremendously. He drove down before spring training started each year with Estelle, did some Florida fishing with other former players, relaxed at the barbecues she put together for old pals, and worked hard with Dodger youngsters.

Most of the players who made it as big league stars, Garvey, Lopes, Russell, Cey, Wes Parker, and Bobby Valentine, whose career was cut short by a broken leg, gave Dixie Walker much credit for their hitting success. "I came up trying to hit every pitch over the fence," Valentine once said. "Dixie taught me that there was a lot of space out there for doubles and triples."

Walker worked easily with all of the Dodgers in those Vero Beach days, the white players and the African American players, the free swingers and the contact hitters, the confident kids and the shaky ones. "He also developed a lot of friendships with the other coaches," Susan Walker says. "He was very friendly with Jim Gilliam and I know he often talked about him, what a fine fellow he was."

Gilliam, an African American infielder who succeeded Jackie Robinson at second base for the Brooklyn Dodgers, played for Brooklyn and Los Angeles from 1953 through 1966 with seven Dodger pennant winners. "I think it had a lot to do with the fact that Gilliam was probably the only Los Angeles coach who actually went back to the Brooklyn days, something Dixie was always very fond of talking about," said Susan Walker's husband, Ed. "There's no question Brooklyn was Dixie's favorite place to play."

Dixie Walker's biggest pal during those Dodger days at Vero Beach was the team owner Walter O'Malley. O'Malley was born in New York City on October 9, 1903. He attended Jamaica High School in Queens, New York, and graduated from Culver Academy in Indiana, a fashionable private school later attended by Yankees owner George M. Steinbrenner.

O'Malley graduated from the University of Pennsylvania and from Fordham University law school in New York. After several successful business ventures, O'Malley became the attorney for the Brooklyn Dodgers in 1943, succeeding Wendell Wilkie, the failed 1940 presidential candidate against Franklin Roosevelt's third term bid. He watched with much joy as Dixie Walker won the National League batting title with the Brooklyn Dodgers in 1944.

He led a coup against Branch Rickey, the man who had brought Jackie Robinson into big league baseball in 1947, and took over leadership of the club in 1950 when Rickey resigned from the Dodgers and moved on to Pittsburgh. O'Malley's hatred of Rickey was so personal that he banned the mention of the former Dodger leader's name in the office and fined any staffer who slipped up and mentioned the name Branch Rickey.

The Dodgers prospered under O'Malley, with pennants in 1952 and 1953 and the only Brooklyn World Series title in 1955. He saw the slippage of attendance from 1.7 million in 1946 to just over a million in decaying Ebbets Field by 1956. He made his move for a new stadium in Brooklyn's downtown, turned down by Triborough Bridge and Tunnel Authority head and parks commissioner Robert Moses. Moses suggested a site in the borough of Queens, once occupied by the 1940 World's Fair and now the location of the New York Mets old park called Shea Stadium. The new stadium, opened in 2009, is called Citi Field.

"If the Brooklyn Dodgers are to move to Queens they might as well move to Los Angeles," O'Malley said. O'Malley urged New York Giants owner Horace Stoneham to accompany him west to San Francisco, opening up baseball for its major twentieth-century expansion and earning O'Malley Hall of Fame honors in 2008.

The move out of Brooklyn forever made O'Malley a Brooklyn villain, and writer Pete Hamill once derided O'Malley by saying the three most villainous twentieth-century figures were Hitler, Stalin, and O'Malley. "If a shooter had two bullets in his gun and Hitler, Stalin and O'Malley in the room whom would he shoot?" Hamill asked. "O'Malley twice."

Despite the distress in Brooklyn, the move to Los Angeles and the building of baseball's most beautiful stadium in Chavez Ravine made O'Malley one of the game's significant figures. The financial success and the on-field triumphs made O'Malley the power behind the baseball throne of Commissioner Bowie Kuhn, an attorney he knew in New York.

O'Malley was the lone baseball owner who had no outside business interests as he operated the Dodgers. He turned the presidency of the Dodgers over to his thirty-year-old son Peter in 1970. He died in 1979 after treatment for cancer and heart difficulties.

O'Malley married his high school sweetheart, Katherine Elizabeth Hanson, in 1931 despite Kay Hanson's bout with laryngeal cancer, a disease that resulted in the loss of her larynx, a setback that prevented her from speaking above a whisper the rest of her life. He kept her name alive in Dodger circles by calling the club's private plane the *Kay O'Malley 1* after his beloved wife of forty-eight years. She died in 1979. A few weeks later, on August 9, 1979, Walter O'Malley died at the Methodist Hospital in Rochester, Minnesota.

"Walter and Dixie were really good friends," Peter O'Malley said. "My dad had a special affinity for anyone who went back to the Brooklyn days with him."

Alf Van Hoose, *Birmingham News* columnist and sportswriter, described a golf match on the Dodgertown course between Dixie and O'Malley in March of 1971. "The turning point in the big galleried match came when an O'Malley shot plunked a seagull in flight," Van Hoose wrote, "causing loss of distance and a losing bogey."

Van Hoose quoted a Los Angeles reporter also reporting on the match, "Under the old Audubon Society rules (written by O'Malley) this would have given the Dodgers president a birdie."

Walker and O'Malley had a mock argument about the shot and O'Malley, Dixie's boss, really groaned when Walker told the press the boss's shot was strictly "for the birds."

It was all in fun for Walker as he spent that delightful decade in his later years working for the Dodgers.

14
Dixie, a Baseball Lifer

It had all started for Dixie Walker as a seventeen-year-old in the Piedmont League in 1928. Through all his playing time with the Yankees, the White Sox, the Tigers, the Brooklyn Dodgers, and those final seasons at Pittsburgh, Walker saw it all as a temporary job.

Injuries can end a playing career in a moment and Walker came close several times. Then there are the days when a batter doesn't hit or he can't catch up to a fly ball or second base seems so much farther away than it used to. "I always thought he would do something else," says Susan Walker. "He knew the end could come quickly and I think that's why he had the hardware business, worked the farm, built houses, had the liquor store in New York, and invested in so many different things. He always invested carefully and he was always careful with his money. I really think he looked on baseball as a means to some other professional end. His major goal was supporting my mother, supporting the family, keeping things in order."

The baseball pension Walker helped create in 1946 and 1947 also guaranteed that he would never have to accept any position he didn't want to when he was through playing baseball. He enjoyed managing in the minors and coaching in the big leagues. He enjoyed scouting because it kept him in the game but he mostly enjoyed his last working years in baseball as a Dodgers hitting instructor. "I used to love to sit around with him after we worked out," Steve Garvey once said. "He would just light up when he talked of those old days in Brooklyn. You could look in his eyes and see the emotion."

After Mickey Mantle retired as a Yankee legend in 1969, a reporter asked him what he thought he would miss the most. Hitting a baseball five hundred feet, winning a game for the Yankees with a home run, seeing his name engraved on a Hall of Fame plaque, or having the fans salute him wherever he appeared? "I think it will be just sitting around the clubhouse and kidding around with the other guys," he said.

Sportswriters can sit around a clubhouse with ball players or listen to their conversations or watch them exchange tales of the past. They can never cross the line. They can never really be a part of it. Unless a man has stood at home plate in a big league game or felt his stomach twist when he faced a fast pitcher or experienced the shock of a line drive crashing into his glove he can never really understand it all.

More than eighteen thousand men have earned their way into big league games in the more than 139 years professional baseball has been played. Maybe 10, 15, even 30 million youngsters have dreamed that impossible dream after they hit a ball in Little League or caught one in their own backyards.

Then there are the baseball lifers.

These are the men like Dixie Walker who play the game well enough to spend many years in a big league uniform. Afterward, they are lucky enough, because of skill, personality, intelligence, friendships, or a combination of those things, to earn their keep for many more years, in uniform or out, connected to the game, still able to visit those clubhouses, thrilled that middle age has not separated them from the love of their lives. The baseball lifers.

Dixie Walker was sixty-two years old, a baseball lifer, when he was honored by the Alabama Sports Hall of Fame in 1973. Along with football legend Harry Gilmer; Alabama football hero Johnny (Hurry Up) Cain; baseball star Luke Sewell; University of Alabama executive Jeff Coleman; and football great Wu Winslett of Horseshoe Bend, Fred

(Dixie) Walker was elected to the Alabama Sports Hall of Fame. He was inducted at a 1973 dinner at the Birmingham-Jefferson Civic Center Exhibition Hall before thirty-five hundred people.

The Alabama Sports Hall of Fame had been created five years earlier, during the administration of Governor Lurleen B. Wallace. Governor George C. Wallace had backed the creation of the Hall of Fame during his administration. "Since the legislation providing for the creation of the Sports Hall of Fame was enacted during the term of my late wife," Wallace wrote in the dinner program, "it is a particular personal pleasure for me to participate in the ceremonies surrounding the 5th annual Sports Hall of Fame."

The dinner was held on February 16, 1973. On May 15, 1972, some eight months earlier, Governor Wallace had been shot five times by a man named Arthur Bremer, who later claimed in his book *An Assassin's Diary* that the assassination attempt was motivated by a desire for fame. Bremer had considered shooting President Richard Nixon but turned to Wallace because he was more easily accessible on the campaign trail. One of the bullets lodged in Wallace's spinal column, leaving him paralyzed for the rest of his life. He died September 13, 1998, at the age of seventy-nine.

"Alabama's Sports Hall of Fame Board takes great pleasure this year in dedicating this banquet and this program to our esteemed Governor, George C. Wallace," wrote sponsors in a tribute page in the event's program. "Governor Wallace, who was shot down in Laurel, Maryland, on May 15, while fighting for the State and country that he loves so dearly, was recently named one of the world's ten most admired men by people in the United States in a Gallup Poll survey. Since becoming Governor of Alabama in 1963, Governor Wallace has been named to this elite group five times in the annual Gallup Poll. Governor Wallace has probably had more influence on the direction of this country toward constitutional government than any other Chief Executive in modern history. At the same time he has given Alabama administrations that will long be remembered for their accomplishments in the areas of education, mental health, industrial development, highway building and sound fiscal management. It was largely through Governor Wallace's efforts and direction that the Sports Hall of Fame came about. Legislation creating the Alabama Sports Hall of Fame was passed and signed during the administration of the late Governor Lurleen Wallace."

Wallace had always been interested in sports. He was an outstanding boxer in his high school days in Clio, Alabama, followed most other sports, earned a law degree from the University of Alabama in 1937, enlisted in the U.S. Army Air Corps in 1942, flew combat missions over Japan, served under General Curtis LeMay (his vice presidential running mate in 1968), served in the state government as an assistant attorney general and as a judge (he was called the Little Fightin' Judge in recognition of his boxing days), and was elected governor in 1962.

He took his first oath of office standing on the gold star in Montgomery where 102 years earlier Jefferson Davis had been sworn in as president of the Confederate States of America. His inaugural speech included this promise: "In the name of the greatest people that have ever trod this earth, I draw the line in the dust and toss the gauntlet before the feet of tyranny, and I say, segregation now, segregation tomorrow, segregation forever." This was some fifteen years after Jackie Robinson had integrated major league baseball with the Brooklyn Dodgers.

Wallace was soon identified as the nation's leading segregationist. He ran for president as an Independent in 1968 and as a Democrat in 1972. He was shot by Bremer at a political rally in 1972 in Maryland, recovered well enough despite the paralysis to continue as governor until 1979, and stayed politically active throughout his life. Bremer was sentenced to fifty-three years in prison and served thirty-five years. He was released on parole on November 9, 2007.

In his speech at the Sports Hall of Fame banquet program, Wallace wrote, "I convey my congratulations to those who have been selected to be enshrined in the Hall. To each one goes my deep appreciation for all that they have meant to our state and its citizenry."

Twenty years after he become eligible for the Baseball Hall of Fame in Cooperstown, Dixie Walker was inducted into his adopted state's Hall of Fame for all of his accomplishments both on and off the field. The *Anniston Star* sportswriter George Smith wrote a piece about Walker that was printed in the Alabama Sports Hall of Fame program. "If it is by a man's works that he is truly judged, then the works that really set Dixie Walker apart from all the others who have contributed to Abner Doubleday's sport is a thing called the players' pension plan. . . . Any baseball player, present, past or future, given to serious thinking will tell you Dixie Walker, more than anyone [else], was the father of the players' pension plan," Smith wrote.

The *Anniston Star* columnist could not imagine that modern baseball players guaranteed up to $185,000 in an annual pension would not recognize Dixie Walker's name. It is not for lack of information about Walker or lack of Dodgers tradition. It is more because the selfishness that typifies professional athletes. "I'm for number 1," Pete Rose, the game's hit leader would often say.

Most players embrace that concept as they recognize that professional baseball is a transitory career. Despite the millions being made by most players (the annual average salary in 2009 was $3.2 million) the life span in the game is less than three years.

Smith's article continued, "Dixie doesn't remember how the idea got started, but there had been talk and he ended up right in the middle of the discussion. Some connections with an insurance executive had a lot to do with Dixie coming up with the plan, and briefly, he was named the chairman by the players in both leagues.

"There was a meeting with the owners in 1946 in Los Angeles, the plan was accepted and today baseball's stars enjoy one of the finest retirements in the land.

"Leo Durocher, for example, put in 20 years and, at age 65, began drawing $22,000 per year.

"This brief summary tells nothing of the hours and days and weeks and months Dixie Walker devoted to the betterment of his peers in the nation's pastime," Smith wrote.

Smith went on to list Dixie's baseball totals, 1,905 games played, 2,064 hits, lifetime batting average of .306 among his on-field accomplishments. "[Those figures] today would earn Dixie somewhere in the very classy neighborhood of $200,000 per year," Smith wrote in that 1973 article. Baseball salaries for many years had been limited to $100,000 a season, a scale reached by the game's few stars, Joe DiMaggio, Stan Musial, Ted Williams, Bob Feller, Willie Mays, and a handful of others. None had made more than that.

In 1966 two Los Angeles Dodgers pitchers, Sandy Koufax and Don Drysdale, held out against the club together through most of spring training. They had each been paid $100,000 a season, the agreed-upon maximum salary owners would offer. After some bitter comments by both sides, the two future Hall of Fame pitchers were able to break that artificial barrier: Koufax accepted a salary of $125,000; Drysdale, $110,000. That broke open the floodgates for baseball salaries with Willie Mays, Henry Aaron, and Mickey Mantle among others crossing that $100,000 limit.

In 1976 a new free agency pact was signed by baseball owners and players, under the leadership of Marvin Miller, the executive director of the Major League Baseball Players Association. Salaries have continued to escalate ever since. The high in 2009 was $26.2 million dollars a year, Alex Rodriguez's salary with the Yankees for the next ten seasons.

Smith ended his article by listing some of Walker's many baseball accomplishments, including the World Series teams he played with in 1941 and 1947; the All-Star teams in 1943, 1946, and 1947; his 1944 National League batting title; and his position as one of the ten Brooklyn Men of the Year elected by the Brooklyn Rotary Club in 1946.

"It is a talent," Smith wrote, "that still brings gainful employment. Dixie is now the batting instructor for the entire Los Angeles Dodgers organization.

"And here tonight," Smith's article concluded, "he rightfully joins Alabama's Sports Hall of Fame."

Dixie Walker, with wife, Estelle, daughter Susan and son-in-law Ed sitting at his side, quietly accepted the honor. That year the Baseball Hall of Fame at Cooperstown elected Roberto Clemente, who had died in a tragic plane crash, Mickey Welch, a nineteenth-century pitcher, and George Kelly, an early twentieth-century slugger.

Almost twenty-five years after his playing career ended in 1949 and five years after his eligibility expired among the baseball writers, those voting on Hall of Famers, Dixie Walker did not receive a single vote. If his fame was fading in the north and even old Brooklyn fans had trouble reciting his deeds by the middle 1970s, Dixie Walker's status remained significant in the south.

Alf Van Hoose, an old Dixie pal, continued to write warmly about him every chance he got. Van Hoose even wrote a column in the *Birmingham News* on May 20, 1975, comparing Dixie in his role as a Brooklyn baseball icon with the current talk of the town in New York City, Joe Namath, the guy Jets owner Sonny Werblin signed off the campus of the University of Alabama. Namath went on to energize the AFL's New York Jets, led his team to a Super Bowl win in 1969, and was the force behind the merger of the old National Football League with the up-start AFL. "Youngsters will doubtless scoff but time was once in hard-ground New York that Dixie Walker was much more a sports idol than Joe Namath was to be, in another sport, 20–30 years later," Van Hoose wrote.

Van Hoose described a phone conversation he had with Walker shortly after Namath was honored in Birmingham. "The Squire of Old Leeds Lane," Van Hoose wrote, "has just returned from overseas vacationing, Ireland, England, Scotland, Holland, Belgium, France and Ireland once again [Estelle's influence]. He's seen less baseball than any spring in 48 years. By choice."

Van Hoose explained that Walker's absence from much of spring training that March was part of his new schedule in semiretirement. "After many nine-months per-year professor terms with Los Angeles Dodgers batters, Dix went to owner Walter O'Malley (and 30-year crony) and requested semi-retirement. That was last winter. O'Malley and Los Angeles manager Walter Alston weren't jubilant about Walker's wish but they conceded to old friendship."

Van Hoose spelled out Walker's new schedule in the Dodgers organization. No more big leaguers to tutor. Now he and Estelle would travel around the country to Dodgers minor league camps and Dixie would work with 18-, 19-, 20-year-old kids struggling to escape the minors and move up to the big club in Los Angeles.

"Dixie will help Dodger farmhands each summer," wrote Van Hoose, "but Steve Garvey, Ron Cey, Willie Crawford, Bill Buckner, Davey Lopes, Bill Russell, Joe Ferguson, et al. [have] graduated from Walker teaching."

Walker explained his reason for wanting semiretirement in the phone call with Van Hoose. "They know all I know and I told Peter [O'Malley] that," Walker said. "I just wanted to spend more time [at] home, more time with Stell and the family, and take it easier. My bosses finally agreed."

Van Hoose went on to describe Dixie's impact on Brooklyn baseball and compared it with the loud noise and wide path Namath was making in professional football. "Personality-wise, they're poles apart," Van Hoose wrote. "Namath is brash, flippant, flamboyant. Walker wasn't and isn't. Namath was promoted into a jet-setter, the hair bit, mustache, high roller, womanizer, palace-apartment guy. Walker would have been horrified with any of that. But performing professionally, they were more alike than unlike. Both had rare charisma," Van Hoose wrote.

"Both, undeniably were winners. Walker sparked teams slightly more consistent than Joe's. Neither was ever bashful about his abilities, personal or team. Neither would allow management to browbeat them. Both spoke out, Walker to such stormy tyrants as Leo Durocher, Larry MacPhail and canny Branch Rickey.

"League brass never cared for either man, really. Too controversial. Neither was an umpire-officials baiter—the Billy Martin-Durocher breed—but both Walker and Namath caused high and mighty uneasiness.

"Nothing perturbs management more than a hint of unionization. It has always been so. And probably will be. Baseball owners and their hired commissioner brag loudest now about the game's pension plan. They should. It's industry's finest.

"But who remembers when a few courageous players stuck necks and careers on the block and said to the game's kings and princes, 'Do or don't.' Dixie Walker was the rebel leader, the player statesman.

"Namath was never timid around [Pete] Rozelle [football commissioner], either. And his salary demands have surely helped his colleagues.

"Joe got all the attention Monday in Birmingham," Van Hoose wrote of the banquet honoring the University of Alabama legend. "And probably couldn't have cared less. Walker got none. But he felt ditto as Namath."

In the last few years of the 1970s, as the Dodgers won pennants in 1977 and 1978 but lost the Series to the Yankees, and in 1981 when the Dodgers won the pennant and finally beat the Yankees in the World Series, Dixie Walker would have his name mentioned in occasional stories. Comments by many of the Los Angeles hitters he helped—Garvey, especially, but also Lopes, Russell, Cey, Steve Sax, Lee Lacy, Mike Scioscia, Steve Yeager, and Dusty Baker—would appear in the press, especially after winning games.

Lacy, a sixteen-year major leaguer with a .286 lifetime average, said at a 2008 baseball card show in Secaucus, New Jersey, that he owed a lot to Dixie Walker. "He really helped me with my hitting," said Lacy, an African American former infielder. "We spent a lot of time working together in the batting cage."

But Dixie didn't need glory any more. He had had plenty of that in his more than a half century in the game. He still gained recognition, mostly in the Birmingham area, with the Alabama Sports Hall of Fame induction and smaller speaking events before enthusiastic crowds.

The baseball years were almost over now for Dixie Walker. He would take a rare scouting trip to look at a youngster as a favor to Peter

O'Malley and new Dodgers manager Tommy Lasorda. Occasionally he showed up at a big league park to give the Dodgers an opinion on a player considered for a trade. Rarely he would take the opportunity to look at a youngster in a high school or college game, mostly near his Birmingham home.

There were no young names that would achieve stardom later that would be connected to Dixie in those late days in the 1970s, but he certainly would pause and reflect when he saw a kid swing a bat, especially from the left side. Maybe there was a kid with that closed stance he had made so famous, maybe even with that quick swing that lined so many baseballs off the wall and the screen at Ebbets Field. He could reminisce about dumping a line drive into the short porch at the Polo Grounds, breaking the hearts of the fans of the New York Giants—he hit twenty-one career homers against the Giants—and sending joy flowing again through the bars in Brooklyn. Fans often called him "the Giants Killer."

When he attended old-timers' games, there was always talk about the days in Brooklyn and that 1947 season. "I remember once talking to Dixie at Shea Stadium during a Mets old-timers' game," said Robert Rosen, a statistician for the Elias Sports Bureau, the keeper of baseball's records. "Dixie said he always regretted the Jackie stuff but that's the way things were in those days and he was a southerner. But he said he admired Jackie very much both as an athlete and a man and said he sympathized with the awful things he had to take when they were 1947 teammates."

But it was over now, the thrill of the swing, the cheering, the emotions, the smell of the grass, the wafting odor of hot dog, and the paper wrappers he often wrestled with in right field. Dixie Walker was giving up the game he loved on his own terms, in his own time, under his own rules. Some forty-five years after he and Estelle Mary Shea first met, he was now her complete loving property.

15
Estelle Carries the Torch

They were together all the time now, Dixie and Estelle Walker, moving slowly around the country, seeing this sight or that, visiting old friends, checking out the scenery, sharing the grandeur of the country and the closeness of their love.

"They were in the Northeast, in Waterbury, Connecticut," recalls Susan Walker, "and they pulled into a rest stop. My father did all the driving when they were together, so he liked to take a quick nap at times before they moved on. He was asleep in the driver's seat and she was sitting in the passenger seat, looking through a book and just enjoying the relaxation."

A car pulled up in the area and three or four kids, teenagers probably, got out of the vehicle. One carried a beer can and another had an open bottle. They walked by several cars and put a scratch on a car or pulled the windshield wiper and bent it from another vehicle. "My mother watched all this with increasing anger. The kids moved farther along the parking row, laughing and pulling at windshield wipers and just carrying on," Susan said.

Suddenly, Estelle was out of the red van, moving toward the car the kids came in and grabbing at their windshields wipers. "She told me later that she just pulled on the windshield wiper as hard as she could and bent them the way the kids had bent so many of the other windshield wipers in that lot. Then she woke my father up and they moved on. She just wanted to teach those kids a lesson," Susan says.

Now in her own grandmotherly days, Susan Walker cannot recall as much as she would have wanted to know about her father. It is a lifelong regret. "I wish I had known more about him when he was alive," she says. "I really didn't appreciate all he had gone through in his life and all he had done for his family."

There were some sweet memories that did come rushing back as she searched for tales about Dixie. "He and I used to sit at the breakfast table when I was in high school and talk about God, heaven, and angels," Susan recalls. "He was always searching for an answer regarding the afterlife. Once I remember he taught me how to waltz in our living room. He would sit and listen to me play the piano after dinner. He never got to go to any of the school operettas I was in because most of the time he was away in spring training or with one team or another at that time of the year.

"I have always felt that both he and I were shortchanged out of sharing each other's lives because of his career," Susan says. "He was always very disciplined, hard working, critical, and focused. My mother was very accepting and loving, so I naturally gravitated toward her. I think about it now and I can't believe my mother never told me how well known and successful he was in baseball. The People's Choice. I guess I never even heard the term until I was a married woman with children of my own and we were living in New Jersey and some friend or other would mention it when they found out I was Dixie Walker's daughter. I think my mother was just protecting me from the public eye and helping me live a normal life."

Susan thought back to those days more than five decades ago. "He was constantly teaching when he spoke to us children," she says. "I now know how hard it was for him to step in and out of our lives. He tried but really did not understand children as he had never really had a childhood of his own. Most of the time I spent with him he was working on the house, repairing the shingles, working on the yard, puttering in his garden, fixing this or that, painting one room or another, or I was trolling quietly in a boat while he fished."

Susan recalls being with her father many times while he fished. It was never a very pleasant experience. "I wasn't allowed to talk. He just concentrated on catching the fish. He was as intense about that as he was about most everything else," she says.

"We never went out to dinner or on family vacations because he was always traveling and eating out while he was away in baseball and didn't want to do any of that when he was at home," she says. "I have to admit now, all these years later, I never really knew him. I feel sad about that. My mother kept me very busy with softball [Susan played in a friendly game and whacked the ball farther than any of the men], volleyball, voice lessons, piano lessons, ballet, tap, toe, jazz, gymnastics, ballroom dancing, performing in those operettas, modeling lessons. She kept me so busy that I never really had time to think about a father who wasn't there."

Susan recognizes that her father was away making his living, supporting his large family. "I know we had a nice house in Mountain Brook, a suburb of Birmingham, nicer than most of our neighbors and we traveled more to his baseball locations as I was growing up, but I never had any real close friends because we would go up north each summer to be with him. I was away so much from home and my mother watched over us so carefully. I was never permitted to stay over at anyone else's house or even play at other homes. It was my mother's way of protecting me and maybe keeping people away from our family because my father was so well known. I think all of that helped form my personality and made me more careful in my choice of friends even as an adult," she says.

"In his last few years of retirement he started working on a book of his own about famous people dealing with some handicaps in their own lives and he began reading historical novels, something he certainly never had time for before," she says. "He grew grapes on an arbor in our backyard and made wine in those huge glass containers. I still have one and use it to collect loose change. He took up wood carving and did a lot of fishing and hunting with his dog. He never would own a dog that couldn't hunt. One time my mother bought my sister and me each a cocker spaniel. He came home and gave them away to my grandparents because they couldn't hunt. He traveled a great deal with my mother in his last years and researched his ancestors in England. He also took his first trip to Ireland with my mother so she could research her family background. Toward the end of their lives together, they had this camper and traveled west with it. They had a wonderful time. My mom would go fishing with him for company but she always hated it and only did it to please him. She simply wasn't an outdoors woman," Susan said.

Religion was a vital part of Estelle Walker's life. She was a devout Roman Catholic. She said the rosary every day of her life as her mother had taught her and belonged to a special order of women who prayed throughout the day.

After Dixie and Estelle were married by a justice of the peace in Westchester, New York, in 1936, Estelle's mother never again talked to her. It was an especially painful part of her life.

"My second son was born in 1967," recalls Susan, "and we wanted my father to act as a stand-in for the godparents at my son's baptism. He was not allowed because he was not baptized. This was the first baptism my father had ever attended. He later asked me a lot of questions about baptism."

Susan said her father was very hurt by that event and later was baptized in a Presbyterian church. "I think in his later life my father was just searching for God," she said.

Susan said that her father became friendly with the local Catholic priest, Father Cazalas, at Our Lady of Sorrows Church in Homewood, Alabama, not far from their family home. "That was my mother's parish and my father would often go fishing with Monsignor Cazalas and Father Murphy. At one point Father Cazalas asked Dixie if he would ever divorce my mother. My father hotly denied that he would ever think of

doing that. The priest then petitioned the Holy Father for a dispensa-
tion to marry my mother and father in his church. It was granted and my
mother and father were married in the church, which meant my mother
was no longer excommunicated and could receive the sacraments again.
That made her very happy. My father would often take her to mass on
Sundays and sit outside in the car reading the sports pages, waiting for
her. Sometimes he would actually go inside the church and listen to the
prayers. He was not a member of the church but he was buried from the
church in Birmingham with the Catholic Mass of the Dead."

Susan recalls that Our Lady of Sorrows Church was the same church
she went to every Monday after school with her mother for a novena
to Our Blessed Mother and the same church school she was put into
without her father's knowledge when she was in the fourth grade. "I had
been in a public school in nearby Crestline up until that time and when
my father came home from a trip and found out about it he was very
upset," Susan said. "My mother stood her ground and wouldn't budge
and they had quite a row about it. He really didn't like it that I had been
put in a Catholic school, especially when he was away and had nothing
to do with it, but she just said that it was the way it would be with me.
True Irish grit. I think later in life he softened on the issue and recognized how important it was to her that the children be raised Catholic.
She contributed every week to the Propagation of the Faith. Through
his actions in later life, it was clear what an effect my mother's example
set for him. He didn't have a chance of not going to heaven with her in
his life. It's no wonder he kept searching for God."

Dixie and Estelle Walker shared many joyous moments in the last
two or three years of his life. They made those trips to Europe, learned
about their own heritage and family connections, and visited historic
places throughout the British Isles. They also took open-ended trips out
West, visiting the Grand Canyon, Yellowstone Park, and Hoover dam.
They shot dozens of rolls of film and enjoyed showing them off to friends
and family when they returned home to Birmingham.

Dixie continued to hunt and fish, often with brother Harry, his lifelong pal who coached college baseball at the University of Alabama at Birmingham after his own professional days ended. "I'd go over to his house in those days," Harry Walker once recalled, "and we would sit around and talk about things that we loved. We could talk a lot about hunting and fishing, we both loved that so much, you know just picking out some spots we had hunted or fished and what we got and what kind of a day it was, whether it was too hot or too cold or the rain was coming down or the wind was blowing. Sure, we talked a little baseball, the years we won batting titles and all that. Mostly he wanted to talk about the Brooklyn Dodgers. I don't think he was very happy with those other teams he played with, the Yankees, the White Sox, the Tigers. He only wanted to talk about the Brooklyn Dodgers, the 1941 Dodgers that won a pennant after a long streak without a victory and the 1944 team when he won the batting title and kept the interest alive in the team for all those wild Brooklyn fans. And he talked of 1947 when I won the batting title and how proud he was of his little brother doing that. And how proud he was of winning a pennant that year, too, and getting so close to winning a Series just before the Yankees took them."

They were very close, Dixie and Harry Walker, and it sometimes seemed odd. Dixie had a soft, gentle voice and picked his words carefully. Harry had a sharp voice, a little screechy and ran on endlessly about almost anything, especially how to hit a baseball, to other players, coaches, even inquisitive sportswriters. A quick question to Harry Walker would almost always elicit a long answer.

Late in 1981 Dixie Walker began feeling some awful stomach pains. He tried laxatives but they didn't help. He had spent so much of his early baseball years involved with doctors, being checked for shoulder pain or backache or leg cramp. He was often kidded by the press for his inability to play every day because of this injury or that. At least he escaped the nickname of Hall of Fame infielder Luke Appling of the Chicago White Sox. He was called Old Aches and Pains. Appling had the last laugh when he hit an exhibition game home run off Hall of Famer Warren Spahn in 1982 in Washington. He was seventy-five years old.

Spahn applauded him as he rounded the bases. Appling died at the age of eighty-three in 1991.

Estelle insisted that Dixie get a checkup despite his baseball-induced aversion to doctors. After a series of tests it was determined Dixie Walker was suffering from stomach cancer. The doctors were optimistic that the cancer could be confined to the stomach area and treated aggressively with chemotherapy. "The treatments made him weak and very tired," said Susan Walker. "We saw him as much as we could. He didn't complain but it was easy to tell from looking at his face and watching him struggle around the house that he was in great pain. We prepared for the worst."

By early 1982 the cancer had spread to the gall bladder, kidney, and colon. It was clear the end was near for Dixie Walker.

The Los Angeles Dodgers had stayed in touch with Dixie and the Walker family. I received a call one day from a representative of the publicity department of the Dodgers. The young man said Dixie Walker was critically ill. Dixie, realizing that he was in his final days, had agreed to talk with some newspaper people about his time in Brooklyn. I placed a call to Dixie at his Birmingham home.

"I wanted to find out how old Dixie was doing and I called the other day," I wrote in my column in the *New York Post*. "When I found out I cried. Then we talked of those glorious days in Brooklyn and we both cried."

Dixie's voice was thin and it was clear he did not have enough energy for a long conversation. "I just got back from one of those chemotherapy treatments," he said. "I'm real weak. It's hard to talk."

Then he was talking clearly, seemingly energized by those sweet memories, about his Yankee days as a teammate of Babe Ruth and Lou Gehrig in the 1930s, his moves to Chicago and Detroit, and the classic trade to Brooklyn. "I won the batting title in 1944 with a .357 average," he said, as a reminder to younger readers of his Brooklyn status. "Some people said the big boys were in service. I never thought about that. I finished ten points ahead of Stan Musial. That was good enough for me."

His voice seemed to strengthen as he continued. "I had a lot to do with getting the pension plan started," he said, with great pride in his voice. "Johnny Murphy [the former Yankee pitcher and later Mets GM] represented the American League and I represented the National League. Johnny asked me to speak at the owners meeting about our pension. We wanted money from television the way we had gotten it from radio rights. The owners didn't want to listen. Happy Chandler spoke up and said the owners had to consider the plan of the players and I had to be allowed to talk. I thought of that when Chandler was named to the Hall of Fame."

My column continued, "The other historic event occurred in 1947 when Jackie Robinson joined the Dodgers. Walker asked to be traded. It was a move done with deep feeling, with dignity, with the weight of much southern history. Walker was sent to Pittsburgh for the next season."

"That was 35 years ago," Dixie said. "I've said all I'm going to say on that subject. I'll add just one more thing. Jackie Robinson was a great ball player."

"Dixie Walker was a great ballplayer," I wrote in my *Post* column. "A great man. The Peepul's Cherce in my borough of Brooklyn. The guy who gave us hope for the future and entertained us in Ebbets Field with his shots off the right field screen.

"I'm not ashamed to say I loved the man. I told him that over the phone. Then he cried. There was no more to say. Then I cried for a good long while."

There was no separating the legend of Jackie Robinson, who died in 1972, from any mention of Dixie Walker, especially in these final days of his life. It was included in a column around that time in the *New York Times* written by Pulitzer Prize–winner Ira Berkow, in local columns in Birmingham and Georgia papers, in national stories from the Associated Press, in most radio and television comments about the ailing Brooklyn hero.

Robinson's status had grown from the baseball fields he played on to the historic documents he was mentioned in. When Martin Luther King was assassinated in 1968, Brooklyn teammate Don Newcombe talked of King visiting at his Los Angeles home twenty-eight days before his death. "We talked a lot about Jackie," Newcombe said in a 2008 interview. "King recognized that Jackie had really started the movement for equality well before Martin got out there in the early 1950s. I remember when King was a young preacher, not very well known, and he sat on our bench in Brooklyn with Jackie and Campy and myself. He kept telling us what he thought he could do in the future and Jackie just urged him on."

Famed broadcaster Tom Brokaw, who ended his career as the anchor and managing editor of the *NBC Nightly News* in 2004, told a tale of his one and only meeting with Jackie Robinson and the impact Robinson had on him and on the country. "I was a kid growing up in Pickstown, South Dakota," Brokaw said in a 2005 interview for my book *Brooklyn Remembered: The 1955 Days of the Dodgers.* "The army engineers had built the town by dams and bridges over the Missouri River. We were all St. Louis Cardinals fans in our family in 1947. The Cardinals represented the western most city in the big leagues then. We heard on the radio that the Dodgers had signed a Negro player. I was seven years old."

Brokaw's father, Anthony (Red) Brokaw, and his maternal grandfather, Jim Conley, were construction workers and helped build those projects over the Missouri. "We were working-class people," Brokaw said, "and the Dodgers seemed like a working-class team, in their small park in Brooklyn, with all those players who seemed like working-class guys. This wasn't a team like the Yankees with the sainted Joe DiMaggio and later the great Mickey Mantle. You know, the Yankee success and their stars. It just never ends. Brooklyn was different. Brooklyn was always an underdog team and there was so much pressure on this new Negro player. We were all for him."

In 1968 Brokaw was a Los Angeles newscaster and he had arranged for an interview with presidential candidate Nelson Rockefeller, New

York's governor, in the Los Angeles NBC studios. "Rockefeller opened the door to the studio with that friendly smile of his and the 'Hi ya, fella, greetings," Brokaw recalled, "and I looked up to see that Jackie Robinson was coming into the studio just behind Rockefeller."

Robinson was working for Rockefeller's nomination then, which eventually went to Richard Nixon. "I walked right past Rockefeller and stuck out my hand and Jackie took it. I was embarrassed that I had passed by Rockefeller," Brokaw said, "but it was the one and only time I met Jackie Robinson."

When Robinson died in 1972, Brokaw did an essay on him and on his baseball career on NBC and spoke of how much he admired him. "I pointed out that certain rights were denied to him just because of the pigmentation of his skin. That was horrible. He was truly one of the great figures of the twentieth century."

Brokaw told many of the same stories about his affection for Jackie Robinson on January 20, 2009, the day Barack Obama was inaugurated as President of the United States. "I know what Jackie meant to his people, black people in America, and when you think about it, to all people," said Brokaw. "He lifted the country in so many ways. I was good friends later on with Rafer Johnson [Olympic decathlon hero] and he always talked about Jackie. He said that most black people in America just looked at Jackie as the most inspirational figure of his time." Much of the emotion that people felt about the presidency of Obama, as the first African American leader of the country, seemed the same.

Brokaw did not mention Dixie Walker's name at the time of that 2005 interview but hardly an article at the end of Dixie's life failed to mention Robinson.

Dixie's condition worsened in the early weeks of May 1982. He was in and out of St. Vincent's Hospital, Estelle always at his side, as the pain spread throughout his body. This great athlete, once tall and handsome, was now a damaged shell of a human being.

Fred (Dixie) Walker died at six thirty in the morning on May 17, 1982, at St. Vincent's Hospital. The immediate cause of death, as listed on the death certificate was liver metastasis and gastric cancer.

In the *New York Times* obituary (May 18, 1982), sportswriter Sam Goldaper, who had known Dixie from his Dodgers days, wrote, "Fred (Dixie) Walker, whose popularity with Ebbets Field fans in the 1940s brought him the nickname The Peepul's Cherce, died yesterday of cancer in Birmingham, Alabama. He was 71 years old.

"Walker compiled a .306 average during 18 seasons in the major leagues, and won the National League batting title in 1944 with .357.

"He signed a minor league contract at 17 with the New York Yankees. Although he lacked smoothness, he was such an outstanding prospect that the Yankees envisioned him as the successor to Babe Ruth after he had batted .350 while playing for the Newark Bears of the International League. He was a pull hitter with terrific power and promise, had speed and was a good fielder with a fine throwing arm," Goldaper wrote.

Goldaper described his many injuries and pointed out that the Yankees gave up on him with the arrival of Joe DiMaggio in New York. He told of the trades to Chicago, Detroit, and finally Brooklyn. "Although he had been hitting for a high average," Goldaper wrote, "his career seemed nearing an end because of the string of injuries. But he became a celebrity in Brooklyn. He had some of his best games against the New York Giants, and as a result, endeared himself to the Brooklyn fans."

Goldaper quoted Dixie's brother, Harry Walker, former big league player and manager now coaching baseball at the University of Alabama at Birmingham, "He loved those days in Brooklyn."

Goldaper then moved on to the connection between Jackie Robinson and Dixie Walker. "When the Dodgers broke baseball's color barrier by signing Jackie Robinson, Walker became a figure of some controversy. In 1947, during spring training, the club announced that it was bringing Robinson up from the minors. Walker thereupon wrote to Branch Rickey, the club president, asking to be traded.

"The letter did not mention Robinson's name, but Walker acknowledged in a recent interview that he had been under pressure from people in his home state of Alabama not to play with Robinson. He denied, however, that he had been in the forefront of a move to block Robinson. 'I've been called the ringleader to try to stop Jackie from playing with

Toronto Maple Leafs

the Dodgers. I was no ringleader.' He said he came to respect Robinson for the way he handled the abuse hurled at him, and called him, 'as outstanding an athlete as I ever saw.' Walker was traded to Pittsburgh in 1948, and ended his playing career with the Pirates the next year. He later rejoined the Dodger organization as a scout and batting instructor. He also managed several minor league teams."

Walker's obituary in the *Times* filled two columns on page forty-six and got much more space than that of the business school dean of Hofstra University, a local Long Island, New York college; or the coauthor of books for Broadway musicals; a famed female journalist; a publisher; a pianist; or a stunt pilot.

The *Times* obituary seemed to focus more on the turmoil of the 1947 season than on Dixie's splendid career and significant contributions to baseball's pension programs. It was another example of the media's ability to create a lifelong image with a few words, an image so hard to undo.

Dixie's long illness devastated Estelle and the family for many months. It consumed the daily events of their lives and controlled their schedules.

Now it was over.

The funeral for Dixie Walker—the great Brooklyn star, the leading National League batter of 1944, the People's Choice—was unpretentious as he had requested. "There were some television cameras outside, a few radio reporters, and a couple of local media people but it was not noisy. It was very dignified and sad," said Susan Walker.

Father Murphy, the priest at Our Lady of Sorrows Church, conducted the services. Harry Walker sat grief-stricken and quiet in the front row of the church with his wife and children. Estelle Walker never let her emotions get the better of her as she sat stone-faced before the altar.

"Even though he had been in the hospital for close to a month by then," Susan Walker said, "my mother never expected him to die."

Estelle received expression of sympathy from many people. The Stankys attended the funeral. The O'Malleys and Toronto owner Jack Kent Cooke sent prayer cards. The Los Angeles Dodgers sent a large spray of flowers with a baseball bat in flowers spread across the front.

Jack Kent Cooke

"Mom came back to New Jersey with us so she wouldn't have to be alone in the house," Susan recalls. "She was very appreciative and often thanked me for doing that." Before she left she gave away most of Dixie's clothes, many baseball-related documents. She destroyed all his love letters. Estelle thought they were too intimate for any one else to see, including her own children.

"They had many friends in baseball but that was their life," Susan said. "I wasn't part of that life. My mom went home to Birmingham when she felt she could cope with all the details accompanying his death. She was only seventy-one."

Dixie was buried in the Walker family plot in Elmwood Cemetery. "My grandfather, grandmother, older sister, Mary Ann, younger brother, Sean, and my mom and dad are buried there," said Susan Walker. "My brother Steve and I each have two plots in the Walker area. There is a very big granite headstone with the name WALKER engraved on it. I will probably never use the two cemetery plots for Ed and me because I wish to be cremated and thrown into the ocean in Bethany Beach, Delaware, where we have enjoyed so many wonderful vacations with our own family.

"Mom and Dad are side by side with her on the left side, next to his heart, at her request. Mom and Dad were both buried from the same church where Ed and I were married, where Dad walked me down the aisle proud as punch and Mom enjoyed the event as if it were her own wedding, making up for her quick, unexciting marriage before a justice of the peace all those years earlier."

A few months after Dixie's death, Estelle Walker resumed her life, independent now, freed of the obligations of handling her husband's needs, able to make her own decisions, travel as she chose, visiting with Susan Walker and her family and her other children. She went to Ireland once or twice a year to research her family history.

"She drove until she was in her late eighties," recalls Susan Walker, "and she enjoyed visiting her friends and having them visit with her at the family home at Mountain Brook. She would entertain elegantly now for friends and family with that Irish linen she had acquired on some of her trips and the marvelous silver tea service she had purchased. My mother was a very special, elegant lady with impeccable manners and so much Old World charm. She had always fulfilled his needs, waited on him, served his meals as he liked at the dining room table. Now she did more of the things she enjoyed for herself. The church became an even more important part of her life and she would volunteer at the schools and work in the classes with the nuns, helping the children with their reading or writing, playing games with the smaller ones, and sharing the joy of their classes."

Estelle Walker visited Susan Walker often in New Jersey, went on vacation trips with them to Florida; to Delaware; to South Bend, Indiana, for Notre Dame events; and to other locations.

She broke her back while on a trip to Ireland and spent one month in an Irish orthopedic hospital, coming home to be put in a full body cast. It barely slowed her down. On another occasion, in her late eighties, she broke her pelvis after a fall, but after surgery she insisted she was well and told Susan after a visit, "Go away, I'm fine."

Her eyesight, which had troubled her for years, began failing as she neared ninety and Susan realized she could no longer care for herself safely. "In the earlier days when Dad was still at home," Susan Walker said, "and I was having babies she would come up unannounced, do all sorts of chores around the house to help, and leave when she felt we had everything under control by ourselves. Now, after he was gone and my children were grown, she would stay longer, participate fully in our lives with our activities and our friends. At the end we just didn't want her home alone. We never really discussed it but she stayed with us the last three years of her life. She still kept the Mountain Brook home on Old Leeds Lane. After she died, it was sold to a young couple with two small children. She would have liked that."

Estelle Walker died in 2002, some twenty years after Dixie Walker had passed away. They now lie together for eternity at Elmwood Cemetery, the spirited Irish girl from New York and the gentle southerner from Birmingham.

Dixie and Estelle Walker are gone now and except for family and friends, his name no longer comes up at Dodgers reunions in Los Angeles, baseball card shows, or Baseball Hall of Fame events. James Gates, the Hall of Fame librarian, said the last time Dixie Walker received any Hall of Fame votes was 1969—twenty years after he retired, in the fifteenth and final year of his Hall of Fame eligibility among the vote of baseball writers. That year he received only 9 votes from the more than 550 sportswriters casting ballots. He got 1 vote in 1962, the year Jackie Robinson was inducted into the Hall of Fame; 6 votes in 1964; and 6 in 1968.

"Votes among the veterans committee are not recorded," said Gates. "Only the elected winners are announced."

Marvin Miller is not yet in the Baseball Hall of Fame despite his revolutionary work with the Major League Baseball Players Association. Dixie Walker, despite an exemplary playing career and his creation of the vital pension plan, resides outside Cooperstown with him.

"Dixie volunteered for two overseas USO trips in World War II," wrote Jack Kavanagh in the 1993 edition of SABR's *Baseball Research Journal.* "He went on the tough Aleutian tour and reached outposts polar explorers such as Admiral Richard Byrd had barely made. The group, which included Frank Frisch and Stan Musial, narrowly escaped being buried under an avalanche at one remote location. The next time Dixie signed up he visited the China-Burma-India theatre. It was warmer but equally dangerous."

The measure of a man's life, his contributions, his impact on his profession, cannot always be calculated only in numbers.

History's Verdict

There are ten former members of the Dodgers whose uniform numbers have been retired by the club: two managers, Walt Alston, number 24, and Tommy Lasorda, 2; three pitchers, Sandy Koufax, 32, Don Sutton, 20, and Don Drysdale, 53; and five regular every-day players, Pee Wee Reese, 1, Duke Snider, 4, Jim Gilliam, 19, Roy Campanella, 39, and Jackie Robinson, 42. Except for Sutton's, all the retired numbers were first worn in Brooklyn.

Number 11, worn by Dixie Walker in Brooklyn from 1939 through 1947, was last worn by a Los Angeles Dodger coach, Manny Mota.

Except for Gilliam, all the individuals who have had their numbers retired are members of the Baseball Hall of Fame.

Of the five regular players, only Robinson, with a lifetime mark of .311, had a higher career batting average over his ten big league seasons than Walker's .306 average (.310 in the National League) over eighteen seasons.

There were streets named for all ten players whose numbers have been retired by the team in the club's longtime spring training site in Vero Beach, Florida. A street was also named for Dixie Walker, who never actually trained with the Dodgers in Vero Beach.

In the chronological history of the Dodgers given in the team's media guide, much is made of Larry MacPhail's acquisition of first baseman

Dolph Camilli in 1938 and the one-season stint by Babe Ruth as a Brooklyn coach. There is no mention of the 1939 arrival of Walker.

"Outfielder Pete Reiser was dynamite in 1941," the media guide reported. "Reiser led the league in batting, runs scored, total bases, slugging percentage and triples while teammate Dolph Camilli topped the league in home runs and RBIs and was honored as the National League MVP." Dixie Walker, who batted .311 in 148 games for the 1941 Brooklyn pennant winners, was not mentioned.

"The Dodgers in 1942 won four more games than in the previous year but finished second to the St. Louis Cardinals. Over the next three years, the Dodgers finished third, seventh and third, respectively. During World War II, many Dodger players were called to military duty." Walker's name was missing again. There was no mention of his 1944 batting title or his 1945 RBI title.

"With the end of the war in 1945, Brooklyn came back in 1946 and put together a big season, going 96–60, and finished tied for first with the St. Louis Cardinals," the media guide reported. There was no mention of Walker's .319 batting average that year or his 116 runs batted in.

"In 1947 the Dodgers won the National League pennant over the Cardinals by five games. That was not the only big story of 1947 as Jackie Robinson became the first African American to play in the big leagues," the guide reported. Walker batted .306 that year in 148 games but was not mentioned in the report.

Dixie's name appears only twice in the record section of the Dodgers guide, once for being the Dodger with the tenth highest average ever for the team, his .357 in 1944 for the league crown (Babe Herman has the highest mark, .393 in 1930, and in another baseball miscarriage of justice has failed to make the Baseball Hall of Fame) and for finishing in a tie for tenth in the team's history in batting average. Walker's Brooklyn average was .311. Jackie Robinson hit .311 in his ten Brooklyn seasons, linking the two together again.

Former Dodgers owner Peter O'Malley's Web site (http://walteromalley.com/) about his former team and its heroes has almost no information about Dixie Walker. There are photos of Dixie and Estelle with the 1943 birth of Susan in Rockville Centre, another picture of Dixie in his familiar batting stance, and a photograph of Dixie dressed in a handsome suit with an Indiana Jones fedora.

There are several more pictures of Dixie in action at Ebbets Field, batting, fielding, and sliding and a few articles about a 1943 holdout and late reporting date at the Brooklyn spring camp at Bear Mountain, New York, an earlier article about Dixie's challenge for a regular everyday job on the club, and a 1943 cartoon from the *New York World-Telegram* by famed cartoonist Willard Mullin. There are no 1947 articles about Dixie Walker and Jackie Robinson on the Web site.

There is no explanation by the Dodgers or by any baseball official as to why Dixie Walker's name seems to have disappeared from baseball memorabilia. His standing in the game as a major star and his contributions to the security of all future players from his own time forward through the pension plan certainly qualify him for the game's highest honors.

While the National League's rookie award is now named after Robinson and his uniform number has been retired throughout the game (only Yankee reliever Mariano Rivera still wears number 42 via a grandfather clause) no mention of Walker's contribution is ever heard.

Robinson's status in the game can never be diminished. Walker's significance should be touted.

Rev. Jesse Jackson put Robinson's significance in perspective in a 1987 interview. "I was a small boy growing up in Greenville, South Carolina," Jackson recalled. "The Brooklyn Dodgers flew into Greenville to play an exhibition baseball game, and we all rushed to the airport to welcome them. These were the famous Brooklyn Dodgers of Jackie Robinson, Roy Campanella, and Don Newcombe, and we had to see them, hopefully touch them, reach out to them. It was raining very hard but we didn't care if the game was cancelled as long as we could see our heroes.

"The players came off the plane and into the small lounge in the airport to use the bathroom facilities, and we waited and waited for our heroes. Jackie Robinson did not get off the plane. I waited for many minutes and soon the white players were walking back to the plane and the plane was taking off again and we were terribly distraught that we had not seen Jackie. 'Why can't we see him, why can't we see him?' One of our leaders, Reverend James Hall, came over to us and told us, 'Jackie Robinson can't get off the plane because they won't let him use the bathroom. It was for whites only.' I remember that like it was yesterday.

"Jackie Robinson was our champion, our hero, and this was another way the white man cut us down. Jackie Robinson rose above segregation, rose above discrimination; he was a man of dignity and honor. When he came into baseball and assumed that pioneering role, he knew he was responsible for people, for all the people, he knew he had to be good and force people to respect and honor him.

"In 1947, people were dealing with those old-fashioned pseudo-psychological ideas of inferiority. Black people were taught by whites that they were inferior, that they were cursed by God to be lesser humans. It is one of the devices used to justify slavery, to explain the injustices of the time, to keep blacks oppressed in our country.

"Now along comes Jackie Robinson, this proud knight in baseball armor, and he was not inferior. He showed that it was talent and intelligence and skills that could lead a man out of poverty and persecution. He was a marvelous player   dynamic, exciting, a true Renaissance man with a variety of abilities. It destroyed so many racist concepts about the shiftless, lazy black man. He literally lifted black people out of depression by his success. He was a therapist for the masses by succeeding, by doing it with such style and flair and drama. He helped level baseball off, to make it truly a game for black and white, with excellence the only test of success," Jackson said.

It was such lofty talk about Robinson, about what he meant to America, both black and white, about what he accomplished that seemed to force the name of Dixie Walker further and further into the background. In every dramatic scenario, there is always a hero and a villain. But sometimes the villain has to be "created" or blown out of proportion or vilified for the sake of contrast. Robinson was clearly the hero, creating descriptions and emotions that have rivaled those inspired by Washington, Lincoln, FDR, by Alexander Graham Bell and Thomas Edison, by Generals Pershing, MacArthur, and Eisenhower.

Dixie Walker was an important member of the Brooklyn Dodgers in 1947 when Robinson arrived on the scene. He was from Birmingham, Alabama. He had been born in 1910 in the southern state of Georgia. The press focused on him as the villain—with or without evidence. No matter what occurred in the next thirty-five years of his life, he would always be linked to Robinson as a negative in this cultural revolution. His family would carry that burden long after he was gone.

Marty Adler was an enthusiastic fan of the Brooklyn Dodgers. He grew up to become the assistant principal of Public School 208 on Bedford Avenue, a short distance away from the site where Ebbets Field once stood. Adler created a Brooklyn Dodgers Hall of Fame where artifacts from the glory days of the Dodgers could reside in his home; later they were transferred to the lobby of the new minor league ball park in Coney Island.

He also pushed hard to have his school named after Jackie Robinson. "I wanted kids in the school to know and understand who Robinson was," he said. "I thought this would be the best way."

All Baseball Hall of Famers including Robinson, Reese, Snider, Campanella, Koufax, would automatically be enshrined in the new Hall of Fame of the Brooklyn Dodgers. Each year a committee of Adler and his pals would consider candidates for election to the Brooklyn Hall of Fame, a shrine without an actual building. Dixie Walker, the People's Choice, was mentioned early and often as a candidate for the Dodgers Hall of Fame, which was created in the 1980s.

"Each year somebody would bring up Dixie's name and each year somebody else would knock it down," said Adler. "There wasn't much discussion about it. He just didn't get elected." Adler didn't recall any arguments about his decision to keep Walker's name from the rest of the honored Dodgers. "Well, you know," he said, "it had to be about the Jackie thing. I guess everybody felt the same way. It was that Dixie, you know, just had that, whatever you want to call it, a reputation that he was one of the guys."

It was all vague. It was all mysterious. It was all without any logic or reason. This was Dixie Walker they were talking about, the most popular player in Brooklyn at his time, the batting champion when there were so few heroes in Brooklyn, a guy who helped bring a couple of pennants to Brooklyn, the man who saw to it that ball players of the 1940s and 1950s wouldn't have to go on welfare or have their families borrow money to bury them with some degree of dignity.

Twenty years after that memorable 1947 season, the Dodgers brought Jackie Robinson and Dixie Walker and other members of that team, Duke Snider, Pee Wee Reese, Gene Hermanski, Bobby Bragan, Clyde King, Ralph Branca, to an old-timers' game in Los Angeles.

Robinson was much heavier than in his playing days, white-haired, having trouble with his knees, his back, and especially his eyesight, as he wore his old uniform with 42 on the back. He really didn't have a baseball connection any more. He was more interested now in politics, in private business, and in the civil rights movement.

Walker was tall and trim, balding now, still pretty fit for a man in his late fifties, still active in baseball, soft spoken, clearly enjoying being back in a ball park with so many men wearing uniforms that said Dodgers across the chest.

They all sat together on the Los Angeles bench, shaking hands with each other, chatting easily, throwing around tales from long-ago, laughing together, enjoying the warm sun on this perfect California day.

Dixie Walker played for the Brooklyn Dodgers at Ebbets Field from 1939 through 1947. He played there again as a visiting player with the Pittsburgh Pirates in 1948 and 1949.

The Dodgers moved out of Brooklyn to Los Angeles after the 1957 season. Ebbets Field was torn down in 1960. Soon after, a subsidized housing complex was under construction at that site.

There are thirteen hundred apartments in the twenty-one-story building that had been home to the Brooklyn Dodgers from 1913 through 1957. Dixie Walker played there from 1939 through 1947; Jackie Robinson played there from 1947 through 1956. Now, mostly minority families live there at the Ebbets Field Apartments with rents running from seven hundred to twelve hundred dollars a month for the larger three-bedroom apartments. Empty apartments are rare.

Three color photos sit on a wall in the rental offices of the Ebbets Field Apartments. One shows Jackie Robinson in an exciting rundown at third base. Another shows a picture of the crowd at the 1952 World Series at Ebbets Field. The third is a glowing photo of a 1954 Brooklyn game at night. A black and white photo, on another wall, shows a 1960 scene of a construction crew working around the dugout when Ebbets Field was being demolished.

A cornerstone reading 1962 inside a stitched outline of a baseball sits on the edge of the building. Eight words are cut into the brick wall: This is the former site of Ebbets Field. Sad.

Dixie Walker never made it back there after his playing days were over. "I would be in New York occasionally," he once said, "but I never got back to Brooklyn. It was just one thing or another when I was in town. I always wanted to do that but the opportunity never really presented itself."

Now the location is home for some forty-five hundred people, most of them living on government assistance. Few of them have any recollection of the ball park that used to be there or the baseball history at the site. But there are some who have not forgotten. "I remember Ebbets Field," says Phyllis Kusinitz Cash, a grandmother and retired New York City schoolteacher. "It was a landmark, like the Statue of Liberty. I wasn't a baseball fan but I remember the name of Dixie Walker. I'm sure every kid growing up in Brooklyn did."

She also recalled the 1947 arrival of Jackie Robinson in Brooklyn with the Dodgers and the controversy surrounding it. That played out in a strange way in her own home a few years later. "My parents were born in Europe and came here as small children. My mother always lied that she was born here, especially during the World War II days, when she was concerned people would look on her as an outsider or even think about sending her back to Europe. That frightened her. She did everything to proclaim that she was a true American.

"In the early 1950s I dated a young man who was a Columbia Law School student. He had a friend, an African American, who was also a Columbia Law School student. My date wanted to come over and pick me up at my home one day. He said he would bring his friend along. I told my mother that my date and his black friend would be coming by. She wouldn't hear of it. She just believed that 'true' Americans wouldn't have a black man in their home. She would do anything to advertise herself as a true American and in those days that meant no contacts with blacks. She's gone now. I wonder what she would think of the United States having an African American president."

Jonathan Eig, in his splendid book on that historic year in baseball, *Opening Day: The Story of Jackie Robinson's First Season*, wrote, "Rickey also recognized that Walker, despite his nickname, had turned out not to be much of a rebel. In fact, after spring training, he put up no resistance at all. He did nothing to disrupt or distract the team as far as anyone could tell. He did nothing to offend Robinson. He never failed to play hard. When it counted, he put the team first."

Perry Dornstein, a retired physician from Brooklyn, now living in a Philadelphia assisted living facility, recalled Dixie Walker as his favorite Brooklyn Dodger player. "I played right field in my high school days, wore number 11, even ran in the outfield and skipped over the foul line like Dixie did before getting to the dugout. I had a better arm than Dixie but he could hit a sweet ball. Who knew from racism in the clubhouse in those days? I still liked him as a ballplayer."

Marty Hanfling, a retired Manhattan businessman and musician, lived near Ebbets Field for many years. He could recall as a youngster of seven or eight hearing the noise of the baseball crowd and seeing the sky brighten above his apartment when the lights were turned on at Ebbets Field. "We all wanted to play for the Brooklyn Dodgers," he recalls. "We all wanted to be Dixie Walker in the 1940s, to get in the batter's box in Brooklyn, assume that closed stance of his, hold that bat back and high over your head, and smack one against the right field wall along Bedford Avenue. Especially against the Giants. When we played stickball we took the name of the Brooklyn players and I was always Dixie.

"I remember listening to Red Barber call out Dixie's name on his radio broadcast and you could hear the sound of the crowd just growing larger and larger as Dixie neared the plate. 'Here comes the pitch, Dixie swings, and there's a line drive to right. It's off the wall. Here comes Pee Wee in to score and here comes Lavagetto.' He was everybody's favorite, the People's Choice, that's what we all called him, that's what they wrote in the papers, Dixie Walker, the People's Choice. He was everybody's favorite. What a player. He's in the Baseball Hall of Fame, right?"

Well, no, he's not.

Index